LIBRARY OF RELIGIOUS BIOGRAPHY

Edited by Mark A. Noll, Nathan O. Hatch, and Allen C. Guelzo

THE LIBRARY OF RELIGIOUS BIOGRAPHY is a series of original biographies on important religious figures throughout American and British history.

The authors are well-known historians, each a recognized authority in the period of religious history in which his or her subject lived and worked. Grounded in solid research of both published and archival sources, these volumes link the lives of their subjects — not always thought of as "religious" persons — to the broader cultural contexts and religious issues that surrounded them. This volume includes a bibliography and an index to serve the needs of students, teachers, and researchers.

Marked by careful scholarship yet free of academic jargon, the books in this series are well-written narratives meant to be *read* and *enjoyed* as well as studied.

D0939464

San Diego Christian College
2100 Greenfield Drive
El Cajon, CA 92019

LIBRARY OF RELIGIOUS BIOGRAPHY

William Ewart Gladstone: Faith and Politics in Victorian Britain
David Bebbington

Aimee Semple McPherson: Everybody's Sister • *Edith L. Blumhofer*

Her Heart Can See: The Life and Hymns of Fanny J. Crosby
Edith L. Blumhofer

Orestes A. Brownson: American Religious Weathervane
Patrick W. Carey

Thomas Merton and the Monastic Vision • *Lawrence S. Cunningham*

Billy Sunday and the Redemption of Urban America • *Lyle W. Dorsett*

The Kingdom Is Always but Coming: A Life of Walter Rauschenbusch
Christopher H. Evans

Liberty of Conscience: Roger Williams in America • *Edwin S. Gaustad*

Sworn on the Altar of God: A Religious Biography of Thomas Jefferson
Edwin S. Gaustad

Abraham Lincoln: Redeemer President • *Allen C. Guelzo*

Charles G. Finney and the Spirit of American Evangelicalism
Charles E. Hambrick-Stowe

Emily Dickinson and the Art of Belief • *Roger Lundin*

The Puritan as Yankee: A Life of Horace Bushnell • *Robert Bruce Mullin*

Prophetess of Health: A Study of Ellen G. White • *Ronald L. Numbers*

Blaise Pascal: Reasons of the Heart • *Marvin R. O'Connell*

Occupy Until I Come: A. T. Pierson and the Evangelization of the World
Dana L. Robert

God's Strange Work: William Miller and the End of the World
David L. Rowe

The Divine Dramatist: George Whitefield and the
Rise of Modern Evangelicalism • *Harry S. Stout*

Assist Me to Proclaim: The Life and Hymns of Charles Wesley
John R. Tyson

286.7092
M652W
R878g

Eng
14.08
534

GOD'S STRANGE WORK

William Miller and the End of the World

David L. Rowe

William B. Eerdmans Publishing Company
Grand Rapids, Michigan / Cambridge, U.K.

© 2008 David L. Rowe
All rights reserved

Published 2008 by
Wm. B. Eerdmans Publishing Co.
2140 Oak Industrial Drive N.E., Grand Rapids, Michigan 49505 /
P.O. Box 163, Cambridge CB3 9PU U.K.

Printed in the United States of America

14 13 12 11 10 09 08 7 6 5 4 3 2 1

Library of Congress Cataloging-in-Publication Data

Rowe, David L.
God's strange work: William Miller and the end of the world / David L. Rowe.
p. cm. — (Library of religious biography)
Includes bibliographical references.
ISBN 978-0-8028-0380-1 (pbk.: alk. paper)
1. Miller, William, 1782-1849. 2. Millerite movement — History.
3. End of the world — History of doctrines — 19th century.
4. Bible. — O.T. — Prophecies — History — 19th century.
5. Adventists — History. I. Title.

BX6115.R68 2008
286.7092 — dc22
[B]

2008003712

www.eerdmans.com

To David Arthur

and all the shepherds of our public memory

Contents

Foreword

In the early 1840s the ground was shifting under many parts of the Christian world. In Scotland, tensions over the influence of lay patrons were moving inexorably toward the breakaway of a "Free Church" from the nation's established Presbyterian Kirk. In Berlin the young Karl Marx was aligning himself with the atheistic wing of Hegel's followers and coming to the conclusion that churches were important mostly for how they obscured the class struggles that were the key to all of history. In the Netherlands, an archivist and political pamphleteer, Groen van Prinsterer, was brooding over the corrosive effects of the French Revolution on church, state, and society; soon he would issue an anti-Revolutionary manifesto that continues to influence Calvinists in many parts of the world. In England, Charles Darwin continued to make public reports on the strange creatures he had encountered on his recently completed round-the-world voyage while in private he worked on a grander theory to explain how this profusion of species had come about. In the islands of the South Seas, in China, in India, and on the coast of South Africa, intrepid missionaries were just beginning the momentous process that would one day transform Christianity from a mostly Western religion into humankind's first truly global religion. And in Low Hampton, New York, a Baptist farmer by the name of William Miller had convinced thousands of his fellow Americans that the End of the World was at hand.

In a recently published general account of American history during the years 1815-1848, Daniel Walker Howe has explained in exquisite detail the dizzying pace of change experienced by American citizens during this era. The title of Howe's book refers to the first message transmitted over Samuel F. B. Morse's newly invented telegraph in 1844; his subtitle spotlights the rapidity of change: *What Hath God Wrought: The Transformation of America, 1815-1848* (Oxford University Press, 2008). This volume carefully describes the communication and transportation revolutions that, in league with accelerating economic activity and a tumultuous political history, were creating a new America. For over three pages in this outstanding general history, Daniel Walker Howe deals at length — and sympathetically — with "Father Miller" and why his message about the End of the World "resonated" so strongly "with a powerful strand in Anglo-American culture" (290).

It was, to be sure, an age of larger-than-life religious figures who, in the rich loam of America's democracy, seemed to be everywhere sprouting into leadership. An age of political democracy was also an age of religious democracy. Charles Grandison Finney turned his abilities as an attorney and his own intense experience of conversion into a mighty engine of revival and reform. Joseph Smith, a dreamy youth who grew up not too far from William Miller in upstate New York, was emerging as a prophet to his Mormon followers and one of history's great charlatans to his detractors. Alexander Campbell and Barton Stone were energetic Presbyterians who grew dissatisfied with partisan ecclesiastical infighting; from humble starting points they created a whole new tradition of "Disciples" and "Christians." John Humphrey Noyes dreamed of a utopia where commerce, society, and family would be marked by community sharing instead of cutthroat competition — and, for several decades, actually put it in place. In this environment of creative populism, it is strange that one of the era's most effective populist religious leaders has never received thorough biographical attention.

David Rowe's balanced and carefully researched treatment of William Miller remedies that oversight. The book's mastery of a large but underutilized corpus of papers and printed material skillfully addresses the need for a careful academic study. But because the book is so well written, so insightful about the milieu in which Miller worked, and so patient in showing the natural fit between Miller's faith and the faith of many others in his generation, the book becomes much more. Rowe's book is, to be sure, a gift for professional students of this period in American history and of the Adventist traditions that sprang from Miller's work. But its humane treatment of an intriguing figure along with a complex crux in American history makes it a captivating story for a much broader audience.

Most of all, this book provides a realistic answer to one of the great mysteries in the American history of Christianity: how did a self-taught farmer's biblical calculations about the impending End of the World become so convincing to so many other pious, Bible-loving, and faithful Christian people? David Rowe's story provides a series of convincing answers to that question. It ranges widely: because William Miller was so thoroughly a part of his era's great transformations, this biography considers warfare (Miller was a captain in the War of 1812), politics (he was tutored by Matthew Lyon, one of the era's most resilient political radicals), communications (the publishing machinery that publicized Miller's biblical conclusions was a marvel of the age), psychology (Miller's diary offers a firsthand look at an extraordinary individual), and much more. What becomes clear after only a few pages is that the wide range and patient skill of this book has, at last, provided the material for answering that most intriguing question.

David's Rowe's biography of William Miller is being published alongside Ronald Numbers's biography of Ellen White, founder of the Seventh-day Adventist church. The combination of two unusually fine books on these two unusually significant individuals is cause for celebration by all who value the past, but also by those who realize how much the kind of past opened up by such books continues to explain the present.

Mark Noll

A Note on Quotations and Citations

In all quotations I retain the original spelling and syntax so far as clarity will permit. When spelling of a word in the original document makes it difficult to decipher I edit the spelling in appropriate ways, always indicated by brackets. The vast majority of Miller letters are located in the Jenks Memorial Collection of Adventual Materials at Aurora University, but other letters appear in the Vermont Historical Society and at the Center for Adventist Research at Andrews University. To avoid both unnecessary duplication and confusion, letters contained in the Jenks Collection will be indicated as Miller Letters, while correspondence from the other two collections will be cited as Miller Letters VHS and Miller Letters AndU. Also, when citing letters to and from William Miller I use his last name only; citations of correspondence from other members of the family employ the full name.

Introduction

The word *strange* appears frequently in discussions of William Miller and the Millerites. Strange were the ideas he promoted: Jesus would return to the earth physically at any moment but no later than "sometime in 1843" to purify the world with heavenly fire, raise the righteous dead, and reign personally over the world for a thousand years, when the wicked dead would rise to damnation. The man was odd, too — unschooled, unprepossessing, a farmer already past middle age with no credentials in theology and no experience at preaching. Commentators described him as "quaint in expression" and "northern-antique" in manner and appearance.[1] Stranger still was the public's response. Thousands of people both at home and abroad believed him. Some merely waited expectantly and passively, but many others uprooted themselves and their families, unsettling churches and neighborhoods to prepare for the great event.

Strangest of all was the outcome. Despite the serial failure of his predictions, the movement gained in popularity, and frenzy. Even with a final denouement in October 1844 and published confessions and apologies from the movement's leaders, Adventism survived to spawn several denominations, national and global, shape several others, and contribute to two of the most significant move-

1. Sylvester Bliss, *Memoirs of William Miller: Generally Known as a Lecturer on the Prophecies, and the Second Coming of Christ* (Boston: Joshua V. Himes, 1853), 149, 249. Apollos Hale write the first three chapters, but the book is generally cited with Bliss as the sole author.

ments in American religious life, fundamentalism and Pentecostalism. Even Miller found his work astounding. At the end of his life, reflecting on the crusade that bore his name and in awe of what God had accomplished through it, Miller called Adventism "this work, this strange work."[2]

Of course, it was this very strangeness that attracted attention, and Millerites exploited it effectively to market their vision. But its long-term impact was negative. Memory keepers have not been kind to William Miller. In his own day, popular commentators described him as demented, dishonest, and divisive, and that reputation lingers in the work of writers who have maintained and refined it, repetition adding to the memory a patina of authority. Clara Endicott Sears is the best example. In her book *Days of Delusion: A Strange Bit of History,* she included Miller among those who "venture from the beaten track of thought and get bewildered in labyrinths of their own making . . . seemingly sensible people who suddenly accept preposterous theories and become fanatics and run hither and thither propounding vagaries." While generally sympathetic to Miller personally, she described his movement as a "strange religious hysteria."[3] Millerites' antics, gleaned from the memory and tradition of their descendants, fill her pages. We read of devotees donning ascension robes preparing for the moment when they would rise in the air to meet Jesus, climbing to roofs and mountaintops to be closer to him as he descends, giving away property, committing crimes, going mad. The same stories have colored college history lectures for decades. Why would anyone believe otherwise of Miller and his followers when in our own day Jim Jones, David Koresh, and Heaven's Gate have made the dangers of apocalyptic speculation terrifyingly real?

While Miller's critics have made light (and dark) of him, more sympathetic memory keepers have provided an equally distorted portrait of the man. To his theological and spiritual descendants — Adventists, dispensationalists, fundamentalists — Miller was a messenger from God, a powerful preacher, courageous leader, fulfillment not only of God's prophetic promise to sound the alarm in

2. Bliss, *Memoirs,* 368.

3. (Boston: Houghton Mifflin Company, 1924), 5.

the last days but of the democratic dream that in America even the simplest citizen can discern truth and act on it. Defensive apologia began at the height of the Millerite movement. In the early 1840s Miller penned brief autobiographies that Joshua V. Himes, the movement's *abbé grise,* printed in his book *Views of the Prophecies and Prophetic Chronology*[4] and in inaugural issues of two newspapers, the *Signs of the Times* and *The Midnight Cry.* This provided the core of an expanded memoir arranged by Himes and written by two Adventist colleagues, Apollos Hale and Sylvester Bliss, in 1853, four years after Miller's death. While eschewing any need "to eulogize him, nor to apologize for him," Himes wanted to present the difference between "the actual position of Mr. Miller and that which prejudice has conceived that he occupied . . . as an act of justice to Mr. Miller." Twenty-two years later the Seventh-day Adventist James White produced a similar volume using most of the same material as Bliss. But because his denomination was founded on a radically different interpretation of the Great Disappointment than the sects supported by Himes and other more moderate leaders, it added material reflecting his denomination's position. An additional memoir appeared in 1910, again mostly incorporating information from Bliss. Francis D. Nichol's 1944 *The Midnight Cry: A Defense of the Character and Conduct of William Miller and the Millerites,* occasioned by the centennial anniversary of Millerism's "Great Disappointment" and the popularity of Sears's book, was more interpretive, but, as the subtitle reveals, equally apologetic. Like his predecessors, Nichol employed a "sympathetic approach" to discover "the real truth regarding" Miller and his movement.[5]

Apologia can correct imbalance, and to a certain extent these

4. Joshua V. Himes, *Views of the Prophecies and Prophetic Chronology, Selected From Manuscripts of William Miller With a Memoir of His Life* (Boston: Joshua V. Himes, 1842), 7-14. Himes intended the memoir for the first edition of this book, published the previous year, but Miller was seriously ill that year, which undoubtedly delayed its writing.

5. Bliss, *Memoirs,* iii-iv; James White, *Sketches of the Christian Life and Public Labors of William Miller, Gathered from His Memoir by the Late Sylvester Bliss, and From Other Sources* (Battle Creek, Mich.: Seventh-Day Adventist Publishing Company, 1875); Francis D. Nichol, *The Midnight Cry: A Defense of the Character and Conduct of William Miller and the Millerites* (Washington, D.C.: Review and Herald, 1944), 16.

did. But hagiographies *in fine* are equally one-dimensional. All, promoters and detractors alike, have viewed Miller through the single reflex lens of Millerism, the man thus becoming the projected image of the movement for good or ill. If Millerism was deluded, then Miller must have been deluded. If Millerism conveyed God's prophetic truth, then Miller was an agent of that truth. Historians, whose job is to sharpen our focus, have not done him that service. Virtually alone among the many religious innovators of the day — the Mormons' Joseph Smith and several of his principal followers, the Oneidans' John Humphrey Noyes and other utopian leaders, the New School's Charles Grandison Finney, the Restorationists' Alexander Campbell and Barton W. Stone — William Miller has never been the subject of a scholarly biography, despite the impact his prophetic career has had on American and world religion. No doubt the volume of published memoir and critique made a more intentionally "professional" biography seemingly unnecessary. Miller's career must have been embarrassing to progressive and nationalist historians who narrated America's advance, not its failures. Too, he lacked the dramatic persona of the day's other world shakers, who effectively marketed themselves as prophets and messiahs, titles he studiously rejected.

In truth, the lack of historians' attention would have been to Miller's liking. He was a most reluctant messenger. For fifteen years he avoided speaking out, and even then he worked hard to get others to preach the approaching end of the world instead of himself. When in 1840 a cadre of effective leaders assumed management of the popular crusade Miller had launched and nurtured for nearly ten years, he gladly deferred to their ardor and expertise. On the other hand, he saved almost everything he wrote (ironic for a man who expected the end of the world), which enabled a more complete and realistic likeness of the man. Early writings included a diary from his youth, an arithmetic book filled with computations and exercises in penmanship, speeches, poems, acrostics on the names of friends and neighbors, and a "Book of Fortune" with astrological and other musings. Service as an officer in the War of 1812 produced military records that survive in the Vermont Historical Society. Careers as sheriff and justice of the peace in two communities produced blot books and accounts, and he stored hundreds of duplicate warrants and other documents in an attic barrel. His apocalyptic crusade produced other records. Miller maintained a "textbook" listing the place, date, and Scripture citations of all his lectures and sermons from 1834 to 1844. He kept drafts and manuscript copies of his articles and licenses to preach and character affidavits that he carried on his tours. Miller and his sons managed his correspondence effectively. Sometimes he copied letters before sending them, and many letters he received were also copied, written out by one of his children before forwarding them to Miller when he was away lecturing.[6]

Himes gathered these letters and others from Miller's correspondents to prepare the memoir of his life, and he kept the collection until shortly before his own death in 1894. This raises reasonable questions about their validity and reliability, particularly given the apologetic purpose they were made to serve. There is no evidence of tampering with the letters or censuring content to avoid embarrassment, but we will never know if any letters were discarded as inappropriate or inconvenient. A more supportable concern is the extent to which copying may have produced errors. Some letters show words crossed out with substitute phrasing written above, letters inserted into words, sometimes duplications of phrases crossed out, as though the scribe were making corrections to assure the accuracy of the copy. In the collection are two copies of a letter (or an original and a copy) to Miller from Benjamin Marshall of Northwest Bridgewater, the first with a paragraph crossed out and the second with that paragraph and another line from the first removed. The letter is simply an invitation for Miller to preach, and there is no obvious significance to the excised material. One of these sentences offered to pay Miller's expenses.[7] Given the frequent public charge that Miller was making money from his lecturing, perhaps the edi-

6. We know that William S. Miller at least, Miller's eldest son and secretary, copied letters to Miller received at home before forwarding them in case they might be lost. On one occasion William S. wrote, "I send this to you as it will save copying off as I am in a great hurry and must close." William S. Miller to Miller, February 20, 1843, William Miller Correspondence, Jenks Memorial Collection of Adventual Materials, Aurora University, reproduced in *Millerites and Early Adventists* (Ann Arbor, 1977), section 5, reel 11 [hereafter cited as Miller Letters].

7. Benjamin Marshall to Miller, December 3, 1839, Miller Letters.

tor wished to avoid adding to public suspicion. But similar offers appear in letters throughout the collection. So while the editing raises questions, its effects seem to have been benign.

As a whole the written record provides ample evidence to do Miller *historical* justice by reversing the lens through which we view him. Miller was not the reflection of the movement he created, and to a great extent, particularly after 1840, it did not reflect him. Long before the public came to know Miller as prophet and preacher, he was a son and brother, husband and father, farmer and scribe, squire to his neighbors and patron to his congregation, war veteran and politico, by turns Calvinist and deist and Baptist. The world was coming to an end in 1843, but in 1816 the crops had to be planted and the sheep sheared, the hogs butchered and the apples pressed for cider. Impersonal forces revolutionized the circumstances of life for Miller and his family, as for all Americans. Sufficiency agriculture gave way to the market economy; Jeffersonian republicanism succumbed to Jacksonian democracy; roads and railroads connected Hampton to the ocean; free will linked the believer directly to God. But titanic change was gradual, and visible mostly in hindsight. Undergirding it all was a rhythm of life rooted in continuity. The New Heavens and New Earth might come in thunderous clouds heralded by universal cataclysms, but the life they promised looked familiar, like "taking comfort" on the farm. It evoked homely assurance of family and hearth, contentment and safety. So it would be in the re-created, restored, and redeemed world, living under the personal reign of Jesus as God's adopted children and heirs.

It was an ancient promise, but under Miller's preaching it became tangible, to many something startlingly new. How easy it was to conflate message and messenger when so many would-be messiahs and prophets were plying their wares. Rejecting such lofty presumptions, Miller struggled to describe the role he was playing. During his life's progress he had received several titles, each one adding cumulatively to his public and private personae. The first of sixteen children, he would always be first son and oldest brother. War service added the distinction of military rank, at first "Lieutenant" and then "Captain"; prosperity and community service layered on it the several meanings of "Esquire." As his new religious career developed, followers insistently addressed him as "Reverend," which endured despite his dislike for it, and critics dubbed him "Prophet Miller," a title he categorically rejected. All these were imposed on him, and each reflected qualities of the man, whether he liked them or not.

Ultimately, one title came to suit him, in the sense both that he liked it and it was appropriate. Early in the life of the Millerite movement, followers began to call him "Father Miller," proffering both the deference and the affection due a patriarch. Like Father Abraham, he received a promise and then led his people into a new spiritual landscape. For that they were grateful. What they could not have guessed was that by thus titling Miller they assuaged the wrenching doubts that were the central dilemma of his life. Once a rebellious son, could he be a fit father? An untrusting man, could he be trustworthy? In the light of both facts, was it possible for him to be faithful to an unseen, unknowable God? These struggles contextualized every important event in his life: his choice of partner, his political and military careers, and his conversion. They affected every relationship — with his parents, his wife, his children, his country, his God. And in each phase the word *faithful* took on new meaning: obedient, humble, manly, loyal, and finally trusting.

Of this lifelong wrestling, Millerism was but the last, albeit the most public, product. Focusing directly on Miller necessarily leaves other parts of the story indistinct. The reader will not find here the history of the Millerite movement per se; that has been told already. Neither will we engage in debate over the place his exegesis occupies in millenarian theology except as it revealed and reflected these life issues. Detailing his hermeneutic has been of interest to others, but theological niceties never meant much to him. Eschewing our own preoccupations, we must let Miller speak for himself, to identify for us his deepest concerns, most nagging fears, and greatest hopes. If by doing that we find that he is both less and more than what we have thought, that is what often happens when we allow historical figures to speak for themselves.

This task comes to me through many years of "conversation" with Miller, beginning with research for a Ph.D. dissertation at the University of Virginia in the early 1970s. Since then the call of other duties, interests, and preoccupations distracted. But a felt need to tell his story (or "tell it to the world," as Miller would have said) never ceased to nag, and continual happenstance over two decades — what my faith community calls "god-coincidences," kept opening doors to the work. Not least of these was the wonderful courtship that led William B. Eerdmans to become its publisher. Instrumental throughout that process has been Ronald L. Numbers. We first met at a symposium of established historians and new Millerite scholars at Killington, Vermont. Ron and Jonathan Butler co-edited the publication of those papers as *The Disappointed: Millerism and Millenarianism in the Nineteenth Century.* Our acquaintance refreshed nearly twenty years later at just the point when Ron was working with Eerdmans on a new edition of his biography of Ellen G. White and my life of William Miller was well beyond the talking stage. Linking the two books has done me great honor. The knowledge that his new volume was awaiting the completion of my manuscript spurred my writing, not only in the pace of production but also my desire to justify his confidence and support. Perhaps because of the obstacles he faced initially in his own work, Ron has been a mentor to other historians, and for that I, and others, are grateful.

Other connections from that Killington experience recurred. The late David T. Arthur's work on Joshua V. Himes was one of the first scholarly approaches to Millerite personalities. But more important than his historicism was his careful shepherding of the Miller papers and collection at Aurora University. It may not be too much to say that that invaluable archive exists today because of his championing of it. I am grateful to have reconnected with him at Aurora just before his death in November 2005. James R. Nix came to the Killington conference with plans not only to hear the papers but to visit, purchase, and restore the William Miller farm just across the state line in New York. He could not have known that my career as an historic preservationist, before becoming a full-time academic, had led me to visit the farm on the way to the conference and prepared me to help initially with a historic assessment of the house. Now Executive Director of the Ellen G. White Foundation and a board member of Adventist Historic Ministries, Nix has greatly assisted my research. One of the delights of this work has been its tendency to keep throwing us together as historians, friends, and fellow ministers, though in different mansions. Finally, it was at Killington that I first met Vern Carner, whose drive, creativity, and money inspired and fueled so much of the burgeoning interest in Millerism in the mid-1980s. Thanks to him University Microfilms produced the large collection *Millerites and Early Adventists,* sections of which my university purchased for my research. It was Miller's letters and Millerite newspapers in that collection that kept drawing me back to him.

Since then many other agencies have nurtured our conversation. Chief among them are the principal stewards of William Miller documents and artifacts whose staffs made me welcome at their facilities: the Jenks Memorial Collection of Adventual Resources, Aurora University, and its three consecutive curators, Doris J. Colby, David T. Arthur, and Susan Palmer; The Ellen G. White Foundation and its executive director, James R. Nix; James Ford and the Center for Adventist Research at Andrews University; and Paul Carnahan, Librarian, and the Vermont Historical Society. The American Baptist Historical Society gave me ready access to their wonderful collection of association minutes and newspapers. The Massachusetts Historical Society granted permission to use the Joshua V. Himes Collection, Loma Linda University the Paulinus Millard Day Book, the library of Colgate Rochester Crozier Divinity School the Augustus Hopkins Strong Papers, and the Division of Manuscripts and Special Collections of the New York State Public Library several collections related to the history of Washington County and the Town of Hampton. The Poultney [Vermont] Historical Society, the Rutland County [Vermont] Historical Society, the Washington County [New York] Historical Society, the Washington County Historian's Office, and the Berkshire Athenaeum in Pittsfield, Massachusetts, diligently searched their holdings for treasures that helped establish the context for Miller's early life and family history.

As a wise historian once said to me, "There are no loners in this business." Developing working relationships is always the most satisfying part of the work I do, and so many, in addition to those I have mentioned, deserve public thanks. Michael Campbell, Associate Director, Del E. Webb Memorial Library, Loma Linda University, shared both his medical expertise and research on Miller's illnesses and a digitalized version of the *Midnight Cry* from the Adventist Digital Library sponsored by the Archives and Special Collections at Loma Linda; Fred Bischoff provided an initial version of the digitalized *Signs of the Times,* Words of the Pioneers CD-ROM; Alice and the late Alv Voorhies and Chet and Bettie Jordan were gracious and helpful hosts during my several visits to the William Miller Farm. Joy Rohrieg was preparing the database of Miller letters during my last visit to the Jenks Collection and shared much of her detailed knowledge about them. Tara White produced photographs of portraits of William and Lucy Miller at the Miller farm for this book. Ron Numbers, John Vile, and the Reverend Timothy Jones kindly provided insightful critiques of the publication proposals and drafts of the manuscript at various stages. David Bratt proved to be an ideal editor of the manuscript. Of course, it with me and not with any of these that credit for any errors must lie.

Finally, this book appears in great measure because of the support in many forms of Middle Tennessee State University. These include release-time grants and a semester-long non-instructional assignment for research and writing, assistance for research trips to New York, Maryland, and New England, and the purchase of microfilm and other essential research aids. Responsible for much of this assistance in time and money are John McDaniel, Dean of the College of Liberal Arts, and my History Department leaders, Thaddeus Smith, former chair, and Janice Leone. Truly all my departmental colleagues must share in the credit for any good thing to come from this book, for they are the ones collectively whose collegiality continues to make this a wonderful place to work.

CHAPTER ONE

Whereby I Might Please God

It was the moment he had always feared. William Miller sat at his desk, looking out the east window toward the Green Mountains in neighboring Vermont, speckled by autumn colors that enriched the late October landscape. Jesus was to have come yesterday, last night, this morning. Miller was to have risen in the air along with his wife, children, grandchildren, the remaining faithful in his Baptist church to be with Jesus as heavenly fire rained to purify the world of all corruption, watching as his father and mother rose from their graves in the family cemetery just down the hill, resurrected saints joining the living Elect safe from the purifying apocalypse. It was for this vision that he had staked everything to sound the alarm and promote the promise. But underlying its grandeur had always been the risk. What if he helped prepare the world for Jesus' return, not sometime in the distant future but *now,* and it didn't happen? So many already called him a charlatan, a dupe, a maniac; what would failure confirm? Others had sacrificed even more than he for the promise. What would happen to them? To their faith?

Truly it was faith most at stake now, not just for them but for Miller himself. Preaching the approaching end of the world had bound him to God as surely as Abraham's walking out of Ur into the desert. Action had proven him obedient, humble, a worthy son of the Heavenly Father, redeeming the disappointment he had caused his earthly parents. Jesus' failure to appear must now raise old doubts about himself. God's promise sustained by prophecy had shown God to be rational, dependable, loving, trustworthy. Was God now arbitrary, serendipitous, even cruel, making him as unworthy of his worship as Miller had once believed? Neither of these truths was affordable. But what *had* gone wrong?

The arena where he now wrestled used to be friendly, but not so anymore. Miller's predicting the end of the world had divided the community, setting neighbor against neighbor, Baptist against Baptist, shrinking his safe world to the house he had built nearly thirty years before, just up the hill from the farm his parents had pioneered. Indeed, here was the first and deepest challenge to his faithfulness. Generations of ancestors had set the measure of civic duty; patrimony's call to serve and protect the community had impressed itself on Miller's life from the beginning. Since the 1640s Miller men had been hardworking craftsmen and farmers of social and military rank, their wives producing children prodigiously. It was Thomas who initiated William's long family heritage, mixing duty, heroism, and rebellion. Reportedly an English cooper, he emigrated to Massachusetts by 1649, disembarking in New Salem and settling a plot of land in what was then frontier Springfield. That year he married Sarah Marshfield; they had thirteen children, ten surviving to adulthood. Moving from the sixth seat in the meetinghouse to the fifth seat in three years signifies a certain growth in respectability,[1] but Thomas also had a rebellious streak. In 1650 he was sentenced to fifteen lashes (remitted to a fine) for striking an Indian, and he was fined ten shillings for disturbing the peace.[2] During King Philip's War he gave his life helping protect his family and neighbors from marauding Indians.[3]

Of the next two generations not much is recorded except for the memory that they were military men. Thomas's fourth child, John (1657-1735), was an ensign, though in what service we do not know, and John's oldest son, Joseph (1700-1760), was a captain, probably in

1. Lewis Nolan, *Nolan-Miller Family History* (Memphis: Highland Press, 1997), 197. Nolan is quoting Henry M. Burt, *The First Century of the History of Springfield, Mass., 1636-1736.*

2. Dorothy Offensend, "William Miller, Prophet in the Wilderness" (unpublished manuscript, Washington County Historical Society, Fort Edward, New York), 2. See Jill Lepore, *The Name of War: King Philip's War and the Origins of American Identity* (New York: Vintage Books, 1998).

3. Nolan, *Family History,* 201-2.

the colonial militia. John and his wife Mary had eight children, the oldest of whom was the first in four successive generations to bear the name William (the Adventist founder was the third in the line). In 1747 William moved west to Pittsfield and married, and in 1752 he purchased one hundred acres straddling the Housatonic River, thereafter known as the Miller farm, a flat, fertile piece of ground west of Pittsfield's center. The property extended to the Hancock line, where Shakers would one day create a community less than two miles south. Unlike his forebears, who tended to be long-lived, William was dead by 1758, leaving a family of five with a meager legacy.[4] But he contributed another story of heroism to family lore, escaping a harrowing Indian attack during the Seven Years' War.[5]

Only from stories could William II, born in 1757, and his three siblings have known their father. It was David Ashley, Mary's second husband, who was the real paternal authority in his life. Like Miller forebears, he held a military title, Captain, and he fought for American independence in the Revolution. Fighting the war was a family affair. William's brother Elihu had joined the militia in 1768, and William, a private, served briefly on at least five separate occasions, fighting side-by-side with Ashley at the Battle of Bennington in 1777. The previous year he had marched to New York City to help relieve pressure on Washington's troops but was forced to retreat along with the Continentals.[6] It was during this evacuation that he added his own chapter to family lore. As his son later recounted the story, William II was sick in the hospital, making travel difficult.

4. Nolan, *Family History,* 316-17; Rollin H. Cooke, Pittsfield Families, Berkshire Athenaeum, Pittsfield, Mass., vol. 7, 114; Edward R. Knurow Collection, Berkshire Athenaeum, Pittsfield, Mass., 7:433-34. The Knurow Collection is a rich resource. Knurow was an indefatigable researcher who compiled thousands of pages of notes on Pittsfield history gleaned from public records. After his death many volumes of these notes were housed in the Berkshire Atheneum, forming the Edward R. Knurow Collection. Miller's appear in 7:427-429, 435.

5. Sylvester Bliss, *Memoirs of William Miller* (Boston: Joshua V. Himes, 1853), 6; Colonel John Worthington submitted an affidavit regarding this event to the provincial Secretary noted in James Edward Adam Smith, *History of Pittsfield (Berkshire County) Massachusetts From the Year 1734 to the Year 1800* (Boston: Lee & Shepard, 1869), 1:104. See Knurow Collection, 7:496 for information about a brother, George, killed in the war.

6. Cooke, Pittsfield Families, 1:46; Smith, *Pittsfield,* 1:480, 489, 487.

> When his companions, in the retiring movement, sought shelter in a barn, during a storm, he was left helpless under the drippings from its roof, until his sad condition moved the compassion of a fellow-soldier, in better health than himself, to come to his relief. This true soldier entered the barn; he crowded together those who filled the already crowded floor, and thus made room for his almost dying comrade, Miller; and then he bore him gently to the rude place of repose he had prepared for him.[7]

It was a minor engagement in the war that changed William's life. In June 1777 the British general John Burgoyne invaded the Champlain Valley and threatened Fort Ticonderoga, and local militias quickly gathered to help defend the fort and then to protect the retreating troops. Among them was William II's Pittsfield militia unit. The British soon broke off engagement to march to defeat at Saratoga while the defenders went home, but the unsettled terrain in eastern New York through which they passed impressed William as a land of opportunity. Marching with him was a Baptist preacher, Elnathan Phelps. The two families were probably acquainted in Pittsfield (William had been baptized as an infant, though in what tradition we do not know), but they soon became close. In 1781 William married Elnathan's daughter, Paulina, and they set up household on the Miller farm.[8]

Paulina's family tradition had much in common with her husband's. Like him, she had lost a parent (her mother died in 1774) and gained a stepparent (Elnathan remarried two years later). And she brought to the Miller family her own patriotic credentials. Grandfather William Phelps was a member of the Pittsfield Committee of Safety and served as a militia captain, and her father was wounded in the French and Indian War.[9]

She brought something new to the family as well: its first connec-

7. Bliss, *Memoirs,* 3-4.

8. Smith, *Pittsfield,* 1:497; Offensend, "Miller," 2; Knurow, 7:436. According to these notes, William was baptized April 17, 1757; Nolan, *Family History,* 317.

9. Nolan, *Family History,* 315; Steve Condarcure, "New England Genealogy," (http://newenglandgenealogy.pcplayground.com/f_66.htm#70), 2005; Oliver S. Phelps and Andrew T. Servin, *The Phelps of America and Their English Ancestors* (Pittsfield, Mass.: Eagle Publishing Company, 1899), 1:189-90.

tion to evangelical religion. Pastor Phelps's career accounts for it in large part. After settling in Pittsfield in 1761, he and other family members founded the Baptist church there, and throughout his career he earned a reputation as a church planter, founding congregations in Orwell, Vermont, and Hampton, New York, among others. Phelps was well known "for the plain, scriptural character of his preaching, through the whole section of country extending from western Massachusetts, along the line of Vermont and New York, to Lake Champlain."[10] More than institutional religiosity, Paulina contributed a personal piety that may well have been new to the family. In Hale's recounting, Miller testified to the strength of her spiritual power and influence. Perhaps this reflected the mid-nineteenth-century assumption that religion belonged in the "proper sphere" of women.

But in the decades following the Revolution, rising evangelical culture encouraged personal piety. The Baptist and Methodist churches were growing rapidly, soon to outstrip the Congregationalists, Presbyterians, and Episcopalians in numbers. *Conversion* was coming to mean a change of heart to love God as much as a bending of the will to obey him, and revivals increasingly were the preferred means to bring it about. Political culture shifted with the times, too. Citizenship required virtue, and the new nation called on republican women to teach it to their children.[11]

The conjunction of religious inspiration, political impulse, and strong personality ensured that Paulina Phelps Miller would play a powerful role in the lives of her children. They came quickly and frequently. On February 15, 1782, Paulina bore the first of sixteen children, a boy who inherited the name William, now traditional in both the Miller and Phelps families. Though the third in as many generations, this William Miller titled himself "junior." His parents called him Bill.[12] In quick succession followed Joseph, who died in his

10. Phelps and Servin, *Phelps of America,* 1:189-90; Bliss, *Memoirs,* 5.

11. Mark A. Noll, *America's God: From Jonathan Edwards to Abraham Lincoln* (Oxford and New York: Oxford University Press, 2002); see particularly chapter five, "Christian Republicanism," and chapter nine, "The Evangelical Surge."

12. Cooke (Pittsfield Families, 1:114) notes that a Bill Miller appears on a local census of 1786, and family stories about his youth have his parents calling him that as well.

eighth month, and Paulina, the last of their children born in Pittsfield.[13]

Sometime in 1786 the Millers left their Massachusetts farm for a new home to the north in Hampton, New York, on the border with Vermont. Financial reasons may have inspired the move. The American Revolution and its aftermath saw hard times in western Massachusetts, like the rest of the new nation. Farm prices had been good in the first two years of the war, but eliminating British trade created shortages in wool, saltpeter, and molasses, and that led to higher prices for commodities that farmers had to buy. Local production would fill the gap (among other things, Miller raised sheep on his new farm), but developing new production systems took time. As is so often the case in war, inflation robbed currency of its value, especially in Massachusetts. The new state government had inflated the currency by printing money to the point that its value disappeared. Seacoast shippers and financiers, largely creditors, worked to stabilize the value of the money supply, but it came at a cost. The state essentially swapped new bills of credit for the old currency, establishing a very high value for the new notes. This meant the state treasury had to raise funds to back up the bills of credit. Existing taxes rose, and new taxes appeared. Worse, the state now required them to be paid in coin rather than in kind, removing scarce money from the hands of citizens in this already cash-strapped region. Those who were unable to pay their debts to creditors or tax collectors saw their property and possessions auctioned off at sheriff's sales, an increasingly common sight in the early 1780s.[14]

William II and his neighbors did not stand by idly as this happened, which may have provided a pressing reason for them to leave town. Miller was a patriot, but he was also a rebel. His generation had endured almost constant war and political turmoil, beginning with the French and Indian War of the 1750s and 1760s, conflict with the British from 1763 to 1776, and then the War for Indepen-

13. Nolan, *Family History,* 317-18. Nolan's information about the next two generations comes from a genealogy compiled by Phillip Phelps, Miller's descendant, and maintained by his daughter, Mrs. Hazel Stannard, Fairhaven, Vermont.

14. See Lee Nathaniel Newcomer, *The Embattled Farmers: A Massachusetts Countryside in the American Revolution* (New York: Russell & Russell, 1953 and 1971), particularly 109-38.

dence. Violence had proved an effective solution to the danger of external enemies and arbitrary authority. If mobs and militias could stop the British from collecting taxes, they could work as well to obstruct forced sales by Massachusetts sheriffs. Farmers' protests were not new, and the militia organization provided a ready means of taking mob action.[15]

Twice Miller attacked a deputy sheriff, and it got him into trouble. In September 1782 Prosper Polly was in the process of confiscating a farmer's oxen when a mob, including Miller, attacked him "with Clubs, staves, knives, fists . . . unlawfully, riotously." They beat him up, released the oxen, drove them off, and then scattered. But fourteen of the men were identified and arrested. Miller stood trial with the others, the jury found them guilty, and the judge fined Miller forty shillings. If he paid the fine, the punishment did not restrain him. Within a year he was arrested for rioting a second time. Deputy Polly may have found a more effective way to punish his attackers: in 1784 he sued seven of them for damages and won a hefty award of twenty pounds plus court costs. There is no record of an attempt to collect the fine or of his paying it, but in April, two weeks before the suit was heard, Miller sold sixteen acres (probably the same land he had inherited from his father) for forty-five pounds, perhaps to cover the cost.[16] Meanwhile, tension in the region continued to build until the winter of 1786, when it exploded in Shay's Rebellion, a full-scale revolt against Massachusetts authority.[17] But by then Miller had left the state.

Regardless of his reason for moving, he knew where he was headed: to Washington County, New York, the area that had so impressed him on his march to Ticonderoga. Many Massachusetts men were moving into that undeveloped country. The town of Hampton hugged the border with Vermont, the Poultney River serving as boundary for town, county, and state. The land there was flat and prone to flooding, but the soil was rich and wooded, good for

15. Newcomer, *Embattled Farmers,* 109-38.

16. Knurow Collection, 7:410-14; 36:429; 7:49. Interestingly, four years later Millard sold the same land to David Ashley, perhaps Miller's stepfather, who then moved to Hampton and established a homestead within a mile of Miller's.

17. See Leonard L. Richards, *Shay's Rebellion: The American Revolution's Final Battle* (Philadelphia: University of Pennsylvania, 2002).

farming and full of timber suitable for housing. He did not buy land but leased a hundred acres for an initial annual rent of twenty bushels of wheat.[18] Young Bill may have celebrated his fourth birthday in their new home, a new sister, Sylvia, joining them in September.[19]

While settling a new territory is a solitary enterprise, the Millers did not leave family and friends behind for long. By 1787 Elnathan Phelps had moved to Orwell, Vermont, where he helped found the Baptist church. One of young Bill's uncles, Abiathar Millard,[20] settled a farm on the plateau above the Millers' home, and by the end of the century aunts and uncles from several sides of William's and Paulina's blended families were living in close proximity. Meanwhile, Ashleys and Guilfords, familiar names from Pittsfield, moved to Poultney, Vermont, a new market town six miles to the south.[21] Some newcomers, attracted by the commercial potential of the river falls at Poultney, developed the hamlet of Hampton Corners, just across the river on the New York side.

The Millers and their neighbors formed a distinct community north of the Corners, eventually taking the name Low Hampton,

18. Hale says Miller leased the land (Bliss, *Memoirs,* 7) while other sources refer to the arrangement as a mortgage. Correspondence between William III and the farm owner in 1814, two years after the father's death, demonstrate conclusively that William II never owned the farm. No later than 1797 the rent had increased to $100 a year. See Wait Robbins to William Miller, March 13, 1814, Miller Letters, Jenks Memorial Collection of Adventual Materials, Aurora University, Aurora, Illinois.

19. Nolan, *Family History,* 317. Miller remembered moving in 1786. Bliss, *Memoirs,* 7; see also Joshua V. Himes, *Views of the Prophecies and Prophetic Chronology, Selected From Manuscripts of William Miller With a Memoir of His Life* (Boston: Joshua V. Himes, 1842), 7. William Miller, "Diary and Book of Fortune, 1797-1803," August 10, 1797, Vermont Historical Society, Barre, Vermont (hereafter cited as Diary).

20. One source cites two unrelated men named Abiather Millard moving into the town. Both were blacksmiths and they married sisters. See "Some Early Hampton, New York, Residents," in G. A. Jackson, *Washington County, New York,* http://www.rootsweb.com/~nywashin/hampton.htm (accessed 2006). A third Abiathar Millard, a doctor, became Millard Fillmore's father-in-law.

21. Henry Crocker, *History of the Baptists in Vermont* (Bellows Falls, Vt.: P. H. Gobie Press, 1931), 133; on Millard, see J. B. Lippincott, *History of Washington County, New York* (New York: J. B. Lippincott, 1873), 371; J. Joslin, B. Frisbie, and F. Ruggles, *A History of the Town of Poultney, Vermont, From its Settlement to the Year 1875, with Family and Biographical Sketches and Incidents* (Poultney, Vt.: J. Joslin, B. Frisbie, F. Ruggles, 1875).

probably named for the Lows, a family of early settlers. Here a second set of mills and a woolen factory arose on another fall in the river less than two miles from the Miller farm. Just across the river from them, in Vermont, Matthew Lyon was developing one of the first industrial towns in America, Fairhaven, eventually hosting iron works, mills of all sorts, and the first plant to make paper from wood pulp.[22] Obviously, while Hampton was a wilderness when the Millers arrived, the frontier stage of settlement was short. Even so, it provided an experience that added to an already-rich family lore. One night, Paulina was "out near their residence, and seeing what she supposed was one of their domestic animals, she approached it, and, as she was about extending her hand towards it, was very soon informed of her mistake, by the frightful growl of a bear."[23] Adventure was memorable because of its rarity; continuity shaped the Millers' lives. Children came at a steady pace: after Sylvia, ten more daughters and three more sons. Ten of those thirteen survived infancy.

William II had joined the local militia by 1788, rose in rank each year, and in 1793 was commissioned a captain, maintaining the Miller men's long military legacy.[24] Radicalism governed his politics here as in Pittsfield, with local circumstances adding their own incentives. Vermont had long been a hotbed of tension. New York and New Hampshire both claimed the territory between the Connecticut River and Lake Champlain, and each sold patents for land to speculators and settlers. In the ten years before the Revolution, New Hampshire settlers contested property with New Yorkers, and when competing claimants showed up to occupy the same piece of land fights broke out. Ethan Allen gathered a force (New Yorkers

22. Helpful descriptors of Hampton are Morris Levy, *Map of Washington County, New York* (Philadelphia: James D. Scott and Robert Pearsall Smith, 1853); Stone & Stewart, *The New Topographical Atlas of Washington County, New York* (Philadelphia: Stone & Stewart, 1866); Allen Corey, *Gazetteer of the County of Washington, New York* (Schuylerville, N.Y., 1849). On Matthew Lyon's remarkable career see Aleine Austin, *Matthew Lyon, "New Man" of the Democratic Revolution, 1749-1822* (University Park: Pennsylvania State University Press, 1981).

23. Bliss, *Memoirs,* 9.

24. Clarence H. Holden, Whitehall, N.Y. Scrapbooks, 1910-1927, 14:317, New York State Library and Archives, Albany, New York. The scrapbooks include a variety of materials, including notes taken from town and state records that sometimes are no longer extant.

said it was a mob) calling themselves the Green Mountain Boys to protect the rights of New Hampshire claimants by harassing New Yorkers and driving them off the land. Only the Revolution prevented the two colonies from going to war with each other. The Green Mountain Boys fought on two fronts, in favor of American independence from the British and Vermont independence from both, keeping both Americans and British off balance. But in the end they sided with union and brought into regional and American politics a radical, libertarian vision of the new republic.[25]

The Allens had supporters throughout the region. One was Matthew Lyon, Fairhaven's developer, a radical republican and political and intellectual ally who was related to Allen through his wife's family and shared his anti-authoritarian views, being a "new man" of the American Revolution.[26] Another was William Miller's stepfather, David Ashley, who opposed tax support to maintain ministers — a radical idea in Massachusetts, where the constitution continued to maintain an established church. In 1789 Ashley petitioned for exemption from the minister's tax in Pittsfield because "he thought it not right to support Mr. Allen [the preacher] with a tax."[27] It may have been through Ashley that William II met Lyon, or perhaps they met after both men moved to within a few miles of each other.

Lyon and Miller became political allies and social friends. The ratification of the U.S. Constitution in 1789 and subsequent disagreements between more libertarian Jeffersonian Republicans and nationalist Federalists led to the rise of political parties, first locally and then nationally. Matthew Lyon promoted Jeffersonian Democratic-Republican societies in western Vermont and eastern New York, and Miller was associated publicly with Lyon's political maneuvering. In 1791 the Fairhaven firebrand ran for Congress, and while he lost that election his Federalist opponents charged him publicly with buying votes and manipulating the electorate. One political enemy charged him with conspiring with Captain William Miller, who was "exercising his men" on election day, and encourag-

25. Michael A. Bellesiles, *Revolutionary Outlaws: Ethan Allen and the Struggle for Independence on the Early American Frontier* (Charlottesville and London: University Press of Virginia, 1993).

26. Austin, *Matthew Lyon,* 12.

27. Cooke, Pittsfield Families, 1:46.

ing him to march his New York militia unit across the Poultney River to vote for Lyon in the Vermont race. The idea was not far-fetched; Vermonters did serve in New York militias, and vice versa. Miller considered the published charge against Lyon to be "groundless . . . so far as he has any knowledge of the business."[28]

In 1797 Lyon finally won his much-desired seat in Congress, and he went to Washington. Brawling with colleagues in the House chamber almost got him expelled. Worse, pro-French views, support for the radical French Revolution, angry talk against American aristocrats (Federalists), and a call for the execution of Louis XVI led to his arrest. The Federalist Congress and President, John Adams, feared a bloody social upheaval in this country modeled after France's and passed a Sedition Act to curtail the activities of Francophile Jeffersonian politicians and newspaper editors. Lyon was their first target. Federalists in Vermont charged him with sedition, and a Vergennes court convicted him, sentencing him to a huge fine of $1000 and a four-month jail term.

Aside from such political excitement, the recording of daily life in young Bill Miller's diary reveals its rhythmic seasonality. Necessity united all — men, women, children, and neighbors — as partners in the perpetual production of food, clothing, and shelter. Gender and age defined responsibilities. Men worked outdoors while women worked inside and close to home, though when necessity called they would work in the fields alongside the men (no household emergency seemed to compel men to join in "women's work"). Children, producers as well as consumers, took up chores early on: gathering eggs, feeding animals, carding wool.[29] For young Bill

28. Joel Hamilton made the charge in *The Farmer's Library*, a Lyon newspaper in Fairhaven published by his teenage son James, on June 17, 1793, and Miller's deposition appeared in the issue of July 1, 1793. (Another deposition from a Hampton farmer, Isaac Harlow, denied that Lyon gave him a fee for voting.) Politics may have been at the bottom of Miller's sudden resignation from the militia. In 1798, as one report puts it, "there was quite a shake-up." One captain was transferred while Miller and a second captain resigned. Holden, "Whitehall Scrapbooks," vol. 21, 108.

29. Christopher Clark, *The Roots of Rural Capitalism: Western Massachusetts, 1780-1860* (Ithaca and London: Cornell University Press, 1990), particularly chapters two and three, which describe rural life and economics in a context very similar to the Millers'.

chopping wood was perpetual, "at the dore," in the woods, at the sap house. In spring the sap rising in the sugar maples initiated the cycle of tapping trees, gathering buckets of sap, boiling it into syrup, and refining it into sugar (on one day Bill "boiled 40 pailfulls sap; gathered 15; shugared 7 pound.")[30] April brought plowing and after that mowing brush, dragging oats, planting corn. Older boys washed sheep, and men sheared them. Summer required hoeing corn, knocking down straw in fallow fields (Bill called it "lodging in the fallow," a term not even used in England by that time), and building fences. In late summer began the reaping, wheat at first and then oats and flax, the last for making linen. Winter was hog-killing season. Out came the huge kettles for boiling the carcasses to soften the bristles, requiring a new round of intensive wood chopping. The day might call for threshing harvested wheat, shelling corn, and always chopping wood — for fire, for rails, for boards. In April the sap rose again, and the cycle refreshed.

Labor was never solitary. All was undertaken in the context of family and neighbors united to provide necessities for the present and, as Christopher Clark puts it, "a determination to set up children in viable households of their own." It was a peculiar kind of independence they sought. The desire to be free from want made them dependent on each other to accomplish it. "However unequally apportioned," writes Clark, "cooperative work by their own members was the chief source of support of families and formed the most important part of the interdependence on which the independence of households rested."[31] One day Bill "helpt uncle Abather hoe corn"; a week later he "plowd in the forenoon uncle Abiather and Mr. Davis helpt." Reciprocal labor was essential for achieving the community's mutual goals, and it bound neighbor to neighbor: "got wood Mr Pember and thaniel west helpt," "I helpt Mr Inman chopt logs," "chopt wood Mr west and son and Isaiah Inman helpt us," "mended fences split rails James McWitty & Isaac McWitty helpd."[32]

30. Miller, Diary, April 5, 1798.

31. Clark, *Rural Capitalism,* 26-27.

32. Miller, Diary, June 22 and June 29, 1798; January 1, 1798; March 26, 1799; March 16, 1799; April 27, 1798.

As Bill grew older, bigger, and stronger, work changed. At first he "held the plow," but within a year he was driving the oxen himself. As oldest son he shared the parental job of introducing siblings, particularly the boys, to farm work, and he took on some responsibility for discipline. Sister Amy left a shoe at school and brother Bill had to go and fetch it. On the way back home he "went through swamp and got a stick,"[33] presumably a flexible willow wand, an ideal tool for teaching children not to be so forgetful. The family planted new kinds of crops — rye, beets, potatoes, beans, apples — in addition to wheat, oats, and corn, and they kept hives of bees for their honey and wax, all requiring new skills. He first mentioned working with flax in April 1799, perhaps because he was old enough to handle the labor, more likely because the family and neighbors began producing it then. Cutting flax, digging ponds for soaking the stems, then breaking them to separate the fibers became a new routine, one more enterprise calling for communal labor.[34]

Growing older also meant working farther afield. The family was engaged in the market, selling surpluses of hay, wood, and livestock, and purchasing luxuries not producible at home — sugar, salt, gunpowder, iron, fine cloth, port wine. At first it was the elder Miller who went off to the city marketing produce, but increasingly Bill accompanied him to Fairhaven, Castleton, Whitehall, Skeenesboro (Whitehall), and Salem.[35] It also meant assuming civic responsibilities. Every man gave one or two days' labor each year (for Bill it was in June) to maintain highways and bridges, as assigned by the highway superintendent. And each summer adult males gathered in local units for militia training in the summer lull between planting and harvesting. Bill thus followed in big family footsteps. Most training was nearby, but occasionally it took him to Granville and "over to the City," probably Fairhaven, or to Castleton in neighboring Vermont. In 1801 he was "chose a co[r]poral," his first military leadership rank.[36]

Bill absorbed the family's political interests, and this tied him to

33. Miller, Diary, March 18, 1798.

34. Miller, Diary, June 7, 1798.

35. Miller, Diary, *passim.*

36. Miller, Diary, September 8, 1801; he eventually attained the rank of sergeant in this New York company (Bliss, *Memoirs,* 18).

a bigger world. He attended town meetings, not only at home but in Vermont. The family subscribed to a newspaper in 1801, probably Lyon's *Farmer's Library* or the *Rutland Herald,* and this kept him aware of elections locally; diary notations included "Election of Abithar Millard" and elections "in [New] York state." The Fourth of July was a day for celebrating. In 1799 he "went out to Casselton [Castleton] to Independence," the next year he attended an "Indian fight" (probably a battle reenactment), and in 1801 he wrote, "this the 25th year of American Independence celebration at Poultney an Oration delivered by James Witherill."[37]

The weekly rhythm made room for the sabbath. Sometimes Bill simply "laid at home" on Sunday, but often there was preaching. Grandfather Phelps had organized a Baptist congregation in his daughter's neighborhood, probably at the Miller home, and he often traveled from Orwell to preach. Paternal Uncle Elihu, an ordained minister, was available too, and by 1799 he became their settled pastor.[38] Absent a preacher, a man appointed to the task (who knew how to read and could recite well) would recite one or two published sermons. Sometimes the congregation "met in conference" to administer the needs of the congregation and to manage personal relationships in the church.

Baptisms, weddings, funerals, and notices of death reveal the rhythm of life: "heard grandfather preach . . . baptized John Lee"; "Jacob Phelps and Susannah Lewis was Marriad Last Sunday Night"; "This night departed in death Betsy Warner wife to Mr. Samuel Warner." Miller was particularly descriptive when noting the death of young people, evincing an early interest in their significance. "[T]his day departed in death a youth late from upper Canaday about 19 francis Davis by name"; "Mr Coggswel child was buried."[39]

Usually news beat an irregular pattern, but during seasons of re-

37. Miller, Diary, April 3 and December 4, 1798; April 25, 1798, and April 30, 1800; April 5, 1801; July 5, 1799, July 4, 1800, and July 4, 1801.

38. Lippincott, *Washington County,* 368-69. References to Uncle Elihu's preaching are frequent in Miller's diary, but they increase in 1799, suggesting he was indeed something of a pastor, though the congregation remained a "house church" until the 1820s.

39. Miller, Diary, June 12, 1799; March 3, 1800; April 10, 1798; July 21, 1798; September 2, 1798.

vival and disease the drumming was more regular. On one weekend, in three meetings, William watched his grandfather baptize "Miss Miller [probably a sister], Mr Inman, Miss Whetford," the next day "Rhoda Stephens, Moses Lee, Anne Whitford," and the next "John Lee." Epidemics could carry away entire generations. One in August and September 1798 took the lives of two neighboring children and made Bill and one of his siblings ill for days. His last entry in the diary records a tragedy. "Judeia Spink Died March 23rd 1802 aged 14 White died March 1802 aged 19; Polly Spink died April 6th 1802 aged 16; Naby spink died April 9th 1802 aged 12." Death was no stranger to his own family. In 1788 Paulina bore a daughter who did not live long enough to receive a name. The family buried her in a field south of the house, the first to rest in what is today the Miller family cemetery. Brother Ira, born December 3, 1799, was never healthy. He "was taken sick" in March 1801, but got better. Then in August he became "verry sick," and the next day Bill "helpt take care" of him — to no avail. On August 4 Bill wrote, "This Day Ira Miller died aged 20 months after an illness of about three Weeks."[40] They buried him beside his unnamed sister.

Bill was paying attention to life's lessons, and Paulina could take credit for a budding religiosity in her son. It was she who had taught Bill how to read using the family's only books — a Bible, Psalter, and hymnal — thus fulfilling her role as a Christian, and a republican, mother. Her work bore fruit. Often after hearing preaching Bill carefully noted in his diary not only the preacher's name but the texts he used, a habit to which he would one day return as a preacher himself. Civics and family heritage united with religion to shape a wider world in which he eagerly participated. Young Bill was aware of fast days proclaimed in Vermont and in the nation as tensions with Britain and France drove the United States toward war. On March 2, 1800, he noted solemnly, "Gen. Washington funeral."[41]

Calvinist culture shaped his youthful religiosity. Early in life he learned its essential lesson: "I was early educated and taught to fear

40. Miller, Diary, August 29–September 3, 1798; June 10, 11, 12, 1799; undated, next-to-last page; March 20, 23, and August 2, 3, and 4, 1801.

41. Miller, Diary, April 18 and May 9, 1798; April 26, 1799.

the Lord."[42] Late in life he recalled that as a boy, he was "often concerned about the welfare of my soul; particularly in relation to its future destiny," and he "spent much time in trying to invent some plan, whereby I might please God, when brought into his immediate presence." He would "do nothing wrong, tell no lies, and obey my parents." He failed at that. The path of sacrifice, "giving up the most cherished objects I possessed," proved equally ineffectual. He couldn't part with any of them.[43] With Paulina and grandfather Phelps stewarding his spiritual welfare, his church experience was conventionally Protestant — preaching and praying. Communion was rare (on only one occasion did he record "had a sacrament"), and while there were revivals, religious "exercises" (demonstrations of charismatic excitement) seem to have been rare, too. At one meeting he "heard Br Atwood tell his vision," and at another "Miss Olmstead got up after meeting and long praising unto the Lord." But it may have been their oddity as much as their spirituality that drew his attention (he once noted going to see "a curious cow").[44] Historians have noted the creative religious enthusiasm that marked western Vermont and eastern New York, making it the first of several so-called "burned-over districts" and the seedbed of new sects.[45] That the fires of enthusiasm burned specially hot in this region or at this time is debatable, but regardless, there is no evidence of the fires having seared Bill Miller.

On the contrary, while religion was important in his early life, more earthly interests grabbed his attention. Bill became a passionate reader. A quest for knowledge was a republican imperative, and Americans, both men and women, were inventive in discover-

42. Miller, Diary, July 10, 1797. Miller intended to write an autobiography, an interesting project for one so young. It was one page long and included mention of the family's move to Hampton. Eight months later the document continued, now as a daily diary.

43. Himes, *Views of the Prophecies,* 9.

44. Miller, Diary, May 11, 1800; August 12, 1798; March 9, 1798; June 15, 1800.

45. See particularly David M. Ludlum, *Social Ferment in Vermont, 1791-1850* (New York: AMS Press, 1966); Randolph A. Roth, *The Democratic Dilemma: Religion, Reform, and the Social Order in the Connecticut River Valley of Vermont, 1791-1850* (New York: Cambridge University Press, 1987); and Whitney Rogers Cross, *The Burned-Over District: The Social and Intellectual History of Enthusiastic Religion in Western New York, 1820-1860* (Ithaca, N.Y.: Cornell University Press, 1950).

ing resources to find it. Most, like Bill, learned to read at home from Bibles and homilies. While some could afford the luxury of academy schooling, most rural youth had to take advantage of local sponsors and mentors, often doctors and lawyers who entered their professions by gathering and reading texts on their own. Thomas Young, an itinerant doctor, mentored Ethan Allen and heavily influenced his political and religious thinking.[46] Similarly, the Miller family's political friends, two of them future members of Congress, became Bill's patrons. These included Dr. James C. Witherill, a Hampton neighbor who moved to Fairhaven about 1788. An active Democratic-Republican, he would serve as Congressman and then as a judge of the Michigan territorial Supreme Court, appointed by President Jefferson. Another was Alexander Cruikshanks, a successful Whitehall farmer.[47]

Most important was Matthew Lyon. Not only did he possess a large personal library from which Bill could borrow, but he owned a bookstore, probably associated with his printing operation. In 1792 he advertised in the *Herald of Vermont* a plan to create a subscription lending library; the Fair Haven Library Society was in place by 1794. Bill's father must have paid the subscription, because he attended the meetings and borrowed books, probably for his son. A library society formed in Hampton in 1796, and it was to this that Bill undoubtedly belonged. In 1800 he "went to Capt Cutlers got a Libra book no. 10" and later that year "went to Library meeting," spelling the word correctly for the first time. Uncle Ashley let him borrow a dictionary for help with new words. Not content always to borrow books, Bill arranged a deal with his father, who let him earn money to buy books by chopping wood during leisure hours.[48]

46. Bellesiles, *Revolutionary Outlaws,* 15 and *passim;* Walter S. Kerry, *Rational Infidels: The American Deists* (Durango, Colo.: Longwood Academic, 1992), 87. See also Richard D. Brown, *Knowledge Is Power: The Diffusion of Information in Early America, 1700-1865* (New York and Oxford: Oxford University Press, 1989) and William J. Gilmore, *Reading Becomes a Necessity of Life: Material and Cultural Life in Rural New England, 1780-1835* (Knoxville, Tenn.: The University of Tennessee Press, 1989).

47. Bliss, *Memoir,* 13. On Witherill see Andrew N. Adams, *History of the Town of Fair Haven, Vermont* (Fair Haven, Vt.: Leonard & Phelps, 1870), 488-91.

48. *Herald of Vermont* [Rutland], September 10, 1792; Austin, *Matthew Lyon,* 81;

Travel and adventure stories thrilled him. The first book he owned was a condensed American version of *Robinson Crusoe* (he thought the word *history* in its title meant this *was* a history), published in 1790. The second was like it, William Rufus Chetwood's *Voyages and Adventures of Captain Robert Boyle,* an early novel published in 1780 with kidnappings and pirates and a romantic rescue of an enslaved English lady in Africa (Bill knew this one was fictional). From Fair Haven he borrowed a copy of Captain Cooke's *Voyages . . . in the Southern Hemisphere,* first published in 1773. All were richly illustrated with woodcuts depicting the sufferings and bravery of the heroic adventurers, and Cooke's *Voyages* included maps and charts of faraway places. This was rich fare, suited to feed the imagination of a youth long nourished by family stories of Indian wars and Revolutionary battles.

Bill's passion for reading created a family crisis. Days filled with chores left little time or opportunity to spend with books, and while there was some leisure during "candle light," the evening hours just before retiring, candles were not to be wasted. So Bill would cut pine plugs, light them in the fireplace, and lie by the fire reading long into the night. One day a sister used some of his "pitch wood" to light a fire. He became furious and "gave her a smart blow." Soon the tables were turned. His father became worried that Bill's spending so much sleep time reading would tire him out, making him unfit for work. So he laid down the law: Bill was to retire the same time as the rest of the family. Bill rebelled. He would wait until everyone was in bed and all was still and then sneak to the fire, light a pine knot, and read "as long as he dared to." This was still a one- or two-room cabin with a loft at best, and inevitably his father caught him. He yelled out, "Bill, if you don't go to bed, I'll horsewhip you!"[49]

There's no sign he ever did, but his hot reaction showed he was serious. The family's survival depended on the work of everyone, and on obedience to the father's authority. Violations endangered everyone. Bill was growing up, beginning to shape an identity, find-

---

Miller, Diary, April 16, 1799, and August 30, 1800; April 2, May 3, May 14, 1799. A Hampton Library, founded in 1796, appears in a list of library incorporations contained in Miscellaneous Records of Washington County, 1:75, Washington County Office Building, Fort Edward, New York.

49. Bliss, *Memoirs,* 12-13.

ing a will of his own. He was the eldest son, preparing to claim a patrimony, surrounded by a growing number of siblings in an increasingly crowded house. Youthful precocity was dangerous to family unity. The passage from dependence to semi-independence required careful negotiation to avoid ruptures in relationships. Fathers who failed to honor their sons' ambitions often paid a heavy price.[50] William and Paulina were wise; they seemed to know that more than anything else Bill needed privacy. And he got it. Sometime after this incident, the family built a larger frame house and provided their teenage son with his own room and candles where he could indulge his passion "in comparative comfort."[51]

It's not clear when that happened, but having a room of his own almost certainly explains the significant projects he undertook in the fall of 1797. Bill Miller began writing, first his autobiography and then the diary. A schoolhouse had already been built nearby, and the seasonal cycle added formal education to the winter months.[52] When he first entered school, Bill's reading skills were so advanced that he easily outpaced the rest of the class. But his handwriting and spelling needed improving, and his diary illustrates growth in both. Poetry attracted him and remained a favored medium his whole life. His diary reveals early, stumbling attempts: "About this time/Nature seams to/Load us mortals with/her golden Treassure/fruit Now is in/its Bloome and all/things seem to Chear and make merry." Writing was a valuable skill, and he became a "scribbler-general" to his friends, writing letters and poems and adding flourishes (a kind of fracture writing examples of which survive in his ciphering book) to their own productions.[53]

50. See Harvey J. Graff, *Conflicting Paths: Growing Up in America* (Cambridge, Mass., and London: Harvard University Press, 1995), particularly chapter three, "Hops, Skips, and Jumps into the Nineteenth Century." Miller's childhood and adolescence followed what Graff calls the traditional path to adulthood. On youthful precocity see Joseph Kett, *Rites of Passage: Adolescence in America 1790 to the Present* (New York: Basic Books, 1977), 42-44.

51. Himes, *Views of the Prophecies,* 7.

52. Miller's 1842 recollection places him in school from 1791, when he was nine, until 1796, when he was fourteen, but his diary records steady attendance in the winters of 1798 through 1800-01.

53. Miller, Diary, August 28, 1799; Bliss, *Memoirs,* 15.

Arithmetic was new to him. In the late eighteenth century Americans learned it by creating a copy book, what Bill called his "sypering [ciphering] Book." As one scholar describes the process, "The teacher dictated rules and problems to be copied into blank books, and the students worked out the answers with varying degrees of individual effort."[54] Bill first mentioned his school book in April 1798, and it has survived, covered in pieces of newspaper. In its pages are exercises in addition and subtraction, multiplication and the dreaded "rule of three" and its many permutations that was so hard to learn. English money — pounds and shillings — was giving way to American pennies and half pennies, dimes and half dimes, first minted from 1792 to 1796, so students had to learn how to convert from one system to the other. Like reading and writing, arithmetic was useful to a republic; "arithmetic would promote the spread of the commercial frame of mind and at the same time foster a citizenry able to reason clearly."[55] So while the problems he copied sometimes projected agricultural situations, they also introduced Bill to the intricacies of borrowing and lending money at interest, travel time and distances covered, and standard weights and measures. He encountered not only farmers but tobacconists, distillers, and West Indies merchants, and, like characters in his novels, they beckoned him to a wider world.

He wanted desperately to respond. The schoolhouse could not satisfy his craving for formal education, for which he now longed "with an intensity of feeling that approached to agony." He had no money for tuition, but his patrons were well off, and the men who encouraged his reading might be willing to pay for his schooling, perhaps at the academy in Castleton, just east of Fairhaven. Dr. Smith was the family's physician, and Bill drafted a letter to him expressing "his intense desires, his want of means to gratify them, his hopes and his prospects, if successful." But before he could deliver the letter his father found it and read it. The letter "somewhat dis-

54. Bliss, *Memoirs,* 10; Miller, Diary, April 29, 1798; Patricia Cline Cohen, *A Calculating People: The Spread of Numeracy in Early America* (Chicago: University of Chicago Press, 1982), 120, 130; William Miller, School Book with Problems, 1798-1804, William Miller Farm (Adventist Heritage Ministry), Hampton, New York, n.p.

55. Cohen, *A Calculating People,* 130.

turbed him for the moment," but annoyance gave way to shame and regret that he could not satisfy his son's ambition.[56]

He must also have seen clearly (if he needed reminding) that his son was becoming an adult, with a mind and a future of his own. Paulina and William had been encouraging Bill's maturation for some time. Besides giving him a private room, they sent him on extended visits to relatives, where he met people, especially girls, his own age. In October 1798 he spent several days with aunts and uncles in Pittsfield. There he helped an uncle build a wall, visited the Shaker community at Hancock close by the Miller homestead, and climbed Saddleback Mountain north of the city. The following March he journeyed to Orwell, where he stayed with Phelps relatives, including his grandfather, a trip he repeated in mid-February 1801.[57] On the fifteenth of that month Bill wrote in the diary, "My Birth day — 19 years old." Aware of his developing maturity, he eagerly developed a social life at home, joining the Masons and becoming a founding member of a Fairhaven debate society. Bill enjoyed the company of other young people, whether hunting squirrels with neighbor boys or attending the singing schools that were held frequently in 1800, many times at his house, drawing young people from around the area.[58] The music he learned to love in these sessions would become a vital part of his own family's life.

Courting was on the young man's mind. In his diary he addressed to an unidentified person "X u B & X u B & verry X u r to me" (dear you be and dear you be and very dear you are to me), and a copied poem revealed developing passions: "O! have you been bathed/ in the morning dew,/the morning rose in infant/bloom display,/ When first its virgin/tints unfold to view,/it Shrinks and scarcely/ trust the blaze of days./So soft, so Delicate, so sweet she came/youth, Damask, glow just/dawning on her cheek/I gazed, I Sighed, I caught/ the tender flames/felt the fond pangs, Dropt with pashion weak." The school book reveals another copied piece, the words of an early traveling-salesman/farmer's-daughter story: "He offered and prof-

56. Bliss, *Memoirs,* 15-16.

57. Miller, Diary, October 4-15, 1798 (two pages of the diary are missing; the trip obviously began some time before the 4th); March 17-22, 1798, and February 10-18, 1801.

58. Miller, Diary, *passim,* January 1799 to April 1800.

fered this fair Lady Bright/Twenty Bright guine[a]s to Lay with her one Night."[59] Adults provided respectable occasions for prospective spouses to meet each other, and Bill's parents made sure he looked respectable by providing a suit of clothes for him from a neighboring seamstress. Orwell relatives arranged a gathering of young people during Bill's stay with them, and there were bees of various sorts, including one that Paulina hosted. But it was at a different kind of social affair that Miller first mentioned his future wife. In April 1801 Bill confided to his diary, "went to Mr. Spinks to rasing a Barn this Day I see L S."[60]

This was probably not the first time he had met Lucy Smith. Ebenezer Smith had moved his family to Poultney from Connecticut about the same year the Millers located in Hampton, and Bliss says the Smiths had relatives in Hampton. That may have included Dan Smith or Peter Smith, both of whose names appear in Miller's diary, or even the family's physician, Dr. Smith. In August 1799 he noted the baptism of a "Miss Smith," and as early as September 1800 he mentioned going "to Poltney [sic]," the reason unstated.[61] Regardless of how they met, Bill clearly was smitten. His diary relates the chain of events: on May 11, 1801, "Lucy Smith came here to day"; on May 21, "I Went out to Mr Smiths in Poultney"; on May 31, "went to meeting and then out to Poultney after Lucy Smith." In June Bill attended a ball in Fairhaven, perhaps with Lucy. In October he visited the Smiths and the next day "Came home from Poultney and plowd the fallow."[62] It was one of the last entries he made in the diary; he had no more time for writing in it, and he had found someone else in whom he could confide. There were two final notices. On January 2, 1803, Bill registered his official betrothal to Lucy, "to be her's and only hers till death shall part us (provided she is of the same mind)." On June 12, according to custom, Grandfather Phelps published the official bans in Hampton, and two weeks later Judge Witherill, Bill's long-time patron, published them in Poultney. On June 29 he and

59. Miller, Diary, February 15, 1799; May 4, 1798; March 24 and April 2, 1801; April 24, 1801; December 9, 1798; December 8, 1799; Miller, School Book, n.p.

60. Miller, Diary, July 14 and November 26, 1798; August 28, 1800; March 21, 1799; November 20, 1800; April 16, 1801.

61. Bliss, *Memoirs,* 17; Miller, Diary, August 7, 1799; September 5, 1800.

62. Miller, Diary, June 2, 1801; October 6 and 7, 1801.

Lucy Phebe Smith were married in Poultney, where they immediately established their household, close to her parents.[63]

Moving to Poultney was more than a physical relocation for Bill. By choosing Lucy Smith to be his wife he was also choosing her family and their friends. For their part, they saw in him an attractive and ambitious young man, a potential leader with gifts they could hone. Bill and Lucy's marriage and ambition would lead them to successful political and military careers and a large family, all of which signaled continuity with his past. Rejecting his own family was not required for any of this to happen. That he did reveals for the first time deep religious quandaries and personality conflicts that would color his life's portrait. Bill got everything he wanted, but for that he would pay a heavy price in spiritual cynicism and shattered family relationships. In a real sense, Bill's first world — or at least his innocence — came to an end.

63. Miller wrote the first official notice of their engagement in his school book, writing her full name, Lucy Phebe Smith. Genealogists have mistakenly cited Lucy's middle name as "Phelps," confusing her with her mother-in-law.

CHAPTER TWO

The Society of a Superior Class of Men

Though small, Poultney offered everything Bill desired and could not get in Hampton. As the oldest son of a farmer, he might have expected some assistance from his father in setting up a homestead of his own, but the elder Miller never owned his own farm, and the large family, like most sufficiency farmers, probably lived uncomfortably close to the edge of survival. After Miller's death in 1812 his landlord claimed to have received only a single lease payment of $100 since 1796, and that from a neighbor.[1]

Poultney proffered greater opportunities for ambitious newlyweds. It was as much a frontier community when Bill and Lucy moved there as Hampton had been for his parents. Two prominent Vermont families, the Allens and the Ashleys, had purchased land in Poultney in the 1770s, but the violent dispute between New York and New Hampshire claimants and the American Revolution impeded settlement. Political life stabilized after Vermont joined the American union as the fourteenth state in 1791, and the population then boomed. At the end of the century nearly seventeen hundred settlers

1. Wait Robbins to Miller, March 13, 1814, Miller Letters, Jenks Memorial Collection of Adventual Materials, Aurora University, Aurora, Illinois. Like most farmers, Robbins did not keep records assiduously. The family may have made other payments he did not record, or perhaps he was simply trying to get more money out of Miller's estate than was due to him. It is clear, though, that the Millers never owned the family farm, and there is no record of their attempting to purchase it. Historians and genealogists have described payments to Robbins as a mortgage, but Robbins refers to the Millers as renters and to the payment as a lease.

had established homesteads, and a quintessentially New England town took shape around a triangular green pointing south to a covered bridge across roaring falls in the Poultney River that over time provided power to mills, foundries, and factories. On the north side of the green, Ebenezer Smith had built the first frame house in the village. From Connecticut he brought his wife Lucy and three daughters: Lucy Phebe (born just three months later than her future husband), Electa, and Aurilla.[2] It was probably in this house that Lucy and Bill were married.

The couple began generating a large family. In April 1805 their first child and son was born, and he received what by now was the traditional name William. It was perhaps to distinguish him from the other Williams in the family that they gave him a middle name, though only the initial S. (possibly for Smith) has survived. Then in rapid succession came a daughter, Bellona, a second son, Ebenezer Satterlee, and just before Bill went off to war a third son, Langdon. The last child to be born in Poultney was another boy, Robbins. In all Bill and Lucy would have ten children, eight of whom lived to adulthood.[3]

Miller supported his family initially as a farmer; other than that, details of daily life are sketchy at best. In the several versions of his autobiography he rarely mentioned the Smiths despite the obviously central role they played in his life for twelve years. Too, the town's records burned in 1862, destroying evidence of any property he may have owned. Still, there are hints. A tax assessment from 1807 reveals Ebenezer Smith to have been a small property owner (worth $112) paying precisely the average amount of tax that year, $1.12. William Miller claimed $49.50 in property and paid taxes of 49.5 cents. As one would expect of a new family, the Millers were not well off, but they weren't poor, either. Seventy-four property owners listed in the roll (from a total of two hundred and eighty five) paid

2. J. Joslin, B. Frisbie, and F. Ruggles, *A History of the Town of Poultney, Vermont, From its Settlement to the Year 1875, with Family and Biographical Sketches and Incidents* (Poultney, Vt.: J. Joslin, B. Frisbie, F. Ruggles, 1875), 21-24, 51-53. Bill's father spent a week there in October 1800, perhaps for business or politics or a combination of the two. William Miller, Diary, October 14 and 23, 1800.

3. Dorothy Offensend, Miller Genealogy, Washington County Historian's Office, Fort Edward, New York.

lower taxes than they. Clearly, he had no difficulty making a living as a farmer. In his ciphering book he recorded amounts of money he received for unspecified service to two local doctors and others and for sales of corn and rye, and by 1808 he owned and was able to sell a small parcel of land.[4]

But farming was not his passion, and it was not to buy land that he moved to Poultney. The heady mix of family lore, fictional adventures, republican rhetoric, and Baptist preaching created a ferment that could lure a yearning spirit. Its character is discernible in a fascinating document surviving from the months surrounding his wedding. As a founding member of the Fairhaven Debate Society he had opportunity to develop and deliver declamations. Three of them survive in a book of writings he titled "The Book of Fortune." One explored the question, "Do we enjoy the most happiness in the present or in thinking of the future[?]" His answer was unequivocal: regardless of how irrational it might seem, "we receive the most happiness from the anticipation." What Miller was anticipating was clear from the examples he used to bolster his argument. The parent "is looking forward with delight to the time when children shall arrive to manhood, hoping they will be benificial to society, beloved & respected by their Neighbours & a friend to their country." More immediately, the lover (writes the soon-to-be groom) "views the approaching nuptials with an elated countenance and a heart gladned by expectation." Revealing a tendency toward sardonic humor early on, he added, "& as I have heard it observed, [he] takes more comfort in his courtship, by anticipation than he does his whole life afterwards through enjoyment." As we have seen, becoming a husband and a parent followed soon after. Notably, though, the first object of his anticipation was something else: "The statesman is looking forward to promotion he feels happy in contemplating on the various branches of trust he expects to enjoy."[5] Miller was ambitious, and so was Lucy.

4. Sylvester Bliss, *Memoirs of William Miller: Generally Known as a Lecturer on the Prophecies, and the Second Coming of Christ* (Boston: Joshua V. Himes, 1853), 19; "The State Tax . . . 1807," Poultney, Vermont, sewn manuscript, Vermont Historical Society; Deed, William Miller to Uriah Wright, April 4, 1808, Center for Adventist Research, James White Library, Andrews University, Barrien Springs, Michigan.

5. Book of Fortune, unpaginated manuscript attached to the Miller Diary, Vermont Historical Society Barre, Vermont.

It was to locate himself in close proximity to influential people that he chose to live in Poultney. Close indeed. Canvassers for the federal census went door to door, proceeding up and down roads and streets in no prescribed pattern, asking a consistent set of questions of each head of household and consecutively numbering each household visited. In 1810 the census taker in Poultney began the enumeration at the Eagle Hotel at the northeast corner of and across the road from the commons. The second household they visited was Ebenezer Smith's. The Millers' was the twenty-ninth household, five away from Elisha Ashley, son of the town's founder, Thomas, whose house stood across the road from the hotel. Thomas's name does not appear in the 1810 census, suggesting he had died, and Elisha probably inherited the house. This would place the Millers very close to Poultney's physical and political center.[6] That is precisely where they wished to be.

Almost immediately the Millers entered what Hale called "the society of a superior class of men," in politics and temperament akin to his Hampton patrons.[7] The Masonic lodge brought him into contact with them. As a youth he had attended at least one Masonic meeting, probably Aurora Lodge, organized in Hampton in January 1793, but it was in Poultney that Miller became a member, joining the Morning Star Lodge and eventually rising in rank to Grand Master.[8] Most important among his new patrons was Poultney's founder, Thomas Ashley. Related to Ethan Allen, he had been present at the taking of Fort Ticonderoga, and like Fairhaven's Matthew Lyon he created a subscription lending library that Miller began to frequent. A leading Democratic-Republican, Ashley sponsored Miller's growth in political awareness and supported his appointment to local offices. So important was his friendship that years later Miller's son wrote of Ashley, "Father always regarded him as a

6. U.S. Government, Bureau of the Census, Manuscript Census, 1810, Poultney [Rutland County], Vermont, 93-94; Joslin et al., *Poultney,* 51; Apollos Hale says that Miller was Thomas Ashley's neighbor (Bliss, *Memoirs,* 19).

7. Bliss, *Memoirs,* 18, 19.

8. Miller, Diary, May 4, 1798; Bliss, *Memoirs,* 21; Joslin et al., *Poultney,* 157; Everts and Ensign, *History of Washington County, New York* (Philadelphia: Everts and Ensign, 1878), 95. The *Farmer's Library* announced the creation of the Aurora Lodge in Hampton and Poultney on August 9, 1793.

sort of a Father." Indeed, since Miller's step-grandfather was an Ashley, there may have been a family connection. Through Ashley, Miller made other significant political friendships, including Judge Henry Stanley, a town founder and Republican organizer; Timothy Crittenden, a Vermont state legislator; Elisha Ashley, Thomas's son; and Daniel Sprague, a blacksmith and postmaster. All were neighbors and would become his patrons.[9]

No one was a better booster of Miller's ambitions than Lucy. The influence of women often lies hidden in nineteenth-century memoirs, befitting a culture that valued only their private, domestic contributions. Occasionally, though, as with Abigail Adams and Mary Todd Lincoln, their own yearnings and public gifts, exercised on behalf of their husbands, thrust through the fog of contemporary maudlin hagiography to reveal a strong character. Town historians reminiscing in 1875 remembered that early in Poultney's history women were "as enthusiastic and determined [about politics] as the men, and their afternoon and evening visits and quiltings were as exclusively partisan as were the meetings of the rougher sex."[10] So it was with Lucy. In a brief description of her, Apollos Hale revealed much: she was "remarkably endowed, by nature and by her industrial and economical habits to make domestic life highly agreeable, and to favor Mr. Miller's promotion and success in the departments of public life to which he was called to move." She took a "deep interest in his improvement and promotion" and set out to "relieve him as much as possible from all the family cares which might call him away from his books. She felt sure that it would not be lost time on his part, or lost labor on her own part." In everything social Bill and Lucy were partners. "The young folks made his house a place of common resort, to which they gathered to spend their leisure hours; while himself and wife became the central unit which drew them together, and kept all in motion."[11]

These were the kind of young leaders Democratic-Republicans recruited and nurtured, and it did not take long for the Millers to at-

9. Joslin et al., *Poultney,* 28, 46, 203, 343-53; William S. Miller to Himes, April 11, 1850, Miller Letters.

10. Joslin et al., *Poultney,* 74.

11. Bliss, *Memoirs,* 18, 19, 21. Joslin et al. confirm the active participation of women in Poultney's political life.

tract their attention. An adolescent penchant for poetry and scribbling now became the boat on which Miller launched a political career. As we have seen, Miller habitually participated in Fourth of July celebrations, and Poultney's rivaled Hampton's and Fairhaven's. Indeed, there were two, sponsored by each of the political parties, a sign of the general partisan nature of life in the village. Democrats gathered at Judge Thompson's Eagle Tavern, Federalists at Parson's Hotel on the opposite corner. "If a dance was gotten up (and there were many in those days), each was known as a Federal or Democratic Ball, and if federal was held at Parsons Hotel; if democratic, at Judge Thompson's." Many people would patronize "only stores, mill-owners, mechanics and professional men of their own party." Politics even determined church affiliation. Congregationalists were Federalists "with one exception," and Baptists were Democrats "with one exception, also." July Fourth was a similarly partisan occasion: "[T]he federalists would celebrate it by themselves, and the democrats by themselves, and if they could spike each other's cannon, steal each other's rum, or do other like mischief, the one to the other, it seemed to be regarded as legitimate and proper, at least, among the younger and more zealous partisans."[12]

It was on these turbulent waters that Miller undertook his maiden political voyage. As the story goes, while hoeing corn one day late in June (probably soon after his arrival in Poultney), words to a poem about American independence came to him. He set them to the meter of the popular tune "Delight," learned undoubtedly in singing school, and wrote out the poem. Someone (perhaps Lucy) must have encouraged him to publicize it, because "he was willing to have his piece seen and used," but only anonymously. Thomas Ashley was grand marshal for the village's celebration, at least the Democratic Party portion, so Miller "took the manuscript, and walked as usual" to his nearby house. Rather than hand it to him personally and thus reveal himself as its author, Miller reached through an open window in the squire's study and placed it near his desk. Ashley read the poem and liked it so well he had copies handwritten for distribution at the festivities. Everyone wondered who the author might be; one of Ashley's friends suggesting sarcastically

12. Joslin et al., *Poultney,* 74.

that an angel in heaven must have delivered it. Baptist Elder Clark Kendrick was helping to distribute copies, and Miller's visible embarrassment when Kendrick handed him a copy gave him away. The revelers sang the song, and the popular response was enthusiastic. "The pious and patriotic emotions of the aged were revived; the ardent responses of the young to these parental emotions found expression in the new hymn; and nothing more was needed, to make its author the popular favorite." The event "secured to him a wide circle of friends, and opened the way for his promotion to office and honor."[13]

As romantic as the story sounds, it is probably true. Written versions of the poem did not survive, but it lingered in family memory sufficiently that one of Miller's sisters could recite several verses of it for Apollos Hale nearly fifty years later. "Our Independence dear," went the first stanza, "Bought with the price of blood,/ Let us receive with care,/ And trust our Maker, God. For he's the tower/ To which we fly;/ His grace is nigh/ In every hour!" That Kendrick should have found Miller out is also likely. Ebenezer Smith was a Baptist, renting a pew at the rear of the meetinghouse the congregation built in the center of the commons just before Miller arrived.[14] William did not become a member of the church, but he undoubtedly attended from time to time, sitting with his in-laws. Kendrick, the congregation's first preacher, certainly knew Miller's preacher grandfather Phelps and uncle Elihu Miller and perhaps Miller's family. He already "had taken a warm interest in Mr. Miller." The poem's pious sentiments would have pleased him, and the time would come when Kendrick would play a significant role in claiming the young man for Jesus.[15]

13. Joslin et al., *Poultney,* 19-20.

14. Mounted on the wall of the church is a sketch of pew renters that G. Ross prepared based on the "First Public Venue" contained in church records that has since disappeared. Smith shared the pew and its purchase price, $105, with two other families.

15. Joslin et al., *Poultney,* 20-21. The Baptist church was founded in 1787 but, with an open communion plan, remained united with the Congregationalists until 1802. That year they separated, politics as much as theology perhaps driving the decision, and Clark Kendrick became the Baptists' first pastor. David Benedict, *A General History of the Baptist Denomination in America and Other Parts of the World* (New York: Sheldon, Lamport, and Blakeman, 1855), 489-90.

Political office followed public acclaim. Although the date is unknown, Miller received an appointment as constable, executing warrants and orders issued by justices of the peace and sheriffs, and in 1809 he became a county sheriff. In each case Miller received fees assessed to defendants, and the combination of revenues from farming and public service placed him in "easy circumstances." He reportedly "kept two horses, one of which he drove, while the other was kept up to rest, week by week, alternately."[16] Advancement was a family affair. In 1805 Hampton town supervisors arranged an appointment of the elder Miller as pound master. Unfenced fields allowed pigs, sheep, and cattle to roam free, damaging property and disrupting travel on the roads. The pound keeper's job was to round up strays, impound them in his barn, notify their owners, and assess fees for any damages they had created and for the costs of impoundment. Two years later and again in 1810 he served as an overseer of highways, ascribing days of labor on the public roads and bridges to males in his road district and making sure they fulfilled their obligation.[17] Local appointments were patronage plums, and likely the same political network benefitted both Millers.

Hagiographers have painted for young Miller a positive political personality. Republican virtue required humility, selflessness, and civility, all qualities Hale, Bliss, and subsequent biographers have claimed for Miller. His public service thus came as a response to the people's call rather than a quest for self-promotion. Like Washington, he became the embodiment of the Roman general Cincinnatus, who left his plow in the field to help defend Rome and then, after achieving victory, returned to his farm, rejecting personal acclaim and power. The biographers also make much of Miller's bipartisanship. As Democratic-Republican constable and sheriff he maintained good relations with the Federalist attorney in town, who re-

16. Bliss, *Memoirs,* 22-23. Miller kept a blot book or log with copies of orders received and executed from 1809 to 1811, housed in the Jenks Collection.

17. Clarence H. Holden, Whitehall, New York, Scrapbooks, 21:121, and 7:188; 7:160, 178, New York State Library and Archives, Albany, New York. Holden included Hampton information in these notebooks. The boundaries of road district 24, of which William II served as overseer, included his property and that of his brother, Elihu Miller (7:176, 182-83).

portedly called Miller "the only honest democrat he knew." Democrats and Federalists served as bondsmen for his appointment as sheriff, evidence that he "enjoyed, in a remarkable degree, the confidence of both the political parties of the day."[18] Given the aggressive political climate, this was quite a feat.

To an extent the portrayal was self-serving, Adventists defending their leader from condemnation in their own day. A humble Miller would not have been guilty of the rank quest for notoriety with which anti-Millerite detractors charged him, and a man who could earn the respect of political enemies in the party wars of the early century could not be guilty of seeking to divide churches, communities, and families. He might almost serve as a witness to brotherly love. In the 1850s, as the nation was splintering over sectional issues, unifying personalities were rare and to be prized. The same year Bliss published Miller's memoirs, 1853, Ann Pamela Cunningham of South Carolina launched a public campaign to purchase and restore Mount Vernon as a shrine to George Washington and to national unity.

But the portrait the biographers paint is realistic. In the libraries of Matthew Lyon and Thomas Ashley, Miller encountered the writings of Enlightenment philosophers — Voltaire, Hume, Ethan Allen, Thomas Paine — and absorbed from them an idealized vision of human character. Reason can govern passions, a concern for the common well-being can curb selfishness, and fraternalism can overrule ambition. Miller was trying to demonstrate these values — humility, self-effacement, consensus. One should serve without seeking acclaim or reward. So in his speeches to the debate society, Miller showed proper deference. "Although I feel myself inadequate to the task, yet I will endeavour to surmount all difficulties and give the Society a short dissertation . . ."; "If I have said any thing amiss I wish the Gentlemen to correct me, I did not expect to teach, or instruct, but to show my simple opinion."[19] Similarly, reason taught that "the practical patriotism of men did not depend so much on the party name they took as on their common sense and integrity. He knew there were bad men enough in each party to ruin the country

18. Bliss, *Memoirs,* 22-23.

19. Miller, Book of Fortune, speech on anticipation, speech on calumny, n.p.

and good men enough in the same parties to promote the public prosperity to the best of their ability."[20]

At a deeper level self-effacement resulted from contrary tendencies in Miller's developing identity. He was clearly ambitious, but he could not appear to be eager for acclaim. He boldly moved away from hearth and home to seek his fortune in a new town, but he reluctantly took public steps to get noticed, a trait that would become more pronounced with age. Human character was capable of reason, but it had a dark side that promoted corruption. The histories and treatises he read from enlightened philosophers taught him that virtue was a rare commodity. "The more I read the more dreadfully corrupt did the character of man appear. I could discern no bright spot in the history of the past. Those conquerors of the world, and heroes of history, were apparently but demons in human form. All the sorrow, suffering, and misery in the world, seemed to be increased in proportion to the power they obtained over their fellows. I began to feel very distrustful of all men." He confided darkly to his arithmetic book, "Friendship and Death remains to mortals here."[21]

Miller was already a skeptic when he married. He preferred anticipation, as he told his debate society, because the future was the only refuge from a dismal present. He knew it was unreasonable to look forward when the present is "all anxiety & care — Disapointments & vexations . . . there is no place in life but what trouble is present, except in thinking of the future." Hope alone allows us mentally to escape to a better tomorrow. "As the proverb says, 'Hope keeps the heart whole.'" The world was becoming a dark and dangerous place, and in more ways than one he sought refuge from its troubles. At the end of his arithmetic book he penned these lines, probably just before getting married:

if all the cares of life conspire,
our head confuse & mudy
To your convienent room retire
Improve your privat study

20. Bliss, *Memoirs*, 22.

21. Bliss, *Memoirs*, 23; William Miller, School Book with Problems, 1798-1804, William Miller Farm [Adventist Heritage Ministry], Hampton, New York.

Then shut you[r] door against all nois
And in your little chamber
you shall possess [celestial] joys
freed from all kind of danger.
for when you are from cares retired
Your Mind both shrill [sharp?] and clear
And with [celestial] joys are fired
no trouble can come near.[22]

The written record reveals no obvious source of trouble for Miller, but there are hints of real tension in the young man's life. In a second speech to the debate society, Miller opined on the destructive effects of gossip on public reputation. Calumny was a "heidious monster, that walks unseen through every country preying upon the characters of men in every station of life like a canker worm destroying the vegetables of Nature." No matter how good a man might be, "calumny is shure to hold somethings up to view, to show that he might have been better, his charity which springs from the best motives is soon talked about; as the offspring of mean selfishness and concealed vice, his bashfull modesty is noted as conspi[cuous] guilt, & his feeble constitution is pointed at as the reward of intemperance." He issued a pointed warning for "the members composing this Society. Beware my friends of hearing any member calumniated, as we have formed ourselves into a body let us protect each member from Injuries he may receive . . . let us try to exterminate every vice that is apt to lay hold of the human mind, such, in particular as prejudice, envy, & deceit."[23]

On his mind was the scandalous, even scatological, nature of political journalism that had scoured the reputations of George Washington and Thomas Jefferson. He could also have mentioned the (to Jeffersonians) unconstitutional jailing of the family's friend Matthew Lyon. But the personal tone of his comments suggests difficulties closer to home. As we have seen, Miller's father had been publicly associated with electoral scandal, and his retirement from the militia seems to have happened in the midst of controversy. Grand-

22. Miller, School Book.
23. Miller, Book of Fortune.

father Elnathan Phelps was a victim of public censure as well. One of the first Baptist preachers in Vermont, he with ten other settlers in Orwell created a Baptist church there in 1787, was ordained its pastor, within a year had built a meetinghouse, and so prospered from a revival in 1790 that they could count over 140 members that year, making it one of the largest congregations in the nascent Vermont Association.[24] Only twenty miles from Hampton, proximity allowed Phelps to help found a congregation and frequently serve the Baptists there as well.

But disaster followed in the wake of revival. In 1791 the congregation brought charges against Phelps and excluded him. He had preached "the sentiment that husbands, or wives, have a right (in certain cases) to put away their companions and marry to others, without any evidence or even suspicions of their former companions having defiled the marriage bed by acts of unchastity with others: and receiving persons that have so done, as clean members in the church." He had also justified a man "putting away an unbelieving wife, and *vice versa,* if they have no other cause, than merely because they are *infidels.* And on the contrary, that they have no gospel right to put away their companions (in case they are believers) though they commit acts of lewdness and unchastity with others, (or what we call adultery.)" For this the congregation removed Phelps as pastor and warned churches in the association "to beware of *him,* and not receive *him* till *he* shall have renounced the above sentiments in a public manner." Regardless of their actions, Phelps remained in Orwell and united with seventeen others who had withdrawn from the congregation to form a separate church not affiliated with the association. By the time Miller paid an extended visit to his grandfather in the spring of 1799 a reconciliation of sorts had been achieved,[25] but he could not have avoided the climate of hostility and hurt feelings during Phelps's frequent preaching stops at their home.

The situation must have aggravated an already festering sore in

24. Benedict, *Baptist Denomination,* 485; Henry Crocker, *History of the Baptists in Vermont* (Bellows Falls, Vt.: P. H. Gobie Press, 1931), 133.

25. *Minutes of the Vermont [Baptist] Association, 1792,* 6-7; Crocker, *Baptists in Vermont,* 133.

Miller's mind. While secular poems and scribblings dot the pages of his manuscripts, there were enough references to Jesus to remind us of his pious upbringing at Paulina's hand. The line "Great are thy mercies Lord and still will they endure" appears in his arithmetic book directly below "Wisdom and virtue and humility are inseperable." But he was beginning to doubt religion's efficacy. He had failed to be good and to sacrifice to earn God's love, and his Calvinist heritage indicated dire consequences. His grandfather's experience indicated the limits of Christian community. Perhaps human nature was as hopelessly corrupt as he preached. One of Miller's diary poems hints at inner turmoil: "JESUS! And Shall it ever be/ A Mortal man ashamed of thee!/ Asham'd of thee whom angels/ prais, whose glory Shines/ Through endless days./ asham'd of Jesus Sooner far,/ Let evening blush to own a Star." Lines ascribed to Miller in 1803 reveal a certain angst:

> Come blest religion, with thy angel's face,
> Dispel this gloom, and brighten all the place;
> Drive this destructive passion from my breast;
> Compose my sorrows, and restore my rest;
> Show me the path that Christian heroes trod,
> Wean me from earth, and raise my soul to God![26]

Confusion, even melancholia, was not uncommon among pious youth. What deepened Miller's anxiety was long-standing cultural tension in his family between the political radicalism of the Millers on the one hand and the Calvinist piety of the Phelpses on the other hand. He was being forced to choose between religion and reason, his heart and his head, and, though he never phrased the conflict in these terms, ultimately between his mother and his father.

The senior William was not a religious man. As Hale put it, "the

26. Miller, Diary, December 1, 1799; Bliss, *Memoirs,* 27. A manuscript version of the poem appears in the folder "Poems and Acrostics," Jenks Collection. It is dated 1847, but the handwriting suggests it was written much earlier than that. Miller always used quotation marks when copying someone else's writing, so it is not difficult to tell from this, as well as from the quality of writing, which pieces came from his pen. The manuscript of this poem has not survived, but the handwriting is superior to pieces he penned in these later years.

father yielded, at least, his assent and respect to that name [Jesus] which had won the heart and added to the graces of [Paulina]."[27] With a preacher brother living close by and father-in-law Phelps only twenty miles away, it was convenient for William II to let the Baptists use his house for services, making it an unofficial meeting-house for the congregation. But his religious proclivities probably veered toward those of his political associates. Matthew Lyon, David Ashley, Ethan Allen, and other Jeffersonians were skeptics about revealed religion. Rational philosophy required empirical verification for belief and action; notions lacking it passed for rank superstition. A liberated mind was unshackled not only from myths but from the institutions that promulgated them to promote their own power. So rationalism was both anti-theological and hostile to ecclesiastical authority. In each case it contradicted the foundations of revealed religion that required faith (the "evidence of things unseen") and maintained itself through authoritarian churches with ordained clergy.

One man in particular, Thomas Paine, earned the condemnation of theists in general and Calvinists in particular. Applauded for his 1776 pamphlet *Common Sense,* which helped patriots define their cause as a fight for independence, his 1794 attack on revealed religion and "priestcraft," *The Age of Reason,* earned him condemnation as a "lilly-livered rogue," "a drunken atheist," and a "detested reptile."[28] No wonder. Of the Bible he wrote: "Whenever we read the obscene stories, the voluptuous debaucheries, the cruel and torturous executions, the unrelenting vindictiveness, with which more than half the Bible is filled, it would be more consistent that we called it the work of a demon, than the word of God. It is a history of wickedness, that has served to corrupt and brutalize mankind; and, for my part, I sincerely detest it, as I detest everything that is cruel."[29] Ethan Allen used similarly inflammatory rhetoric, while Lyon and other rationalists expressed the same ideas in more palatable terms. But they all shared a preference for rational over re-

27. Bliss, *Memoirs,* 5.

28. Quoted in Kerry S. Walters, *The American Deists: Voices of Reason and Dissent in the Early Republic* (Lawrence: University of Kansas Press, 1992), 209.

29. Thomas Paine, *Age of Reason: Being an Investigation of True and Fabulous Theology* (reprinted Cutchogue, N.Y.: Buccaneer Books, 1976), 18-19.

vealed truth. It was this kind of literature that Bill encountered in Lyon's personal library.

The extent to which the elder Miller absorbed any of these attitudes is unknown; there is no evidence of his being a deep thinker in any sense. But he certainly entertained rationalism and revelation under his roof. The last Sunday in September 1799, Elnathan Phelps preached and baptized in their house. A week later the Millers welcomed Matthew Lyon as their guest.[30] One can only wonder about the mixture of feelings young William must have experienced, the conversations between father and mother, parents and grandfather, son and parents. Did Paulina worry about Lyon's religious influence on Bill, caution him, exhort him to faithfulness? She had cause to worry. Already, the evidence suggests, rationalism was providing the medium for his spirituality. In one of his speeches before the debating society, "An Address on Self Love," Miller advised as an antidote to pride's corrosive effect on character the realization that "we are descended from the same parrent, protected by the same Being." While piety prescribed humility by contemplating the graceful action of God, Miller chose to teach the same lesson in rational terms. "We are fed & clothed by the same bountifull Benefactor, we are upheld by the same hand of providence as our neighbours," for all we have "are the gifts of our Creator."[31] No mention here of the Bible's God; Miller's concept of the divine would have pleased Thomas Jefferson.

If rationalism and piety were incompatible, he would have to choose not only between systems of authority but perhaps also among family members. Perhaps this was the tension he sought to escape by fleeing to his "convenient room," freed from "all kind of danger." Moving to Poultney was another way of escaping. Intentionally or otherwise, when he crossed the river to be with his wife's family and friends, he made his decision. The libraries he frequented there put him in touch with an even wider range of Enlightenment writing, and his new associates were "deeply affected with sceptical principles and deistical theories." The town's historians

30. Miller, Diary, September 29 and October 6-10, 1799.

31. The manuscript, included in the Jenks Collection, is undated but is written on the same quality of paper and with the same style of writing and spelling as draft speeches included in his Book of Fortune. So it almost certainly dates from before Miller's marriage in 1803.

ascribed the influence to the Allens, but, regardless, they confirmed that "for nearly half a century after the first settlement, [Poultney] was infidel in its character" and that deism "prevailed in this part of the town . . . years after the Allens and the elder Ashleys were in the graves." Chief among them was Miller's principal patron, Thomas Ashley, and the members of the Library Association. So offensive was the association's infidel influence to Baptist pastor Clark Kendrick that he joined it so he could buy up the offending "old books" and burn them — but not before Miller absorbed as much of the material as he wanted. Within a year after moving to the town, Miller proclaimed himself to be a deist.[32]

Deism comprehended a variety of philosophies, theologies, political cultures, and personal values, so Miller's memoirist was right to ask the question: what did it mean for *Miller* to have been a deist? At its outset deism was a system of ideas circulating among British and French intellectuals at the turn of the eighteenth century. God was, if anything at all, a creator who allowed the universe to operate through the operation of natural law — a *prima causa* and *deus obsconditus* but not a *prima mobile.* Leaves fall to the ground because the force of gravity compels them, not because the finger of God pushes them. Colonials encountered deism as students in Scottish universities, particularly Edinburgh and Glasgow, and through deists' many publications. On this side of the ocean Calvinism and the rising tide of intellectual egalitarianism inhibited its growth, making it a somewhat elitist perspective of well-read provincial leaders like Benjamin Franklin and Thomas Jefferson, who were so averse to dogmatism that they rejected even the label *deist.* Others systematized their views more formally. Elihu Palmer and Philip Freneau held to well-formulated naturalist theologies that eventually would contribute to the rise of Unitarianism. Ethan Allen and Tom Paine more readily absorbed the radical European anti-clericalism that attracted public notice, but they could not rally much popular adherence.

None of this describes Miller. He was not a systematic thinker. He might write an occasional rationalist maxim and allude to na-

32. Bliss, *Memoirs,* 24; Joslin et al., *Poultney,* 31, 36. Apollos Hale dates Miller's declaration to 1804, based on his statement that he was a deist for twelve years and experienced a conversion in 1816 (Bliss, *Memoirs,* 25).

ture's beauty in his youthful poems, but he left behind no philosophical discourse about nature, natural law, or the sources of human character. The only political writing we have from him is a large fragment of a speech to the debate society defending the purchase of Louisiana. No arguments here for the rights of humanity or natural blessings from an augmented frontier. Miller's considerations were entirely practical: preventing a war with France for control of the Mississippi, cementing national unity by securing navigation rights for the southern states, adding at low cost territory that would produce enormous revenues for the national treasury.[33] Nor did he embrace rationalism's optimistic assumptions of human nature — its reasonableness, capacity for self-regulation, and ability to sacrifice for the common well-being.

Rather, Miller's deism flowed, first, from practical needs rather than from intellectual conclusions. From deism, as from piety, he sought returns — assurance, understanding, predictability, and a measure of control over himself and the world around him. This helps to explain a fascination with astrology that was evident in the months surrounding his marriage. Miller filled the pages of his Book of Fortune with prognostications based on calendric and astronomical considerations. If Christmas falls on a Sunday, "then shall the winter be moderate and the spring seasonable," and "he that is born that Day shall be fortunate, and shall thrive in all that he undertakes." The year he and Lucy were born, 1782, Christmas fell on a Wednesday, suggesting that both of them would be "short lived and of a sickly constitution." Similar forecasts follow for the other days of the week. A chart noted evil days of the month, and he copied descriptions of the various astrological houses and nine of the twelve zodiacal signs (he didn't quite make it to his and Lucy's, Aquarius and Pisces). Many in the eighteenth century, religious and secular, dabbled in divination, and in the nineteenth century, as a quality of what one scholar has called the "village enlightenment," its pseudo-empiricism attracted as much practical as mystical interest.[34] For Miller, astrology abetted the same curiosity that sent him

33. Miller, Book of Fortune.

34. See particularly Mark A. Noll, *America's God: From Jonathan Edwards to Abraham Lincoln* (Oxford and New York: Oxford University Press, 2002), 143-45; Walters,

looking for a strange cow and would much later inspire him to visit phrenologists.

More immediately and personally, deism provided Miller with a rhetoric for expressing his frustration with revealed religion. The word *deist,* like the word *pagan* today, had a generic connotation, more descriptive than explanatory. In this sense a deist was a rebel who knew better what to reject than what to accept. This best describes Miller. He was not anti-theistic, but he had come to doubt the reasonableness of Scripture and the authority on which it rested. As he put it, "While I was a Deist, I believed in a God, but I could not, as I thought, believe the *Bible* was the *word of God.*" With its "many contradictions and inconsistencies," the Bible seemed to be "a work of designing men, whose object was to enslave the mind of man; operate on their hopes and fears, with a view to aggrandize themselves." They did this by teaching that the meaning of Scripture was "so dark and intricate that no man could understand it," thereby monopolizing its power and making of religion "a system of *craft,* rather than of *truth* . . . more like the oracles of heathen gods, than like the wisdom of the just and righteous God." Trying to please such an arbitrary deity was frustrating, as he had discovered. Would a loving God "give us the Scriptures to teach us the way of eternal life, and at the same time clothe them in a mantle of mysticism, so that no man could understand them! Reveal his will, which we cannot understand, and then punish us for disobedience! How can such a being be called either wise or good?"[35] Away from the "less cultivated family at Low Hampton,"[36] surrounded by a circle of like-minded friends, Miller was able to vent his spleen.

And vent he did. He now attacked not only the religion that had tormented him but those who purveyed it. The weapon he chose was a sardonic, cutting wit. Again ironically, he undoubtedly honed a natural tendency to sarcasm through the scathing political gossip

---

American Deists; and Craig James Hazen, *The Village Enlightenment in America: Popular Religion and Science in the Nineteenth Century* (Urbana and Chicago: University of Illinois Press, 2000).

35. Joshua V. Himes, *Views of the Prophecies and Prophetic Chronology, Selected From Manuscripts of William Miller With a Memoir of His Life* (Boston: Joshua V. Himes, 1842), 9.

36. Bliss, *Memoirs,* 27.

and calumny he had come to hate. An early example of his talent for sarcastic diatribe exists in a letter he wrote and copied in his arithmetic book to one Horace Old. On June 29, the day Bill and Lucy married, Old created an incident of some sort, undoubtedly at the wedding or the festivities following it. Miller wrote him three days later to "congratulate" him on his "brave courage and cool behaviour, while first in the rear & your agility and swiftness, in retreating from the enemy when in the front, did so much attract my notice that I could not help wondering at the slaughter you would have made had you an army of liliputians to encounter[;] truly your victorious arm would have mowed down thousands while you had waded in blood to the souls [sic] of your feet." After warming up, Miller advanced. "May every revolving year, unfold to you on [the anniversary of] that day an opportunity for you to display your courage, your manners, and genteel behaviour towards strangers. You have now no doubt, Sir, raised your character to a most sublime height. Long will your famous deed of the 29 of June be remembered[,] your prattling children long will tell the shamefull story to their listening hearers how their forefather rob[b]ed them of their honour." Details of the incident are unknown. It's possible Old had been a competing suitor for Lucy's hand; Miller comments that his behavior "disturbed the repose of your sick Lady," probably referring to Lucy and her reaction to the disturbance.[37] Of note here is Miller's tendency to condemn and belittle with hyperbolic false praise and caricature, a talent he would often exercise in his various careers.

He now turned these weapons on his family. To impress his new friends and patrons, Miller demonstrated his abandonment of religion "by performing for their sport, the devotions of the worship to which he had been accustomed, and by mimicking the devotional peculiarities of some of his own family relatives." Principal targets were his preacher uncle Elihu Miller and grandfather Elnathan Phelps. There is no record of Miller's visiting his Hampton family, but they visited him in Poultney. He "received them with affection," Hale says, but behind their back "he was in the habit of imitating, with the most ludicrous gravity, their words, tones of voice, gestures, fervency, and even the grief they might manifest for such as himself,

37. Miller, School Book.

to afford a kind of entertainment for his sceptical associates, which they seemed to enjoy with a particular relish." Private performance it may have been, but some of his sisters witnessed it, and "his Mother knew of it, and it was as the bitterness of death to her."[38] There is no mention of a response from his father. Clearly he had chosen the Smiths over the Millers, and it was causing grief and tension between the two families.

As a youth Miller had solved philosophical and emotional distress by moving away from Hampton to Poultney. Now, as a man, he moved again, this time from politics to the military. By the end of Jefferson's administration in 1809, Vermont needed to bolster its militia. Relations with Great Britain had been strained for years over their impressing Americans into the British navy, occupying forts on American territory, and fomenting Indian attacks on the northwest frontier. They counter-charged that the United States was harboring British deserters in its navy and had failed to live up to treaty obligations to reimburse Loyalists for property confiscated from them during the Revolution. In the seemingly never-ending Napoleonic wars between Britain and France, Jefferson promulgated a policy of strict neutrality, and in response both nations attacked American ships trading with the other side. War loomed with both nations, so to prevent further provocations and to force a change in both the British and French policies Jefferson cut off all trade, keeping American ships at home.

This embargo backfired. It failed to affect Europeans' policies but ruined American shippers and commodity traders who had developed thriving markets in Canada. In fact, black market prices for smuggled potash, lumber, and furs were so high that they enriched producers and tradesmen in New York and Vermont. One of the principal smuggling routes was Lake Champlain, an easy water highway leading directly north to Montreal. There a ton of ash brought as much as $4. Trade in contraband grew so profitable that it became a principal economic enterprise in northern New York, the smuggling so flagrant that in April 1808 Jefferson declared the Champlain region to be in a state of rebellion against federal authority. Indeed, participation in the trade throughout the region was

38. Bliss, *Memoirs*, 28-29.

so widespread that federal customs officials did not trust New York militiamen from the northern counties to enforce the law. So in June 1808 they called in Vermont militiamen from Burlington to cross the lake (none from Miller's Rutland County were involved) and a Potash Rebellion ensued, leading to the deaths of several smugglers and militiamen.[39] Democratic-Republicans controlled Vermont, holding the governorship and both houses of the legislature, and Jeffersonian policies were generally popular. But opposition to the embargo and the economic woes it created and hostility to using state militiamen outside Vermont revived the Federalist Party in the Green Mountain State and even re-fired old dreams of seceding and joining Canada as a semi-autonomous province.

Enemies within and without called for a patriotic response, and Miller stepped up to the plate. In July 1810 he accepted a commission as lieutenant in the Vermont militia. His political friends probably arranged the appointment; Governor Jonas Galusha, a Republican, bypassed a noncommissioned officer who was expecting a promotion and gave Miller precedence.[40] How soon after that he resigned as sheriff is not clear, but his blot book ends in 1811. The following year the United States declared war on Britain, relying as it always had on a combined force of regular enlistees and militiamen to do the fighting. The national government required each state to raise a quota of militia units, and it is a sign of the war's popularity in Vermont that it provided more than three times the assigned number. Lieutenant Miller did his part. He organized a company of forty-seven volunteers from Poultney and surrounding towns, including two Phelps cousins from Orwell and some recruits from New York. The men elected him captain, and Governor Galusha responded by commissioning him in that rank.[41] So, like generations of Miller forebears, William was going to war.

39. *Rutland (Vermont) Herald,* May 28, June 11, June 14, July 2, July 23, 1808; on the unreliability of the New York militia see Richard P. Casey, "North Country Nemesis: The Potash Rebellion and the Embargo of 1807-1809," *The New-York Historical Society Quarterly* 64 (January 1980): 45. See also Allan S. Everest, *The War of 1812 in the Champlain Valley* (Syracuse, N.Y.: Syracuse University Press, 1981), 11-15.

40. Bliss, *Memoirs,* 31.

41. Muster Roll, November 16, 1812, Poultney, Vermont, William Miller Farm [Adventist Heritage ministry], Hampton, New York.

In a military life Miller expected to find what pious religion and civic service had failed to reveal, a sign that humanity was not hopelessly corrupt. "I fondly cherished the idea, that I should find one bright spot at least in the human character, as a star of hope: *a love of country* — PATRIOTISM."[42] In this he would be initially disappointed. War camps are not suited to bring out the best in human nature, including his own. Even before fighting commenced, tragedy struck his family repeatedly, augmenting his melancholy with grief and guilt. Ultimately, though, he would find in the experience of war the assurance he craved, not about human nature but about himself. Battle would challenge his courage, force him to confront difficult truths, and finally provoke a crisis of identity. Once again, he would have to choose, and from that crisis there would be no fleeing.

42. Bliss, *Memoirs*, 23-24; Himes, *Views of the Prophecies*, 10.

CHAPTER THREE

How Has He Visited Me in My Nightly Dreams

Miller went to war, he said nearly thirty years after the event, for love of country. There is no reason to doubt him. True, he was ambitious, and military service offered advancement and a leadership role beyond what he had experienced. But nationalism was running high. British infringements of American sovereignty were many, both on land and sea. The Royal Navy was impressing American sailors into the British service and impounding neutral America's trade goods destined for France, with whom England was at war. They had yet to evacuate some forts on American soil nearly thirty years after the Revolution, and westerners blamed them for arousing Native Americans in the Ohio Valley and arming them to attack white settlers. This was, indeed, a "second war for independence."[1]

Even so, his motives were also deeply personal. War offered Miller the chance to test his character and to discover those nobler qualities of human nature that had so far eluded him in his study of history. That going to war would provoke a religious conversion was beyond his imagining. Rather, the spiritual call he heard was coming from generations of frontier heroes and Revolutionary patriots whose sacrifices were the subject of family legend. All men of the

1. The classic history of foreign relations in the early nineteenth century is Charles Anderson Stagg, *Mr. Madison's War: Politics, Diplomacy, and Warfare in the Early American Republic, 1783-1830* (Princeton, N.J.: Princeton University Press, 1983); a recent assessment of the War of 1812 and its impact on American life is C. Edward Skeen, *1816: America Rising* (Lexington: University Press of Kentucky, 2003).

post-Revolutionary generation sensed paternal voices posing the question Francis Scott Key would put into words: "Oh say, does that star spangled banner yet wave o'er the land of the free and the home of the brave?" Put more personally: Have you kept faith with your fathers? Miller forebears beckoned William to demonstrate the same manhood they had shown — to keep faith with them.

Prospects for him were bright. In the military as in civic life, Miller was a natural leader. For several months the state gathered arms and supplies from the national government (never in the amounts promised), and in June 1813 Miller's company marched sixty miles north along the eastern shore of Lake Champlain to join forces gathering in Burlington in response to a British invasion rumored to be impending. On arriving, he received a very different set of orders. The United States Army, ill prepared for war, was building a corps of officers by raiding state militias of experienced and promising men. Since Governor Galusha was a friend of the Madison administration and a supporter of the war (unlike most other New England governors), he gladly cooperated, and Miller found himself transferred from the Vermont militia to the United States army with the rank of lieutenant. He was to be a regional recruiter in and around Poultney and Rutland County, a job he performed intermittently until he retired from the military in 1815.[2]

Initially life was comfortable. He was stationed in his hometown, though he traveled frequently. As an officer he had the services of an enlisted man as a "waiter" or body servant, and he was promised reimbursement for equipment, clothing, lodging, firewood, and shipment of personal belongings from one posting to another. By locating him close to home, the army was taking advantage of his local popularity and political connections, all of which seemed to pay off initially. Physical requirements of a recruit were minimal. He could be anywhere from sixteen to forty-five years old, but even a minor could enlist as a musician if a responsible adult approved. Other than being "free from sore legs, scurvy, scaled head, ruptures and other infirmities," there were no standards.[3]

2. Sylvester Bliss, *Memoirs of William Miller: Generally Known as a Lecturer on the Prophecies, and the Second Coming of Christ* (Boston: Joshua V. Himes, 1853), 32-35.

3. *Rutland (Vermont) Herald,* July 12, 1812 and February 18, 1813.

The United States offered a premium of $16 and 160 acres of land to any man who enlisted and joined a regiment, along with $15 of advance pay and suits of summer and winter clothing, and Vermont added further inducements. Several receipts for bounty money Miller distributed suggest that early on he had little difficulty finding takers, and in January that year he received promotion to the rank of captain.[4]

But he was bored and morose. Pay came late, and recruitments slacked; in April 1814 he had signed up fifteen men but did not "expect many more." Opposition to Galusha's ordering Vermont militiamen to fight outside the state created a political backlash that resulted in Vermonters' electing an anti-war Federalist, Martin Chittenden, as governor that fall. An American invasion of Canada had backfired. Expecting Canadians to fight for independence from Britain as they had, American forces instead found themselves trapped, captured, and defeated. The future looked grim. Miller wrote to "Robins," an old friend serving on a Lake Champlain gunboat, that a "dark & evil cloud on the political horizon" was passing before his eyes, adding, "I could see nothing but defeat, disgrace, and anihilation of our government." Naval officers were skilled and committed, but he could not say the same for the army.

> Oh! Robins could I be as certain of conquering the land forces[,] could I see that buisy industry, bravery and skill in our commanders as we do amoung our naval heros[,] could I believe our government was determined on the taking of the Canadas[,] that unanimity and Patriotism amoung our citizens which is necessary to reap advantages from our successes — then should I be satisfied

4. The original orders and receipts for expenditures to be reimbursed can be found in the Military Records, William Miller Papers, Vermont Historical Society, Barre, Vermont. The recruiting advertisement appeared in the *Rutland Herald,* July 1, 1812. There is some confusion about the date of the promotion. Hale copied the commission from James Monroe verbatim (Bliss, *Memoirs,* 41-42), but the date he assigned, February 1, 1815, could not have been correct. Herbert T. Johnson in *Roster of Soldiers in the War of 1812-14* dates his promotion January 31, 1814 (St. Albans, Vt.: Messenger Press, 1933), 298. It undoubtedly took time for news of his promotion to circulate; some receipts still refer to him as Lt. Miller as late as April 1814.

> and willingly would I devote the remainder part of my life for the government that I wish to leave uncontaminated by the finger of aristocracy or hand of Monarchy.

War was supposed to reveal the nobler qualities of men, but sacrifice appeared to be futile. Several of the men he had recruited had been killed in Canada "without effecting the object for which they were sent or having the least opportunity of revenging themselv[e]s upon the common foe."[5] And war had become personally frustrating, providing little opportunity to prove himself. During a cross-border foray in the fall of 1813 he had expected finally to see some action, but nothing happened. "[I] cannot tell you of hair-breadth escapes and dismal sights, hdeous yells and war-whoops," he wrote to Lucy, "but so it is. I have seen nothing like an enemy, although I have been into Canada."[6]

So, in hopes yet of proving himself, Miller asked his commanding officer for transfer to a more active duty. In August 1814 he returned to Plattsburgh to command an infantry company preparing once again for an expected British assault. This time rumors proved correct. The British had built a flotilla of gunboats and support vessels on Lake Champlain, including two captured, refitted American ships. The U.S. Navy had responded by constructing its own fleet at Whitehall, located at the southern head of Lake Champlain (since the lake drained north into the St. Lawrence River, this was the upper end). A British land force of slightly over eight thousand veterans of the Napoleonic wars left Canada to join the lake fleet in attacking Plattsburgh, anticipating that by gaining a foothold in the Champlain Valley they could claim it for Canada in peace talks then underway at The Hague.[7] With the New York militia from the northern counties greatly outnumbered, infantry from the U.S. Army and Vermont militia volunteers (Chittenden still refused to order men to cross state borders) rushed to give aid. The swift response created as much chaos as help, but the increased size of the American force

5. Miller to [W. M.] Robins, April 27, 1814, Miller Letters, Vermont Historical Society, Barre, Vt. (hereafter cited as Miller Letters VHS).

6. Miller to Lucy, October 31, 1813, quoted in Bliss, *Memoirs,* 39.

7. Allan S. Everest, *The War of 1812 in the Champlain Valley* (Syracuse, N.Y.: Syracuse University Press, 1981), 166-67.

strengthened defenders' confidence in the face of superior British numbers and expertise.[8]

On September 11, when the British fleet sailed into Plattsburgh harbor, it found an American flotilla prepared to engage. A two-hour battle resulted in an American victory, with the British naval commander dead, his ship captured, and the fleet run aground or so badly damaged that it limped out of the harbor. With the naval battle lost, British land forces immediately retreated north to the border, despite their numerical superiority.[9] Though not a huge battle, it was a significant psychological victory for Americans, coming less than a month after the British had burned Washington.

For Miller the battle was a turning point. Army service had taken him away from family and community for the first time in his life. To stay connected he initiated a correspondence, writing letters to family and friends that not only describe events but, more important, reveal the profile of a personality. He went to war hoping that in sacrifice and courage he would find nobler qualities of human character, and finally he seemed to have succeeded. From Fort Scott on the shore of Lake Champlain, where he was stationed, Miller experienced all the sights, sounds, and smells of the battle. "What a scene!" he wrote to Lucy the following day. "All was dreadful! — nothing but roaring and groaning, for about six or eight hours." Both terrible and sublime were the "roaring of cannon, the bursting of bombs, the whizzing of balls, the popping of small arms, the cracking of timbers, the shrieks of the dying, the groans of the wounded, the commands of the officers, the swearing of soldiers, the smoke, the fire. . . ."[10] Given the rapidity of the British land withdrawal he probably did not have to fire a shot, but a shell bursting "within two feet" wounded three of his men. Victory was heady. From his vantage point he reported to his old friend John Stanley at the critical moment: "It is over, it is done. The British fleet has struck to the American Flagg, great slaughter on both sides — they

8. Skeen, *America Rising,* 116.

9. Everest, *War of 1812,* 179-89.

10. Quoted in Bliss, *Memoirs,* 49-50. This is one of the few letters Hale and Bliss copy that are not extant. They did not always quote letters correctly or completely, but there is no reason to doubt this letter existed or that its contents were essentially as Hale reported.

are in plain view where I am now writing. My God, the sight was majestic, it was noble, it was Grand."[11]

Personal vindication added to patriotic pride. He had doubted his courage and once warned Lucy, "Remember, you will never hear from me, if I am a coward." Now, all his fears were gone. Now it was not to Lucy but again to John Stanley that he wrote in exultation, "I am satisfied that I can fight. I know I am no coward." He intended it as a public proclamation. Perhaps he feared sharing the disgrace of state militiamen, New Yorkers and Vermonters, whose desertions before and during the battle earned sharp rebukes from American commanders. So the Judge must "visit Mr. Loomis [a Poultney tavern-keeper] & drink my health and I will pay the shot." Stanley complied immediately, gathering friends and even some Federalists who gladly drank to the "Honour of Champlain & to your self."[12]

But short-term victory could not allay his years-old, deep-seated melancholy. Friends were familiar with his moods. After venting his spleen against the government and the army to Robins, Miller anticipated his naval friend's response. "I perceive you begin to laugh, and I hear you say, 'Miller you are troubled with *hypocondrical* fits.'" But Robins's letter "served as a nostrum to restore me to my former self — and when I feel the fit returning, I amediately read over your letter and feel my self well." Later he would admit to his mother that he was "too apt to find fault" and knew he appeared "moross and ill natured."[13]

The self-doubt that hounded him transmitted as suspicion of others, and his wife suffered its worst effects. Lucy did not communicate well, and he complained. "I have not heard from you since I came from home. Do write immediately." He received no reply to his excited letter of September 12, the day after the battle, or to a second message in late October. "How unpropitious are these strong winds!

11. Miller to John Stanley, September 11, 1814, Miller Letters, Jenks Memorial Collection of Adventual Materials, Aurora University, Aurora, Illinois [hereafter cited as Miller Letters].

12. Miller to Lucy, September 4, 1814, quoted in Bliss, *Memoirs,* 43; Miller to Stanley, September 11, 1814; John Stanley to Miller, September 21, 1814, Miller Letters, VHS.

13. Miller to Robins, April 27, 1814, Miller Letters VHS; Miller to Paulina Miller, November 15, 1815, Miller Letters.

Or is my Lucy unkind?" She had promised to write him weekly "if she were alive," so he could only imagine the worst. He wrote on the two-month anniversary of the battle, "Have you departed this life, are you gone to the world of spirits. (I almost fancy that while I am writing your unimbodied spirit is hovering around me) or are you so engaged that you could not devote one hour in a week to your humble servant? . . . Shall I ever see my Lucy again? I have often exclaimed 'Ah. No. She would not tell me a falsehood.'"[14]

Dark fears troubled his mind with imagined "engagements" that might be occupying her. Sister-in-law Electa Smith, responding to searching questions he wrote her in November, reassured him. Lucy had been "very glad to hear of your heroism during the battle," and his honor in Poultney shone "as the meridian sun." But his wife looked forward to the time when "your presen[ce] would complete her happiness." William must not think that it was "her gallants" that distracted her from writing, for "she would not take such liberties as this she would think her crime next to a paricide to betray the Inocent." In fact "she smiles with antisapation flattering herself of your returning. likewise you wish to no if she would be glad to sleep with you. I presume she would be your partner in danceing a figure of the nine hair." Lucy would be glad if William would resign and return home, "but that is to your own judgment. you know she is a person that carries two faces under one hat."[15]

This was a mysterious parting statement open to several interpretations — that Lucy was indecisive, that she did not always say what she really thought or felt, or that she was contradictory. Indeed, Lucy's silence is puzzling. It is likely responses from her were at least delayed, given the exigencies of war and terrain that made the transport of mail difficult. That was how Miller biographer Hale explained one letter's late arrival to Miller. But from Miller's correspondence with Electa it is clear he had not heard from Lucy a full two months after his heartfelt battlefield letter to her. The problem was not Lucy's largess but her apparent failure to respond at all. She

14. Miller to Lucy Miller, October 31, 1813, and November 11, 1814, Miller Letters.

15. Electa Smythe [sic] to Miller, November 15, 1814, Miller Letters VHS. While the meaning of dancing a figure of the nine hair is obscure, the phrase is suggestive.

was almost certainly literate, but she may not have been a good writer. Hale used a "large bundle of letters written by [Miller]" to Lucy to help write the *Memoirs,* undoubtedly receiving them from his widow, as he did many other documents. But he did not mention a single letter from her.[16] A collective letter from the family to son George in 1837 includes contributions by his father and his siblings, William S., Lucy Ann, and John, but not a word from Lucy.[17] The fact is that no document clearly from her own hand exists in any Miller collection save, presumably, for an inscription in a Bible she gave to George in 1852.[18] Perhaps she destroyed her letters to William after he died, but it is possible she wrote few, or none.

William might have been more solicitous. Lucy had demonstrated her loving care for him the year before. Stationed at Burlington, in July he contracted camp fever, or typhus, which was sweeping through the army. A local physician established a makeshift hospital in a college dormitory, and Miller became one of his many patients. As soon as she heard of his illness Lucy rushed to Burlington, where she found him convalescing well, but then she fell ill. With William on the mend Lucy "resolved to fly from the infected region" and run the risk of being captured by the British or dying on the road home. Once away from Burlington she recovered her health quickly, but she never forgot the scenes of death, nor the fear she experienced. Now, slightly more than a year later, as the gunboats battled at Plattsburgh, Lucy was nearing the end of another pregnancy, her fifth. This was always a dangerous time for a woman, and knowing that her husband was in harm's way increased Lucy's stress. In fact, she reported decades later that on the day of the battle she had a "presentiment" of disaster, the sensation that a "dark, furious,

16. Bliss, *Memoirs,* 56.

17. William, William S., Lucy Ann, and John Miller to George Miller, February 27–March 7, 1837, William Miller Collection, Center for Adventist Research, James White Library, Andrews University, Berrien Springs, MI [hereafter cited as Miller Letters AndU].

18. William Miller Collection, AndU. Among an assortment of poems and acrostics in the Jenks collection is a song titled "The Sacrifice," and at its conclusion, above a line of musical notation, it bears the initials *L. M.* The script of the verses is William's, so the initials may mean that Lucy wrote the melody. See the folder "Poems and Acrostics."

smothering tornado rushed down on a poor, unsheltered flock of little birds." It made her "nearly frantic with agony" so that her friends "thought she had had a nervous time, or was slightly insane."[19]

But Miller was no more suspicious of his wife than of anyone else. He had come to believe that all humans were hopelessly corrupt, incapable of honest, faithful relationships. He wrote the children, not having heard from their mother, that she must be dead, "and but a little while and your father must follow." So he penned a final testament, passing on as legacy the lessons he had learned. Remember, he said, that "the lives of your parents were short and you know not the hour you will be called for." The world was a cold place, he said, and he wanted them to prepare for the worst. "Meet the frowns of Fortune and learn in your youth to repel the shafts of adversity" and live so that "when you come to die . . . not one reflection pass your mind but that you have lived so as to merit the good will of all good men." Even so, as Miller had discovered, "in this you will find the ingratitude of man." He had "vainly sought the friendship of man, and never could he discover any friendship only where there was a dependence." As an officer he commanded a hundred men "that depend upon me for every comfort" and each one "professes a real love for me." But if he were "a citizen or one of their own rank" he could expect nothing but "common friendship."[20] So it was not just the capacity of others to give him love that Miller doubted, but his capacity to earn it. Thus speaks the man who as a boy long ago decided he would never be good enough to please God. Now death was on his mind, and with it the fear that all chances to prove himself would come to an end.

Death surrounded him. He had seen men killed in battle, prepared their bodies, and buried them, including the body of British Commodore Downie, killed by a cannonball aboard his flagship, the *Confiance,* at Plattsburgh.[21] That battle was not the first occasion for Miller to confront his own mortality; during his first deployment to Burlington in 1813 he fell off the back of a wagon and was knocked unconscious, "laying as if dead for fifteen or twenty minutes." A month later he contracted the typhus that caused Lucy to run to his

19. Bliss, *Memoirs,* 38-39, 48-49.

20. Miller to Lucy, November 11, 1814, Miller Letters.

21. Miller to Lucy, October 28, 1814, Miller Letters; Bliss, *Memoirs,* 53.

side, and in the autumn a sore on his arm so festered that physicians considered amputating the limb. He reportedly prevented it only by threatening the surgeons with his sword.[22]

Though he escaped permanent injury, family and friends did not. In an eighteen-month period, Miller mourned the loss of five close relatives. Two siblings died in close proximity, brother Ira in August 1811 and sister Rhoda the following February. At the end of 1812 the typhus that ravaged American troops at Burlington and struck William raged through the region, claiming a third sibling, sister Anna. Three days later, Miller suffered the sharpest blow of all when his father and namesake succumbed to the disease. The grim news continued: his grandfather Elnathan Phelps was rushing to Pittsfield to help a stricken brother when the disease caught up with him. He collapsed beside the road at Pownal, and although good-hearted townsmen tried to nurse him back to health, he died and was buried next to the local Baptist pastor. It took days for the news to reach Paulina and the family.[23]

The death of so many loved ones, along with the contemplation of his own mortality, caused Miller to reevaluate deism on at least one score. In 1814 his friend Henry Spencer died of camp fever. While he did not react to the loss of family members in letters for two years, the death of this peer prompted long deathbed descriptions to both Lucy and Electa Smith. Clearly his own pain at not hearing from Lucy inspired the discussion, since he ascribed Spencer's demise not to disease so much as to a broken heart, a yearning for "Charlotte" that was not requited.[24] It was also the oc-

22. Miller to Lucy, June 13, 1813, quoted in Bliss, *Memoirs,* 34; Bliss, *Memoirs,* 39.

23. Carolyn R. McCullen and Daniele L. Roberts, *Set in Stone: The Cemeteries of Hampton* (Fair Haven, Vt.: New York Sleeper Books, 2002), 26. Various dates for the elder Miller's death are recorded, but I am using the date inscribed on his tombstone. Likewise, his daughter's name appears variously as Ann, Amia, or Arnia — obviously all differences in transcription. An announcement about the death of Captain Miller and his daughter appeared in the *Rutland (Vermont) Herald* on January 20, 1813, a sign of his relative prominence in the region. A letter from Vera C. Halstead, February 10, 1955, a Phelps descendent, recounting traditional memory of how Elnathan died can be found in file #1125, Vermont Historical Society (VHS), Barre, Vermont.

24. Miller to Lucy, October 28, 1814, quoted in Bliss, *Memoirs,* 54-55; Electa Smith to Miller, November 15, 1814, Miller Letters VHS. Electa refers to Charlotte as

casion, for the first time in writing, for theological rumination. "But a short time," he said to Lucy, "and I shall be no more. It is a solemn thought." What made it solemn was the fear that death was final; his friend Judge Stanley had confirmed that in a conversation in 1812. Like many other rationalists, Stanley believed that death extinguished, or annihilated, human life. Our existence, he said, is like that of a tree "which flourishes for a time, and turns again to earth; and to that of a candle, which burns to nothing." Miller had pondered the idea for some time, but now, with Spencer and so many others dead, he had to reject its comfortless finality. "[C]ould I be sure of one other life," he confided to Lucy, "there would be nothing terrif[ying]; but to go out like an extinguished taper, is insupportable — the thought is doleful." The only option was faith in life after death: "No! rather let me cling to that hope which warrants a never-ending existence; a future spring, where troubles shall cease, and tears find no conveyance; where never-ending spring shall flourish, and love pure as the driven snow, rest[s] in every breast." Do write to me, he again pleaded. "I am troubled."[25]

Once a vehicle for venting frustration with an arbitrary God, deism had itself become arbitrary — cold, comfortless, inconvenient. It explained nothing about eternity and offered nothing in his hour of need. The religion of his youth, on the other hand, posited some assurance of eternal life. Even if salvation's attaining was mysterious and Christianity's God was serendipitous, at least the promise of judgment could hold in check a person's natural inclination to vice. So while passing on aphorisms Miller advised his children to develop a measure of piety as a foundation for a useful life. "[L]ook up to the Supreme Being as the Author of all things," he wrote them. "When you learn his attributes or as much as man is to know you will ever keep in mind that he sees every action of your life, knows every thought and hears every word." Study God's ways, and "in your cooler moments conscience will point to you the road you ought to follow." Perhaps he was reflecting on his own wayward path, devoid of God's guidance, in being more pointed. Don't search "for vain

---

a coquette. Miller recorded Spencer's death in the semi-annual muster roll, August 31–December 31, 1814, Military Records, VHS.

25. Miller to Lucy, October 28, 1814, quoted in Bliss, *Memoirs*, 55.

and empty baubles, it is a more solid pleasure 'to do as you would be done by.'" Don't succumb to adversity "nor be raised up in prosperity for pride is equally as dangerous as cowardice." No matter how fruitless, "endeavor to get the good will of all people for it is better to have the good than the ill will of even a dog."[26]

Obviously some remnant of old Baptist teaching, some echoes of Paulina's and Elnathan's exhorting, could still sway. Now it launched a full-scale barrage. Commanding the attack was Clark Kendrick, Miller's Poultney pastor. As we have seen, he took a direct interest in Miller's spiritual welfare, and intermittent but extended stays at home put Miller in continuing contact with his exhorting. When Miller's militia company first set out from Poultney in 1813, the captain reportedly surprised deist friends by taking Kendrick by the hand and emotionally presenting "his former friend" to the crowd to offer prayers, creating an effect that observers remembered years later as "almost overpowering."[27] Kendrick, too, received a letter from Miller, written the day after the victory at Plattsburgh, marking him with Lucy and Judge Stanley as among the principal people in Miller's life. It was, Kendrick noted, "fraught with sentiments of tenderness, love, and good will towards me, which are [herein] most heartily reciprocated." But it was not until November that he replied, interestingly only ten days after Miller had written his "last will and testament" to Lucy and the children. Kendrick had recently seen a letter from Miller "one evening, in the office," and it may well have been that one,[28] for his comments cannily echoed the advice Miller sent to his children and targeted directly the two issues at the center of Miller's spiritual crisis. His reply has the ring of one striking while the iron was hot.

The first issue for Miller, and the oldest, was personal behavior, the struggle "to be good." As a youth he had meant "to do no wrong, tell no lies, and obey my parents," and, but for the accretion of a more sophisticated language, his sumptuary counsel to the children shows that it remained the standard. It was for Kendrick, too.

26. Bliss, *Memoirs,* 55.

27. Bliss, *Memoirs,* 33-34. The words Hale used to describe Kendrick's comments are similar to the words Kendrick wrote directly to Miller, so Hale may have taken them directly from Kendrick's letter of November 21, 1814.

28. Clark Kendrick to Miller, November 21, 1814, Miller Letters VHS.

"When I heard of the contest at Plattsburgh, I felt distressed for your fate," he wrote. God be thanked that "of his infinite Mercy [he has] preserved you through that tremendous contest." It was not just Miller's physical well-being that concerned Kendrick; he worried about the impact of camp life on Miller's morality, removed from "the peaceful retreats of domestic life, and the privilege of regular Gospel society." It was natural that among soldiers "unprincipled men will be found, such as neither regard the gospel nor the face of the Lord," but he hoped William would not suffer himself to be "polluted, by evil communication."[29] As always, eyes were watching him, whether patriot fathers demanding manhood and sacrifice, frowning Fortune weighing character, or sleepless Jehovah judging behavior.

Examining his life, Miller counted both vices and virtues. While he did not escape camp life unblemished, the experience did not besmirch his character, as Apollos Hale put it, "to a hopeless extent." Before entering the army Miller frequented taverns where local politics was exercised, and in camp "whiskey day" came every three or four days. He seems to have enjoyed wine, and as late as 1845 he accepted a gift of wine from a close friend. But there is no record of his drinking to excess. There is some indication that he smoked or indulged in snuff; again, toward the end of life a beloved compatriot gave him a silver tobacco box. Of course, drinking alcohol and using tobacco were not notorious, as they would become later in the century. Profanity proved a greater problem. It crept into at least one letter, in which he referred to British military leaders as "damned fools," and he confessed that taking the name of the Lord in vain was "a habit I acquired in the service." He also picked up a taste for gambling at cards, a practice he abandoned after returning home.[30]

29. Clark Kendrick to Miller, November 21, 1814, Miller Letters VHS.

30. Miller to Lucy, September 4, 1814, quoted in Bliss, *Memoirs,* 43. In 1845 John G. McMurray, a longtime Millerite from Troy, New York, sent Miller a six-gallon keg of wine as a gift and was annoyed when Miller tried to pay him for it. McMurray to Miller, May 23 and September 2, 1845, Miller Letters. Joshua Vaughan Himes to Miller, November 26, 1846, Joshua V. Himes Papers, Massachusetts Historical Society, Boston, Massachusetts. The quotes are from Miller to Lucy, September 4, 1814, copied in Bliss, *Memoirs,* 43, 61. Hale went to great lengths to excuse his use of the word, attesting to the change in proprieties by the middle of the century.

If personal demeanor alone were the standard, Miller might have judged himself to be very good indeed.

He also could claim to be an honest man; he was what he seemed to be. As a politician he had attracted compliments from Federalists as well as Democratic-Republicans, and the dignity with which his unit buried the British dead at Plattsburgh, particularly Commodore Downie, elicited gratitude from the enemy and from Downie's widow.[31] But his sardonic sense of humor could lead Miller to cruel pranks. Catching a sergeant and some of his men praying in a tent at night, Miller decided to have some fun at their expense, just as he used to ridicule his grandfather's and uncle's piety. Ordering the sergeant to his tent, Captain Miller accused him of gambling, a violation of camp regulations (of which Miller himself was guilty). The man, embarrassed to admit he had been praying, denied the charge but refused to say what they had really been doing. Miller berated him until the man finally "confessed." Surprisingly, Miller took no pleasure from his joke, but was "almost in tears," stricken by "the doubtful course" he had pursued in ridiculing the man.[32] Later he would ascribe his unexpected shame to a budding Christian sensibility. Certainly the incident fit a pattern of events leading to his later conversion, but there was another reason for his pang of conscience: Miller had violated a paternal relationship by betraying the trust a subordinate should enjoy with a commander, much as a son should expect from a father. Authority brings responsibility to model fairness and justice, and violation of that authority discredited leadership. An arbitrary father and officer could no more command respect than an arbitrary God could demand obedience or worship.

Such considerations focused directly on the second source of Miller's depression: his rebellion. As a military officer, Miller was deferential, even obsequious,[33] to his superiors, and he demanded

31. Bliss, *Memoirs,* 53.

32. Bliss, *Memoirs,* 59-60.

33. Miller closed a request to his commanding officer for recruiting funds, "The Colonel will pardon this request I have made of him knowing the confidence of my heart in the soldierly esteem which he has manifested for him and has the honor to be with every sentiment of esteem respect and high consideration dear Colonel your humble and obedient servant. . . ." Miller to Colonel [Elias] Fassett, January 10, 1814,

and received obedience from subordinates. At Plattsburgh he took command of an unruly company of men, forcing him to become a strict disciplinarian. Beginning a letter to Lucy one payday, turmoil in camp interrupted him twice while he went "to still the noise." Drunken clamoring caused him "to punish four or five of them very severely," giving him reason "to believe that they both love and fear me." Picketing was the punishment for one insubordinate soldier; he was made to stand on a narrow stake with his hands stretched and tied to an overhead gallows for an hour.[34] Others received fines for infractions such as selling army blankets, losing weapons, and stealing equipment, while one recruit went to Vermont State Prison for passing counterfeit money. On occasion Captain Miller sent out parties to search out and arrest deserters, and after the battle of Plattsburgh he was present at the hanging of six men.[35]

But he had been a rebel, too, ridiculing his own family and betraying their teaching. Kendrick must have known about this festering wound in Miller's heart, for now he focused directly on it. How good it was to hear, he wrote, that the infidels surrounding him in camp had not corrupted "those moral sentiments, and impressions, which you were early taught by your surviving Mother, and your Fathers, renowned for their piety though they now lie low in the grave. With all that solicitation which the responsibility of my profession and our [Baptist] Society connexion ought to inspire I do most earnestly pray, and exhort you to have their advice, and example in remembrance." The legacy he had received from them Miller must now faithfully pass on. Always remember, wrote Kendrick, that "you are a Husband to an excellent Wife, that you are Father of a number of beautiful children, that you are a citizen whose talents are all appreciated, and how important it is that you should preserve them unimpaired by vice, that

Miller Letters VHS. Even considered as formal address, the rhetoric is excessively fulsome.

34. Miller to Lucy, September 4, 1814, Miller Letters.

35. See Inspection Returns, Military Records, Miller Collection, VHS. Miller described the hanging to Lucy in his letter of October 28, 1814, Miller Letters. For a discussion of military discipline see C. Edward Skeen, *Citizen Soldiers in the War of 1812* (Lexington: University Press of Kentucky, 1999), 47. While mutilation (branding and cropping of limbs) was available to him, there is no evidence that Miller employed any of these punishments.

when God in his Providence shall again direct you to your domestic circle that you return with these unsullied virtues which I hope may ever be invulnerable to the depravity of others."[36]

But how could Miller, having been a disobedient son, hope to be a worthy father? How could he faithfully resume the roles of which Kendrick astutely reminded him by returning to Poultney, a town that had so richly nourished his rebellion? How could he model the behaviors he preached to the children while surrounded by the worldly distractions — fame, reputation, success — that had corrupted him?

The answer was clear: he could not. Once again, he decided to flee, escaping to the one place and the one person best suited to preserve his legacy. In 1815, with hostilities concluding and Miller contemplating retirement from the army, he wrote to his mother for the first time since leaving for war. After causing such deep pain, he struggled to find the words that would restore their relationship. What can I say to my mother, he asked? "[S]hall I tell her that I am well," he wrote, "perhaps that may in some measure, enduce me to write and you to read." He had tried to write often but could not finish a letter. "Alas, I never can think of my mother but the image of my father presents itself to my eyes." The "peculiar state I was in" at the time of his father's death, disrespectful and scornful, "has ever rendered my feelings more poignant, and was to me more distressing. Often, yes Often, have I almost taken my pen in hand to write to my father before I could reflect that my father was no more. how has he visited me in my nightly dreams, how often in [my] imagination have I seen him." He had tried to forget his father and his "former home," but to no avail: "in vain, have I believed that absence and other objects, would blunt my feelings. it is more cutting now than, the first moment I experienced the loss."[37]

His behavior was to blame, to be sure. "I know my conduct generaly has been such to my family, as you disaprove of." But fault rested with the Smiths, too. In fact, he cited their influence as the principal reason for his going astray. "I have had many dificulties to encounter where I now live," he wrote, and he worried that his in-laws would corrupt his children as they had corrupted him. "[Y]ou

36. Kendrick to Miller, November 21, 1814, Miller Letters VHS.

37. Miller to Paulina Miller, May 21, 1815, Miller Letters.

must be sensible that to bring up my family under the partiality of their Parrents and Grand Parrents, would be productive of the greatest evil, their young minds would imbibe feelings that when they come into the world they would, on the first rub in life, loose their spirits and would there after be unfit for society." Just as he had. A youth when first starting out in life "believes all mankind their friend, and esteem them all honest." He wanted his children "to see more of the world, to be aware of the intrigues, and deceptions made use of to decoy the artless and unsuspecting into the snares of vice." In short, he wanted Paulina to be a role model for them, as his father had been his model, leading "in the path of rectitude." So he hoped Paulina would do two things. First, he asked her to visit Lucy and to "transfer as much of the Parential affection as you possibly can from me to [her]" so there may be "a good understanding between you two, the two dearest persons to me on earth." Second, should he "get rid of the Army," he intended to "move on to my farm" in Hampton and place his family under her watchful care. Her "experience in life, will cause you to give Lucy and myself such advice as will be for the happiness of us both."[38]

At last he had discovered the cause of his melancholy — guilt over rejecting his parents and their teaching. And he could locate the twin sources of his treason in the corrosive influence of his in-laws and his own personality. The solution, too, was ready at hand: leave Poultney and the Smiths, return home, and place himself and the family under his mother's tutelage. But his confession and submission are as notable for what Miller did not say. He expressed no desire to return to revealed religion and to the faith that was the bedrock of that maternal wisdom and experience on which he now threw himself. He had sought human nobility in civic virtue and patriotic service and found none, not even in his own courage under fire. In the face of death, deism left him cold and comfortless, and so, apparently, did the Smiths. Rebellion had rendered him unfit to raise his children, so he would return to the womb that bore him, entrusting them all to his mother's teaching and discipline. Elnathan's preaching, Paulina's nurturing, and Kendrick's exhorting had revealed to Miller a foundation that could sustain the build-

38. Miller to Paulina Miller, May 21, 1815, Miller Letters.

ing of a useful and virtuous life. But he could not yet trust that God was either its source or its end. Still, as revivalists would come to understand, conviction of sin is the first stage of conversion, and Miller was well on the road back home, not just to Paulina, not just to Low Hampton, but to God.

According to plan, a month after writing to Paulina, Miller retired from the army.[39] In 1814 he had purchased his father's farm from the landlord and somewhat earlier a fifty-four-acre parcel, probably the adjoining land on the hill to the west overlooking the flat plain on which his father had settled nearly thirty years earlier. Within six months of retiring he had built the house in which he would live and work the rest of his life.[40] Whether he lived in Poultney or Hampton in the meantime is not clear. He and Lucy could have moved in with Paulina, though the accommodations would have been snug. She occupied the house with daughters Anna, Lois, Stella, and Eleanor, and sons George and Solomon, other siblings having died or married. William and Lucy had five children of their own, sons William S., Ebenezer, Langdon, and Robbins (whom the family nicknamed "rifle McDonough" after the hero of the American victory at Plattsburgh), and daughter Bellona. Regardless, the family atmosphere must have been tense. Once-cordial relations with his in-laws obviously had soured, and one can only guess how that affected William's relations with Lucy and Lucy's relations with Paulina. One hint may be a subtle change in the name of their third child, whom they had named for his maternal grandfather. Some time early in his life, perhaps now, Ebenezer Satterlee became Satterlee E., the name he took to his tombstone.[41]

39. Johnson, *Roster,* 298.

40. On the purchase of the elder Miller's farm see Wait Robbins to Miller, March 13, 1814, Miller Letters. Robbins and Miller disputed the payment of back rent, the conversation turning at one point to a possible lawsuit. But the sale seems to have proceeded without difficulty. Washington County, Deeds, James Quinton McFarland to William Miller, February 1, 1814, book AA, page 108. Deeds often went unrecorded in this early settlement period. Hazel Stannard, a Miller descendant in Fairhaven, Vermont, retained an unrecorded deed for Miller's sale of a parcel in 1816 to long-time neighbor Isaiah Inman.

41. A family Bible located in the Miller Chapel, Low Hampton, New York, lists the second son's name as Ebenezer Satterlee, though he always went by Satterlee Ebenezer, and that is the name on his monument in the Poultney cemetery.

True to his word, Miller set out to model his life after his father. Money from his military severance and sale of his Poultney property allowed him to build a commodious house and farmstead. It was a typically Federal-style, two-story structure of clapboard over heavy timbers with a massive central chimney that housed hearths for rooms on both floors. Facing north, a single-story extension off the back of the house hosted the kitchen with its own massive cooking hearth, the remains of which are still visible in the basement.[42] Paulinus Millard, his neighbor immediately to the north, built a house two years later, and his expenditures recorded in a day book illustrate costs that must have been similar to Miller's. Millard's total of $253.45 purchased over 2600 bricks, ten thousand slate shingles, twelve pounds of lead, sawn clapboards, nails, and lime for mortar, adding to the fees of masons, sawyers, and joiners, not to mention five gallons of rum to lighten the labor of neighbors who helped raise the house.[43]

Miller now reentered the local economy of his youth. Self-sufficiency required diversity, and a large English barn, horse barn, "piggery," corn crib, and the remains of what may have been an ash house served all its needs. Millard operated a cider press and a granary at which the Millers processed large quantities of apples and wheat. The family butchered hogs in season. The children now undoubtedly followed in their father's youthful footsteps, their labor cementing bonds of mutual need.[44] Household women churned the cows' milk into butter and worked year-round to keep the family clothed. Men and boys sheared the sheep while women and girls boiled the fleeces, carded the wool, spun it into yarn, and wove it

42. A frontispiece to Bliss's *Memoirs* clearly shows the central chimney plan. After Miller's death in 1849, and probably after Lucy's in 1853, son John, who inherited the farm, remodeled the house in a Greek Revival style, obliterating much of the original plan.

43. Paulinus Millard, Day Book, Del E. Webb Memorial Library, Loma Linda University. The house is illustrated in Everts and Ensign, *History of Washington County, New York* (Philadelphia: Everts and Ensign, 1878), following page 364.

44. Adventist Historic Properties, Inc., "A Preservation Plan for the William Miller Farm, prepared by Crawford & Stearns, Architects and Doell & Doell, Landscape Architects," Syracuse, New York, October 1987; Millard, Day Book. On one occasion Millard pressed seventeen gallons of cider for Miller.

into cloth. There were flax fields for linen, too, the production of which had its own seasonal rhythm. Within ten years improved breeds of sheep and growing textile manufacturing would encourage farmers increasingly to specialize, but for now diversity of production dictated the pattern of life.

Like his father, too, Miller probably intended that Paulina should be principally responsible for inculcating piety in the children even as he became the Baptists' principal patron in Low Hampton. The congregation's history is murky, relying as it does on faulty human memory. Miller recalled that his grandfather Phelps had converted a number of people in Low Hampton, including Paulina, who then created a congregation associated with the Baptist church in Orwell and built a meetinghouse just north of where his new farm would be located. In 1812 an Elisha Miller, supposedly William's uncle, became its pastor. There is no record of the elder Miller's having a brother named Elisha, but in 1816 Elihu Miller, who was indeed his father's brother and a licensed preacher, was serving as pastor.[45] William "became a constant attendant" in the meetinghouse and "contributed liberally to its support." As in his father's day, the Miller farm became "the head-quarters of the denomination on extra as on ordinary occasions." Initially, civic responsibility and an awareness of his social status inspired his leadership. When an ordained or licensed preacher was not present the deacons appointed a layman to read a published sermon that they selected. On those occasions, Miller refused to attend unless "*he* could do the reading," which, under the circumstances, they were happy to allow.[46] All this despite the fact that he was not yet a member of the church and almost certainly was not yet baptized.

Having confessed his sins to Paulina and returned home, he might have expected relief from his melancholy. But it was not so. Despite his military and civic success, Miller was bored, and he felt that "[t]hose things in which I expected to find some solid good,"

45. *Minutes of the Vermont [Baptist] Association.* The Vermont Association did not mention a congregation linked to Orwell's but noted the existence of a Hampton church for the first time in this report. Since Phelps had been disfellowshipped for heresy, the congregation he founded in Hampton was family-based, undoubtedly reflecting his personal theology.

46. Bliss, *Memoirs,* 64.

service to the public and to his country, "had deceived" him. "It appeared to me that there was nothing good on earth. . . . I began to think man was no more than a brute." (Ironically, the Calvinism he condemned would have agreed.) Deism, too, betrayed him, offering no solace when death surrounded him. "Annihilation was a cold and chilling thought; and accountability was sure destruction to all. The heavens were as brass over my head, and the earth as iron under my feet. ETERNITY! *What was it? And death, why was it?*" He tried to reason his way to peace, but to no avail: "The more I thought, the more scattered were my conclusions. I tried to stop thinking; but my thoughts would not be controlled. I was truly wretched; but did not understand *the cause.* I murmured and complained, but knew not of whom. I felt that there was a wrong, but knew not how, or where, to find the right. I mourned, but without hope."[47]

That would change. Continuing depression was but a signpost of a developing conversion, and in September a local revival brought it to fruition. Since the turn of the century, evangelicals had benefitted from periodic religious refreshings, and in 1817 postwar Vermont experienced the second in a trio of such harvests (the others came in 1810 and 1821). Jeffrey Potash has noticed that these were community, not individual, events presaged by a period of congregational "self-conscious reformation" that often produced "'surprising' or 'unexpected' converts," already nominally Christians, to whom revivalists could point as signs of success "in vanquishing the 'infidel tide.'" Particularly notable among the reborn was the presence of young people aged thirteen to twenty-one, the product of converted parents' focusing their attention on their children's spiritual well-being. Conversion was "commonly triggered by a brush with death," and Potash notes particularly the large number of "youth males" whose numbers signaled "a major redirection of the revivalistic focus" not just to youth but to young men.[48] Save for Miller's age, his conversion aptly fits the pattern.

47. Joshua V. Himes, *Views of the Prophecies and Prophetic Chronology, Selected From Manuscripts of William Miller With a Memoir of His Life* (Boston: Joshua V. Himes, 1842), 10-11.

48. P. Jeffrey Potash, *Vermont's Burned-Over District: Patterns of Community Development and Religious Activity, 1762-1850* (New York: Carlson Publishing, Inc., 1991), 140-47.

September 11, 1816, was the second anniversary of the Battle of Plattsburgh, and a regional ball was planned to be held in Fairhaven, Matthew Lyon's former hometown and the scene of Miller's first exposure to deism. As one of the most prominent veterans of that battle, Miller entered into its planning "with all the ardor of a soldier." That evening he and a contingent from Low Hampton crossed the Poultney River expecting a rousing evening of dance and frivolity. The first event, though, was preaching, and the Hampton contingent attended "more from curiosity than from other actuating cause." The selected Scripture was from Zechariah 2:4, "Run! speak to this young man," and the message hit home. Everyone became thoughtful, "incapacitated for any part in the festive arrangements," and the ball was postponed. "The seriousness extended from family to family, and in the several neighborhoods in that vicinity meetings for prayer and praise took the place of mirth and the dance."[49] Repentance (rethinking) had now succeeded conviction.

The following Sunday, the Baptist preacher being absent, the deacons asked Miller to read a prepared homily. If it was coincidental that they chose one "on the importance of Parental Duties," their choice could not have been better targeted. Beginning to read, undoubtedly with Paulina sitting in front of him, Miller was overcome with emotion "with which the entire congregation sympathized," and he was unable to continue. The crisis had come; deism had become "an almost insurmountable difficulty with him,"[50] and with a new set of relations nurturing his growth Miller was ready to flee one more time, now into the arms of a rescuing Lord. "God by his Holy Spirit opened my eyes," he wrote. He was "a Rock in the midst of the ocean of life"; Jesus became "a friend, and my only help"; and the Bible became his lifeboat, "the *perfect rule* of duty . . . the lamp to my feet and light to my path." In it he found "everything revealed that my heart could desire, and a remedy for every disease of the soul." His mind, long pained by doubts and frustrations, now "became settled and satisfied."[51]

As Potash suggests, this conversion was a community, not just

49. Bliss, *Memoirs,* 66.
50. Bliss, *Memoirs,* 66.
51. Himes, *Views,* 11.

an individual, event. Forty people were added to the congregation by baptism that year, including Miller.[52] Like him, they were probably attendants for whom impediments had prevented their joining previously. No matter how communal the reevaluation, though, Miller's conversion was the central event. He was the local surprise, well known both for his skepticism and his sharp wit. Few outside his immediate family witnessed the struggles that produced it or could guess that it bloomed from a residue of piety inculcated in his youth. To all, his was an "unexpected conversion" that justified and verified the others'. Nor could they see the lingering rationalism that would continue to make the noumenal quality of faith troubling for him. All anyone knew was that the lost had been found, and his public conversion could be a potent weapon against infidelity. Now he "immediately erected the family altar," proclaimed the faith "that had been food for his mirth, by connecting himself with the little church that he had despised," and became "an ornament and pillar in the church, and an aid to both pastor and people."[53]

True enough, but the process of conversion did not end. As his words show, so far as Miller was concerned what was transformed was his frame of mind; conversion gave him a new way of thinking about God as a parent and Jesus as a friend. Obviously, his heart had changed, too, to the extent that he could accept God's authority as from a loving father. But *metanoia,* true transformation, required more. He had once rejected God for deism because God's rule made no sense, and he now rejected deism because, while it made intellectual sense, the conclusion to which it led ineluctably — the annihilation of the soul at death — was unacceptable. Essentially, that September Miller chose serenity over reason. Still, serendipity troubled, and while he could accept God's love he was as yet unable to return for it the one thing God required: his unbridled trust. Now ensconced in a community that could nurture it, his conversion would proceed apace, with startling results.

52. *Vermont Association Minutes.* It is not certain that Miller was baptized at this time, but he did formally join the church, and the only two ways to join were by baptism and by presenting a letter of dismission from another congregation. No one joined by letter of dismission that year, so it is almost certain that Miller was baptized, probably by his uncle and presumably in the Poultney River.

53. Bliss, *Memoirs,* 67.

CHAPTER FOUR

A Feast of Reason

Public memory of Miller's conversion, a memory he and his closest Adventist colleagues crafted, makes of it a revolution, a victory of faith over skepticism. It was both less and more than that. As an event, it marked a return rather than an overturning. For Miller as a young man, republican rhetoric had come to mediate the content of piety, and even after converting he never abandoned its terms. On the contrary, it was Miller's inability to live up to piety's expectations that had caused years of frustration and self-doubt. The goal was always clear; the means had eluded him. Rationalism betrayed in the opposite way. While he had succeeded in fulfilling its expectations — civic honor, self-sacrifice for the greater good, personal courage — there were no rewards. Virtue was fleeting, and human nature (including his own) was still corrupt. Reason had no power to effectuate what it authorized. Piety, on the other hand, had at last brought peace, a certain assurance; while he could not rationalize it, the effects were undeniable. Applying the test of functionality, piety won. Miller's reaction to God's saving power, it turns out, was most reasonable, illustrating as much continuity as revision in his spiritual development.

While signifying less than claimed, Miller's conversion points to something more, with broader significance. The product of a community awakening, Miller's spiritual evolution from 1800 to 1816 reflected a transformation in the religious culture of the young republic. The intellectualism of eighteenth-century classicism was slowly giving way to the sentimentality of nineteenth-century romanticism, the slow, difficult evolution producing confusion and profound effects for Protestantism in general and evangelicalism in particular. Miller's capacity to reconcile reason and revelation marked a general rapprochement, what Mark Noll calls a "synthesis of republican ideology, commonsense ethical reason, and Christian theology"[1] in the post-Revolutionary generation. Essentially, America was growing into the Revolution's more radical, libertarian implications in its political, social, economic, and religious life. Gone already was instinctive deference to position, replaced by a kind of civic respectability that someone like Miller earned by virtuous living. A social class ladder on which one could ascend and descend was replacing immutable, inherited rank. *Liberty* no longer meant the capacity of reasonable people to ascribe and contribute to civic order so much as a release from custom and habit that freed the individual for self-improvement. Consequently, *virtue* revealed itself not so much in public, communal conduct as in private morality, signifying the potential of personal character rather than the condition of the common welfare.[2]

Necessarily under review, therefore, was the authoritarian Jehovah who demanded obedience but whose promised reward of virtuous order in this world could not compensate for the terrors of a fate, salvation or damnation, lodged in a serendipitous future. Like Miller, many Americans required an approachable God who rescues and assures, who connects with his creatures through the heart as well as the mind.[3] No wonder, then, that the denominational promoters of the old order should falter as their century gave way to the next. Shibboleths of decorum and structure wilted in the heat of revival as the Spirit beat back the power of the Word. Congregational-

1. Mark A. Noll, *America's God: From Jonathan Edwards to Abraham Lincoln* (New York: Oxford University Press, 2002), 251.

2. Noll, *America's God,* 214-15.

3. The bibliography of evangelical history is enormous. Works that have particularly informed this study are Harry S. Stout, *The New England Soul: Preaching and Religious Culture in Colonial New England* (New York and London: Oxford University Press, 1986); George M. Marsden, *Jonathan Edwards: A Life* (New Haven: Yale University Press, 2003); Nathan Hatch, *The Democratization of American Christianity* (New Haven: Yale University, 1989), and Mark Noll, *The Work We Have to Do: A History of Protestants in America* (New York: Oxford University Press, 2002).

ists and Presbyterians, formalists who required an educated clergy, resident pastors, and structures of authority that stewarded the belief and practice of congregations could not keep pace with the dynamic anti-formalists, principally the Methodists and Baptists, who encouraged lay participation by the uneducated and whose less stringent congregational arrangements assured individual expression and creativity.[4]

Numbers tell the tale. Between 1776 and 1850 the percentage of Congregationalists among total Christian adherents dropped from 20.4 to 4, of Presbyterians from 19 to 11.6, and of Episcopalians from 15.7 to 3.5. Methodists, on the other hand, added so many members in those decades that the 1776 percentage, 2.5, rose to 34.2, and Baptists increased their share from 16.9 percent to 20.5 percent.[5] The War of 1812 accelerated the shift. Anti-formal evangelicals received a boost from their support of the more democratic Republican political system and, consequently, of the war. Formalists, on the other hand, suffered from their opposition and from talk toward the end of the war of New England's seceding.[6]

Miller's conversion was one of thousands contributing to this evangelical tidal wave. That it occurred well along in the process of cultural transformation helps to explain why one of his feet remained planted in the world of his youth while the other guided him toward the future. While his return home to build a patrimony based on his father's model looked like a turning back, his conversion was evidence of something new operating in Miller's life and in evangelical culture. The eighteenth century defined conversion as homocentric, its emotionalism and "exercises" (fainting, weeping,

4. I first used the terms *formal* and *antiformal* to describe distinct pietist personalities in my book *Thunder and Trumpets: The Millerites and Apocalyptic Thought in Upstate New York, 1800-1850* (Chico, Calif.: Scholars Press, 1985), 71-72. Curtis Johnson applied the concept more broadly in *Redeeming America: Evangelicals and the Road to Civil War* (Chicago: University of Chicago Press, 1993), and Mark Noll discusses the distinction in *America's God*, 5, 175-76.

5. Roger Finke and Rodney Stark, *The Churching of America 1776-1990: Winners and Losers in Our Religious Economy* (New Brunswick, N.J.: Rutgers University Press, 1992), 55.

6. William Gribbin, *The Churches Militant: The War of 1812 and American Religion* (New Haven: Yale University Press, 1973).

flailing on the floor, prophesying) the effect of God's grace, freely given, unearned, and irresistible. That groups of people could experience grace at the same time and place and have the same response was simply a sign of an outpouring presaging a great work of Providence — according to Jonathan Edwards, the approach of the Millennium itself. But it was God's work. The only requirement of converts was that they persevere in the grace God had already bestowed. By the turn of the nineteenth century, republicanism had inspired rethinking about conversion as homopraxic if not homocentric, "the analogue to Lockean individualism." Far from sustaining habitual doctrine, it "free[d] individuals from tradition, family, and inherited authority, even as it allowed believers to take in hand the commerce of their own souls."[7] Appearances notwithstanding, in moving back to Low Hampton Miller made all the decisions, built his own farm on his own land, and invested a personal piety into his religious leadership that contrasted markedly with his father's apparent grudging acceptance of religious forms. In other words, he made choices in the interests of his own salvation and that of his family.

If conversion offered opportunities, it also proffered the responsibility to participate in one's own salvation by witnessing to the saving work of God, by defending that work from the assault of infidels, and by living a pious life. Now a new man, Miller determined that "henceforth, wherever he was, he must deport himself as a Christian, and perform his whole duty." Former deist friends mourned the loss of a champion to the Christian cause, and they came to view him as "a powerful, and, therefore, a desirable antagonist."[8] Like Saul/Paul, the new Miller took up the sword and argued the futility of rationalist ideas he had once accepted as dogma. For ammunition he turned to the book he had once scorned as hopelessly contradictory. The Bible became his "chief study," the "lamp to my feet and light to my path." He had read it before, of course, but now it was a new book: "[T]he half was never told me. I wondered why I had not seen its beauty and glory before, and marvelled that I could ever

7. Noll, *America's God,* 214.

8. Sylvester Bliss, *Memoirs of William Miller: Generally Known as a Lecturer on the Prophecies, and the Second Coming of Christ* (Boston: Joshua V. Himes, 1853), 68.

have rejected it." Following his own advice to the children, Miller now set out to know God: "I lost all taste for other reading, and applied my heart to get wisdom from God."[9] Conversion inspired, even required, personal Bible study. Democratizing evangelicalism assured believers that its meaning was open to anyone who approached it in humility, guided by the Holy Spirit. Miller now engaged in a two-year study of the Scriptures, spending "whole nights, as well as days" in the effort.[10]

More than piety inspired this exegesis, though its precise purpose shifts subtly from one recounting to another. Miller's first memoir, in 1842, is short and conveys no details about the post-conversion Bible study, moving directly to its dramatic product. Three years later, in an apology for his error in predicting a time for the second coming of Christ, he was more fulsome. The goal of his exegesis was personal, part of the continuing quest to reconcile rationalism and religion. He had learned as a youth "to reverence the Scriptures as a revelation from God to man" and had become a reader of it "more or less" without becoming "affected by it." At the time he entertained no "serious doubts about its authenticity" though he was troubled by "what I then deemed inconsistencies and contradictions." Even as a deist he continued to believe in a Supreme Being "as brought to view by the works of Nature and Providence," though he discarded the Bible as "the work of designing men."

Conversion brought him back to Scripture, but he still felt "that to believe in such a Saviour without evidence, would be visionary in the extreme." A Baptist brother reminded him that the apparent inconsistencies remained, so how could he be sure the Bible was authentically revealed? "I replied that if the Bible was the word of God, everything contained therein might be understood, and all its parts be made to harmonize; and I said to him, that if he would give me time, I would harmonize all these apparent contradictions, to my own satisfaction, or I would be a deist still." Accordingly, he "deter-

9. Joshua V. Himes, *Views of the Prophecies and Prophetic Chronology, Selected From Manuscripts of William Miller With a Memoir of His Life* (Boston: Joshua V. Himes, 1842), 11.

10. Bliss, *Memoirs,* 69.

mined to lay aside all my presuppositions" (the phrasing in the 1842 memoir is "all commentaries, former views and prepossessions")[11] and for two years working from Genesis through Revelation rationalized and clarified every inconsistency. At its end he had assured himself "that the Bible is a system of revealed truths, so clearly and simply given, that the 'wayfaring man, though a fool, need not err therein.'"[12] He had been a fool; now Scripture presumably authorized him to believe without fear of error.

Apollos Hale cast the story differently in Bliss's 1853 *Memoirs,* transforming the skeptic seeking greater assurance into a warrior liberating Scripture from obscurity. Here Miller demands no evidence for faith, commitment to revelation appearing more determined than in the previous account. The Baptist brother's challenge repeats, but Miller's response is slightly different, suggesting that the Bible will prove itself. If the Bible is a revelation God gave the world "for man's instruction," Miller reasoned, it "must be consistent with itself; all its parts must harmonize" (rather than be made to harmonize) and "consequently, must be adapted to his understanding." The key was to reconcile all apparent contradictions, thus to reveal "with child-like simplicity, [its] natural and obvious meaning." With this purpose in mind he "laid aside all commentaries [the reference to former views and prepossessions is removed]" all the "peculiar and partisan interpretations" of the Bible, and "using only a copy of Cruden's concordance" set out "to correct all interpretations" so that its own pure light would shine "with out the mists which traditionary belief had involved it in." The final doxology remains the same, but the identity of the "wayfaring man, though a fool" is no longer Miller but any Christian who earnestly and faithfully seeks the will of God.[13]

Truth rings more clearly in the first telling. By the 1850s, the effects of failure wrecking the movement, Adventist leaders were at pains to promote Miller as a formulator of what became the standard evangelical understanding that the individual participates in his or her salvation. They thus shifted attention from Miller's odd

11. Himes, *Views,* 11.

12. William Miller, *Apology and Defense* (Boston: Joshua V. Himes, 1845), 4-6.

13. Bliss, *Memoirs,* 68-70; Himes, *Views,* 11.

conclusion to the orthodox methodology that produced it. So we find in the *Memoirs* a lengthy exposition of his "Rules of Interpretation" that led to his dramatic discovery. The rules began with an assumption rather than a question: Scripture *is* consistent. Therefore, one can discover the plain meaning of a prophetic image or figure by comparing how it is used in one verse with how it is used in other verses "such as mountains, meaning governments . . . beasts, meaning kingdoms . . . waters, meaning people." The test of truth was common sense: only interpretations that make sense can be valid; only interpretations that are consistent, i.e., are not internally contradictory, make sense. The reasoning is circular, to be sure, but that did not matter, because the rules did not produce Miller's dramatic belief — they were meant to justify it. Simply put, it was not for his democratic evangelicalism that Miller became famous, and infamous, nor for the theology that underlay it, but for the startling revelation on which he now became "nearly settled." After two years of arduous labor, Scripture opened to him the momentous news for which Christian hearts had yearned through the centuries: "on or before 1843" Jesus would return to purify the globe with heavenly fire.[14]

Never before had Miller expressed curiosity about eschatology, the theology of last things. Both his hermeneutic (method of interpreting Scripture) and the message it uncovered were undoubtedly homegrown. Over the years it would systematize, partly from additional study but largely in response to criticisms, and since memories of how he arrived at his apocalyptic conclusion come from late in his life it is difficult to say how much of what he later taught he had concluded by 1818. That he chose to put aside all commentaries means he must have read some (at least two, as we shall see). He applied one of the central principles of millenarian exegesis, that the word *day* in prophecy really meant a year (based on Numbers 14:34, "even forty days, each day for a year," and Ezekiel 4:6, "I have appointed thee each

14. Miller, *Apology,* 12; Article 15, Statement of Faith, written in a manuscript sheriff's record book, September 5, 1822, Miller Papers, Jenks Memorial Collection of Adventual Materials, Aurora University, Aurora, Illinois. Hale says this was attached to a preaching license the Hampton congregation accorded him, and that may have been why he systematized his creed at this time. Further discussion of its contents appears below.

day for a year"), and he knew this was "in accordance with the opinions of all the standard Protestant commentators."[15]

How and when he learned this is unclear, but he could have used any number of sources. Speculation about "end things" was rife in Christian history and theology[16] and escalated throughout the eighteenth century. Jonathan Edwards saw portents of the end in the enthusiasm of the First Great Awakening, New England divines portrayed the French and Indians during the Seven Years' War as tools of Antichrist, and patriot preachers during the Revolution painted the British and Anglicanism in the same lurid colors.[17] The Napoleonic wars at the end of the century invigorated British apocalyptic. When French armies captured and imprisoned Pope Pius VII in 1798, many Anglicans believed the Beast of Revelation had been overthrown, presaging the defeat of the Ottoman Empire and the return of the Jews to Israel. Antichrist was destroyed and the world was verging on the Millennium. Anticipation produced a number of publications and a series of millennial conferences at Albury, England, in the 1820s. Miller reportedly had two prophetic commentaries on his desk in the early years of the Millerite movement: the Rev. George Faber's *Dissertation on the Prophecies,* published in at least three editions between 1804 and 1811, and an unspecified volume by "Newton," likely Bishop Thomas Newton's *Dissertations on the*

15. Bliss, *Memoirs,* 75.

16. See particularly James West Davidson, *The Logic of Millennial Thought: Eighteenth-Century New England* (New Haven: Yale University Press, 1977); Ernest R. Sandeen, *The Roots of Fundamentalism: British and American Millenarianism 1800-1930* (Chicago: University of Chicago Press, 1970); "Millennialism," in *The Rise of Adventism: Religion and Society in Mid-Nineteenth Century America,* ed. Edwin S. Gaustad (New York: Harper and Row, 1974), 104-18; Nathan O. Hatch, "The Origins of Civil Millennialism in America: New England Clergymen, War with France, and the Revolution," *New England Quarterly,* 3d series, 31, no. 3 (July 1974): 407-30; Ruth H. Bloch, *The Visionary Republic: Millennial Themes in American Thought, 1756-1800* (Cambridge: Cambridge University Press, 1985); and Grant Underwood, *The Millenarian World of Early Mormonism* (Urbana: University of Illinois, 1993).

17. John Howard Smith, "'The Promised Day of the Lord': American Millennialism and Apocalypticism, 1735-1783," in *Anglo-American Millennialism, from Milton to the Millerites,* ed. Richard Connors and Andrew Colin Gow (Leiden and Boston: Brill, 2004), 115-58. Historians have often seen millenarian implications in Jonathan Edwards's writings, particularly in the 1740s and 1750s, but his most recent biographer disagrees with this view. See Marsden, *Edwards,* 265-67.

Prophecies published in 1796.[18] While feeding his millennial speculation, they reached different conclusions than Miller about the nature of the Millennium and how it would come about. Miller's views on that score were clearly his own.

Less direct but more powerful influences surrounded him. One was a popular culture steeped in apocalyptic speculation. The instruction Elnathan Phelps and his mother provided surely included at least reference to the end of the world and final judgment, which were also common themes at funerals, several of which he attended as a youth. The books of Revelation and Daniel appear occasionally in the Sunday texts of visiting preachers Miller noted in his diary. The same year it published the elder Miller's deposition about his militia unit's electoral activities, the *Vermont Herald* published a "Description of the Last Day," a nightmare occasioned by "the death of my comrade [in?] iniquity," and a vision of judgment occasioned by a violent thunderstorm.[19] An unusual darkness at midday on May 20, 1780, and again in February 1808, and the dramatic New Madrid earthquakes that struck the Mississippi Valley from 1808 to 1812 also aroused popular apocalyptic fears. A reflection on "The Solemnities of the Judgement Day" appeared in the *Vermont Missionary Magazine,* published in Miller's hometown, in 1812.[20] He made no public comment about any of this; at that time such stories more likely served as fodder for his sarcasm than sparks to his curiosity.

More dramatic and closer to home were the colorful end-of-the-world sects that sprinkled the region. As a youth Miller had visited

18. Letter of Nathaniel Southard, *Midnight Cry,* October 26, 1843. On the development of British millennialism at the turn of the nineteenth century see Sandeen, *Roots,* 5-22. LeRoy Edwin Froom published an exhaustive catalogue and description of millennial writing through the centuries in his four-volume work *The Prophetic Faith of Our Fathers* (Washington: Review and Herald Publishing Association, 1946-1954). See particularly his comments on Newton, 2:684-86.

19. William Miller, Diary and Book of Fortune, July 16, 23, 1792, Miller Papers, Vermont Historical Society, Barre, Vermont.

20. I discuss apocalyptic responses to natural events in *Thunder and Trumpets* and in "Comets and Eclipses: The Millerites, Nature, and the Apocalypse," *Adventist Heritage* 3, no. 2 (Winter 1976): 10-19. See also Jay Feldman, *When the Mississippi Ran Backwards: Empire, Intrigue, Murder, and the New Madrid Earthquakes* (New York: Free Press, 2005); *Vermont Missionary Magazine,* January 1812, 139-40.

the Shakers outside Pittsfield, hearing something of their belief that Jesus had already come back to earth and instituted the Millennium. Nearby, the Dorrilites maintained a similar community in the 1790s, practicing vegetarianism and, quite unlike the Shakers, promiscuous sexual relations. Shortly before Miller moved to Poultney, the "Wood Scrape" troubled Rutland County. In 1800 Nathaniel Wood, the "Old Man of All" who had turned his large family into a cult, partnered with a would-be soothsayer who used a dowsing stick to search for buried treasure. The only money he found came from the pockets of credulous victims. Wood used the witch stick, now called "St. John's rod," to intimidate his followers and to forecast the future. The end of all things would come on January 14, 1801, he predicted, and he claimed divine power to judge all his neighbors. Up to one hundred people reportedly became followers, and as the day approached the locality became so frightened of what Wood would do to them that the local militia mustered to maintain order. The cult moved on shortly after, three years before Miller arrived, but the newlyweds surely heard stories about them. Again in 1817, as Miller was engaged in his Bible study, a group calling themselves Pilgrims moved into Vermont from the northern end of Lake Champlain in Upper Canada. Camping near South Woodstock, they became notorious for their physical peculiarities. Followers wore animal skins, men shaved their upper lips only, and the faithful refused to bathe, rolling in the dirt as a devotional act.[21]

Evidence about all these groups is largely hearsay and apocryphal, gleaned from old sources that are themselves products of rumor and gossip.[22] None of them contributed to Miller's apocalypticism; like

21. Accounts of these cults appear in David M. Ludlum, *Social Ferment in Vermont 1791-1850* (New York: Columbia University Press, 1939; reprint New York: AMS Press, 1966), 239-50, and Whitney R. Cross, *The Burned-over District: The Social and Intellectual History of Enthusiastic Religion in Western New York, 1800-1850* (Ithaca, N.Y.: Cornell University Press, 1950), 38-39.

22. Possible connection to Joseph Smith and the rise of Mormonism has particularly encouraged the recovery and discussion of this fugitive literature. Barnes Frisbie, who contributed to the writing of Poultney's history, is the principal source on the Wood Scrape. His book, *History of Middletown* (Rutland, Vt.: Tuttle & Company, 1867) has been transcribed on Dale R. Broadhurst's Web site *Mormon Classics: Opening New Horizons in Mormon History,* http://www.sidneyrigdon.com/Classics1

"superstitious" responses to natural phenomena they could only have fueled his ridicule. But in some way the rich seam of popular apocalyptic nurtured many creative innovators. Miller was not the only skeptic and cynic who turned to personal devices to reconcile religious tension. Joseph Smith was born in Sharon, and future Mormon leaders Brigham Young and Oliver Cowdery (whom historians have linked to the Wood cult) were from the region. Another favorite son, John Humphrey Noyes, mixed millennialism, socialism, and sex in his perfectionist communes, first at Putney, Vermont, and later at Oneida, New York.

A second powerful medium for apocalyptic was politics. Millennial rhetoric engaged both sides in the debate over the War of 1812, the American theater of the Napoleonic wars, just as it inspired Anglican prelates. Division over secular policy had turned the denominations into warring camps, playing a crucial role in defining distinct evangelical personalities. Formalists (Presbyterians, Congregationalists, mainline Reformed churches), valuing order over spontaneity, the Word over the Spirit, saw Britain as the principal guarantor of moral order. French defeat in Russia marked Czar Alexander, Britain's ally and "the most pious sovereign in Christendom," as the "holy deliverer," preserving American republicanism from the depravation of French libertines. Caleb Strong, Federalist governor of Massachusetts, called Britain the "bulwark of true religion." Napoleon was "Daniel's infidel king, the tyrannical antichrist," despite his overthrow of the pope, and Madison and his Republican allies were atheists and demagogues. Federalists celebrated American military defeats in the war as proper chastisement and a portent of the victory of righteousness: "The world is rapidly preparing to submit with one accord to the sceptre of the Prince of Peace." The orthodox Vermont Missionary Society agreed: "We live in an age of wonders. The predictions of the Bible, respecting the latter-day glory of the church, are rapidly fulfilling."[23]

.htm (accessed 26 September 2006). Another page on the Web site, "Uncle Dale's Readings in Early Mormon History: Newspapers of New England," transcribes contemporary newspaper articles about rodmen (dowsers who search for buried treasure), the Pilgrims, the Wood Scrape, and other regional religious events.

23. Quoted in Gribbin, *The Churches Militant,* 52-53, 58-59.

Antiformalists, principally Baptists and Methodists, had equally millennial expectations in their support of the war and Republican policy. Far from being the guarantors of order and piety, Britain and Russia were autocratic and despotic. If Americans needed any additional evidence of their antichristian intent they had only to consider that their ally was indeed the pope. Napoleon, in capturing the pope, sparked the hope that "the time is not very far distant, when the waiting posts shall be furnished with the long expected news. 'Babylon is fallen! Babylon is fallen!'" Incorporated in the shibboleth were domestic antiwar supporters of the British cause, Federalists and elitists, "the merchants of Babylon who hang down their heads and mourn." There is no evidence that Miller engaged in this conversation, but Clark Kendrick, ardent evangelical and Republican, could have apprised him of it. His letter to Miller in 1814 expressed delight at the Plattsburgh victory that was "so disgraceful to those of the 'Bulwark of Religion,'" thus passing on a common rejoinder to Caleb Strong's characterization of Anglicanism, traitorous not only to Americans in general but to evangelical Protestants in particular.[24] Miller obviously understood the reference. Indeed, since at the time Miller evidenced no interest in millennialism, one must wonder if it was Kendrick who supplied him with the Faber and Newton commentaries, hoping to spark one.

The third medium, and the most influential, was history. Heroic stories of the past filled his youthful reading, at once sparking the quest for adventure and feeding his cynical view of human nature. Ironically, the American Revolution affected rationalist republicans' view of the past in the same way conversion defined it for antiformal evangelicals: it liberated from habit and tradition, making the nation, like the convert, a new thing. One studied the past to identify the prime force motivating human conduct and to justify the radical newness of the American experiment — political primitivism thus complementing what the new evangelicalism was promoting. Conversion allowed Miller to reconcile fascination with the past and disgust over its lessons just as it enabled him to move beyond his personal sin to a new life. It was not history that justified

24. Quoted in Gribbin, *Churches Militant,* 64; Kendrick to Miller, November 21, 1814, Miller Letters VHS; Gribbin, *Churches Militant,* 24 and *passim.*

the Bible, but the reverse: Scripture explained human failure and offered the final escape from its certitude.

Miller's hermeneutic began with prophecy, which led him to history and finally to chronology. As he read the prophecies of Daniel, Revelation, and Ezekiel, horns and beasts became empires and tyrants, Babylon, Persia, Greece, finally Rome lingering as the Roman Catholic Church. Faber, Newton, and exegetes through the centuries applied the year/day formula, discovering duration between prophecies. Twenty three hundred "days" would elapse between the rise of the first empire and the end of the fourth, which would reign for 1260 "days." Then there would be a great "cleansing of the sanctuary." History taught when prophetic periods began, and contemporary events — the imprisonment of the pope, the defeat of Napoleon, the expected defeat of the Ottomans — pointed to their ending. "Reckoning all these prophetic periods from the several dates assigned by the best chronologers for the events from which they should evidently be reckoned, they all would terminate together, about A.D. 1843." Thus did secular history and mathematics come to the defense of prophecy, making the Bible "a feast of reason."[25] That at least four other writers published similar chronologies from 1768 to 1818 identifying 1843 as the termination date affirmed his method.[26] He did not copy from them; he didn't need to. The method made sense.

Otherwise, his thinking was not as systematic as Bliss later claimed. In 1822 Miller drafted a personal testimony, never completed, reflecting most Baptist congregations' articles of faith. While conventional in form, Miller's was inventive, incomplete, even theologically confused, mixing orthodoxy and rationalism. Most confessions affirmed the events of salvation history, Creation through the Last Judgment, and propounded church ordinances such as baptism, the Lord's Supper, sometimes feet washing and established church order. Miller's intent was to justify the startling

25. Miller, *Apology and Defense,* 11-12. Reference to prophetic periods does not make Miller a proto-dispensationalist. Historical landmarks pointed to the fulfillment of prophecies across salvation history, while dispensationalism posits a fulfillment of prophecy at the end of time, immediately preceding the future apocalypse. Also, Miller never contemplated God's acting in distinct dispensations but always pointed to the one essential act of grace, Jesus' death for human sin on the cross.

26. Froom, *Prophetic Faith,* 4:404.

discovery he would now privately set down in writing for the first time, as though convincing himself.

He began by affirming that "the Bible is given to man as a rule to our practice and guide to our Faith, and is properly the Revelation of God to man." This makes sense, he said, because "reason teaches that if there is a God he would not leave man wholely in the dark as it respects his being, attributes, and laws, and the Bible discribes him, in my humble opinion, the most agreeable to reason of any system on earth." God must exist in three Persons because "[e]very thing in nature have three parts as for instance the Tree[,] bark, wood, & sap etc. water, air, earth[.]" Accordingly God "by his son" created humanity in his own image "with a body, soul, and spirit." Believers receive mercy "in conformity to the Divine plan, founded on the wisdom and knowledge of God." He tried to reconcile predestination and Arminianism. God created man as a "moral agent" capable of choosing to obey or disobey, but God, "knowing from etternity the use man would make of his agency," ordained his Son's death "in the Councill of Eternity" that salvation might come to the world "through such means as God should appoint."[27]

Only after establishing the warrant does Miller walk toward the essential fact. Anyone who believes in Christ "may take him by faith and go to God and find mercy and such will in no wise be rejected." Any who confess will receive forgiveness of sin through the "intercession of Jesus Christ and the sprinkling of his blood in the holy of holies, and upon the mercy-seat and people." Jesus "will eventually take away the sin of the world;" then "all impenitents will be destroyed from the earth" and "sent away into a place prepared for the Devil & his angels." I believe, he wrote, "Jesus Christ will come again in his glory & person to our earth" to accomplish all this. Finally, using words that would shape the rest of his life, he proclaimed to himself when all this will happen: "I believe that the second coming of Christ is near even at the door, even within twenty one years, or on or before 1843."[28] At the end he mentioned baptism and was beginning work on an article affirming the Lord's Supper, but he never finished it. Affirming ordinances was not on his mind.

27. Miller, Statement of Faith, articles 1, 2, 3, 5, 6.

28. Miller, Statement of Faith, articles 7, 9, 12-15.

Later claims of consistency and assurance about his views from the beginning were only partly correct. In 1842 he wrote of his labors, "I found, in going through with the Bible, the end of all things was clearly and emphatically predicted, both as to time and manner."[29] Confirming the accounts in the *Apology* and in the *Memoirs*, as early as this drafted testimony Miller had concluded that there would be two resurrections, "the just believers at Christs Second Coming. And the unjust 1000 years afterwards. When the judgement of each class, will take place in their order at their several resurrections." But despite his proclaimed certitude, his views remained fluid as to both the time and the manner of Christ's second coming. As late as 1831, in his first systematic communication on the subject, he dated the return of Christ for "1843 or 1847 at most."[30] And while Jesus *eventually* would "cleanse the earth from all pollution," there was no mention of the world's burning. Jesus would accomplish God's purpose by "the means he has appointed. All believers by regeneration, sanctification, justification, & glorification."[31] Miller's apocalyptic, like his testimony, was a work in progress.

Despite the fuzziness of details, there was no doubting the effect of his Bible study in creating both conviction and a call to mission. "I believed," he said, adding, "immediately the duty to publish this doctrine, that the world might believe and get ready to meet the Judge and Bridegroom at his coming, was impressed upon my mind."[32] Thus the imperative to action linked with compelling belief. But it took thirteen years for him to heed the call, all the while feeling slothful and cowardly for not responding. His memory of chronology was faulty, as was no doubt the process by which he came to make his first public proclamation. But the obstacles he described ring true. Scripture was not as clear as he thought. For five years "texts would occur to me, which seemed to weigh against my conclusions." Regarding his return Jesus said "of that day and hour

29. Himes, *Views*, 12.

30. William Miller, "[A] few Evidences of the time of the 2nd coming of Christ," manuscript, February 15, 1831, Miller Collection, Center for Adventist Research, James White Library, Andrews University, Berrien Springs, Michigan, 8.

31. September 22, 1822, Miller Papers, *passim*.

32. Himes, *Views*, 12.

knoweth no man"; prophecy seemed to point to the conversion of the world, not its destruction; commentators posited a single resurrection and judgment at the end of the Millennium; Scripture seemed to require the Jews' return to Israel. Personal reticence held him back, too: "I told the Lord that I was not used to public speaking; that I had not the necessary qualifications to gain the attention of an audience; that I was very diffident and feared to go before the world; that they would 'not believe me nor hearken to my voice'; that I was 'slow of speech and of a slow tongue.'" Add to these the fear of public ridicule, the certain end of his renewed political career, and likely rejection and ridicule by his own family. Approaching fifty, "it seemed impossible for me to surmount the obstacles which lay in my path, to successfully present it in a public manner."[33]

Apart from misremembered dates, Miller's long road from hesitation to action was not that systematic. Doubt did not flow like a stream from one landmark to another but swirled like a whirlpool, catching him up and moving him as often in circles as forward. It may have dissipated but it never disappeared. As a youth he failed to reconcile revelation and reason and fled to Poultney to escape the tension; as a man he failed to reconcile the idea of human virtue endowed by nature with the fact of human corruption revealed by history, so he retreated into the army; as a middle-aged man he could not rationalize his role as a father with his past behavior as a son, so he ran back home. Small wonder, then, that it would take years of struggle to commit himself to an idea so odd and to defend it publicly.

Besides, he feared for others as much as for himself. Miller was the patriarch of a large, widespread family. Already the parents of five children, after returning to Hampton Bill and Lucy produced five more — George in 1816, Electa three years later (she lived only three years), an infant son who died at birth, John in 1822, and Lucy Ann three years later. On occasion the household included others, "aliens" and "paupers," perhaps as laborers, perhaps out of charity. Paulina occupied the old farm at the bottom of the hill with daughter Eleanor, son Solomon and, after 1826, his new wife. Other siblings had died or married, dispersing to Vermont and Upper Canada

33. Miller, *Apology and Defense,* 9-10.

and populating nearby towns with names like Bosworth, Adams, Shaw, and Guilford.[34] In this rural community tightly knit by blood, bond, and mutual need, one man's fate touched everyone's.

Protecting the public reputation that came with high social status was another good reason to demur. He was a respected war hero and a Hampton squire. In 1816 he and Seth Peck paid the highest amounts in school taxes out of twenty-two assessable landholders in Hampton,[35] and successful farming maintained him in that elite position. As always, the farm produced as much on-site as possible — wheat, oats, rye, corn, and potatoes. Every fall Paulinus Millard's mill pressed their apples into cider, bushels of grain paying for barrels of the winter drink. Horses for pulling wagons and sleighs shared the barn with sheep (forty of them in 1825) and hogs (ten of those). The farms grew flax and wool, feeding the fulling mill, carding machine, and woolen factory that had sprouted on the banks of the Poultney River. The Miller women then took the yarn and turned it into cloth, in 1825 producing fifty yards of fulled cloth, ten of flannel, and 120 of linen between the two farmsteads.[36]

These same years technology and the market revolution slowly transformed their production. The first steel-shod plow appeared in Poultney in 1825, and the new breed of merino sheep appeared in the region shortly after, each innovation allowing farmers to specialize and encouraging them to expand land holdings. Strong protection for American wool in 1824 and 1828 pushed prices higher, and the Champlain Valley became the hotbed of "the sheep craze."[37] By 1835 Miller owned ninety-six sheep, and son William S. grazed another fifty-three on a ninety-acre farm of his own nearby, granted by his parents. Women's lives changed accordingly; that year only Paulina's

34. Phillip Phelps, Miller Family Genealogy; New York State Agricultural Census, 1825. The census records two male aliens and two male paupers that year.

35. Tax bill, Hampton, N.Y., April 22, 1816, Miller Papers, Vermont Historical Society, Barre, Vermont.

36. Paulinus Millard, Day Book, Del E. Webb Memorial Library, Loma Linda University, Loma Linda, California; New York Agricultural Census, 1825.

37. P. Jeffrey Potash, *Vermont's Burned-over District* (New York: Carlson Publishing, Inc., 1991), 102-5; J. Joslin, B. Frisbie, and F. Ruggles, *A History of the Town of Poultney, Vermont, From its Settlement to the Year 1875, with Family and Biographical Sketches and Incidents* (Poultney, Vt.: J. Joslin, B. Frisbie, F. Ruggles, 1875), 82.

household was producing flannel, and none of the (now three) farms made linen. In addition to farming, William S. took up the profession of tailoring, and Robbins became a shoemaker. Surpluses brought money, and cash appeared more often in transactions. In 1826 Miller used labor, services, and commodities to cover debts to Millard, but in 1830 he "settled all up" with a cash payment of $6.72.[38]

Along with position went responsibility. After returning to Hampton, Miller resumed an active political life, allying now with New York Republicans and becoming a local party operative. So important was he that when the Marquis de Lafayette made a reunion tour of the nation in 1825, Miller was among those invited to dine with him.[39] In 1816 he was elected a school trustee and, with money raised by a property assessment for the first time, helped oversee the building of a school on what would become known as School Hill, adjacent to his own farm. He also served as "poor master" in 1817 and 1818 and town supervisor in 1821, 1829, and 1832. In 1821 he was appointed justice of the peace and then elected in 1827 and subsequently, serving until 1834.[40] Along with the responsibility came a

38. Washington County, N.Y., Deed, January 3, 1834, book NN, 295 (it is possible the Millers bought this farm for their son as he came of age); New York Agricultural Census, 1835; Millard, Day Book, 26.

39. State legislator Melancthon Wheeler included Miller in a "form letter" in 1824 mailed to local Republicans explaining his vote in favor of popular election of presidential electors. Miller had written to express his opinion and to ask his advice about the current field of four presidential candidates. A politician indeed, Wheeler respected John Quincy Adams, was favorably impressed with William Crawford, personally preferred Henry Clay, but found much that favored Andrew Jackson. March 12, 1824, Miller Letters. Miller described his experience in a letter to brother-in-law Joseph Atwood, June 28, 1825, Miller Letters.

40. Tax Assessment, May 11, 1816, Miller Papers, VHS. The tax raised $35.79, plus $1.81 in collection fees. Paulinus Millard's account on the construction noted a total expense of $16.83. Day Book, 26. Holden, Whitehall Scrapbooks, 5:29; see also a deposition Miller provided as poor master for a civil action, May 4, 1817, Miller Papers, VHS. Everts and Ensign, *History of Washington County, New York* (Philadelphia: Everts and Ensign, 1878), 119-20, 364, 366; Allen Corey, *Gazetteer of the County of Washington, New York* (Schuylerville, N.Y., 1849), 190. Miller's justice of the peace "blot book" for 1831-1834 is at the Miller Farm (Adventist Heritage Ministry). Hundreds of receipts, bills, warrants, and summonses from his justice career are housed in the William Miller Collection at the Ellen G. White Estate, Silver Spring, Maryland.

title — *Esquire* — that now became attached to his name along with *Captain.*

The church became a springboard for public action, though gradually. Here were men with credentials and skills that he lacked, and while he did not share his apocalyptic vision publicly, he undertook ministry in other ways. Now patron of the Hampton Baptist congregation and nephew of its new pastor, William inevitably became a leading light. In 1819 and 1820 he was a delegate to the Vermont Association, each year accompanying new pastor E. W. Martin to the annual meeting. The following year the Hampton Baptist Church incorporated at the meetinghouse just northwest of Miller's farm. It was a neighborhood affair: Miller signed the certificate and brother-in-law Hezekiah Bosworth was elected a trustee, along with Seth Peck, Isaiah Inman, and two Harlows. Membership fluctuated but generally increased, thanks to the third wave of religious refreshing in the region. By 1822 it was the sixth-largest congregation of the twenty-five in the association, and it peaked the following year at 133 members. Baptist growth generally led to new associations and reorganizing old ones. In 1827 Hampton and six other churches formed the Washington Baptist Association, and the Hampton church chose Miller to be a delegate that year and the next.[41]

It was an auspicious time for Miller to rise in the ranks. Millennialism was on everybody's mind, one way or another. The end of the War of 1812 had brought little comfort to either side in the millennial debate. The Federalists and formalists not only saw the British defeated but themselves discredited. Discussions of seceding labeled them traitors as well as aristocrats, a reputation the Federalist Party could not survive. Ironically, antiformalist expectations fared little better. America did not win the war militarily, but not losing the war seemed like a victory. Maintaining national integrity at the peace table and promoting national honor by defeating the British at New Orleans caused rejoicing and a sense that God had saved the nation. But the return of Napoleon, reinstatement of the pope, and resur-

41. *Vermont Baptist Association Minutes,* 1819, 1829; Incorporation of the First Baptist Church of Hampton, October 22, 1821, Miscellaneous Records of Washington County, book 1, Washington County Office Building, Fort Edward, N.Y.; Potash, *Vermont's Burned-over District,* 144; *Minutes of the Washington Baptist Association,* 1827, 1828.

gence of European colonial ambitions at the Congress of Vienna provoked lament. Not for the last time, Americans came to believe they had won the war but lost the peace. Like Confederates following the Civil War and, eerily, like Adventists following the Great Disappointment in 1844, faithful evangelicals asked, What went wrong?

Churchmen provided two linked answers: God was chastising his people (somehow they had not measured up), but in doing so God was preparing them for a great purpose. The Holy Remnant, as William Gribbin puts it, was being given "another chance, to make the most of divine mercy, to be the leaven in America's loaf."[42] To prove themselves, evangelicals in the postwar years undertook two campaigns that affected Miller directly. One was to spread the gospel around the world. Luther Rice and Adoniram Judson promoted foreign missions among Baptists, encouraging the formation of statewide conventions to raise money for the support of missionaries. Vermont Baptists responded by forming a voluntary Domestic and Foreign Missionary Society. Hampton Baptists sent money and jewelry annually for its support, and Miller was one of the contributors. In 1824 the association appointed him second vice president. One of the first acts of the new Washington Baptist Association was also to form a missionary society, this one to be attached to the Baptist Board of Foreign Missions. Hampton Baptists continued their support, a fact the association noted in 1832.[43]

Revival suggested that God smiled on their efforts, millennial rhetoric shaping Baptists' celebration. "The time to build God's house, seems to have fully come," wrote one preacher. Miller was present at the Washington Association annual meeting when Archibald Wait wrote in a circulating letter, "Most assuredly, brethren, this is the dawn of that auspicious day of which the prophets so sweetly sung; when the light of the moon shall be as the light of the sun, and the light of the sun shall be seven fold. Already is the situation of Mount Zion beautiful, and soon, very soon, shall she become the glory and joy of the whole earth. May the Lord hasten it in his time."[44] One can imagine Miller's responding, "Amen." A broken

42. Gribbin, *Militant Churches,* 137, 147.

43. *Vermont Association,* 1824; *Washington Association,* 1827 and 1832.

44. *Vermont Association,* 1819; *Washington Association,* 1828.

arm kept him from the Vermont Missionary Society meeting in 1824, but he sent annual dues along with his personal greetings. "[W]hile the Lord gives me breath I hope I shall feel anxious for the cause, and willing to do all that our duty requires." Oh that all Christians "might feel the importance of being co-workers with God. for the time is at hand when the captivity of Zion shall return and her walls will be built up. Let light be communicated. We aught to do much for the translation & printing the scriptures in different languages."[45]

The second campaign was to purify Americans at home by reforming personal behavior. Temperance was their first focus. New ways to farm changed working relationships, individual labor substituting for men's working side-by-side, feeding their conviviality with liquor. It used to take a team of men to cut hay: "Each would go forward in his turn, and thus they would chase each other around until noon, or until the grass on the piece was cut down, not forgetting at each round to stop and take a drink. Rum was then in every hay field." But new mowers meant that gradually all it took was "one man, a machine, and water, no rum."[46] Both the Washington Union and the Vermont Association went on record opposing the use of intoxicating beverages, and the Hampton church formed a temperance society. In 1824 a woman in the church became publicly intoxicated, which sparked Miller to write former pastor Edward Martin searching questions about the duty of confession and the nature of atonement.[47]

A loyal Baptist, Miller endorsed temperance, but he was otherwise uninvolved, for good reason: much of the Miller cider was probably intended for the local distillery to be converted into the popular apple brandy, though by 1855 only the old farmstead was still producing apples. The temperance movement divided some congregations that could not decide whether righteousness required teetotaling or simply restrained use of alcohol.[48] As we have seen, there

45. Miller to Elisha Ashley, October 5, 1824, Miller Letters VHS. Like Miller, Ashley had converted and become an ardent Baptist. Joslin et al., *Poultney,* 203.

46. Joslin et al., *Poultney,* 80.

47. *Washington Association,* 1827, 1829, and 1832; *Vermont Association,* 1831. Miller to Edward Martin, December, 1824, Miller Letters.

48. Joslin et al., *Poultney,* 80-81; Paul Goodman, *Towards a Christian Republic: Antimasonry and the Great Transition in New England, 1826-1836* (New York: Oxford University Press, 1988), 136; New York Agricultural Census, 1855.

is evidence of Miller's drinking wine until late in his life. Having never been an alcoholic or, so far as we know, publicly intoxicated, he does not seem to have become a teetotaler.

In this as in everything else, Miller did nothing to stand out from the crowd. Though the personal and public record of his life in the 1820s is sparse, all the evidence points to a religiosity that was conventional, private belief in the imminent second coming of Christ notwithstanding. His evangelicalism was christological (affirming Jesus' death and resurrection as God's means of salvation), biblicist (embracing the Scriptures as the sole source of authority for belief and action), pious (living faithfully only through a personal relationship with God through Jesus Christ), conversional (preaching transformation brought about by the action of God), ecclesial (locating the Christian life in the context of the faithful community), and eschatological (pointing toward the final victory of righteousness over sin). Despite his millenarian vision of the apocalypse, by supporting missions and reform Miller evinced the standard postmillennial confidence in human capacity to purify the world in preparation for Christ's thousand-year reign. He expressed no concern about the short time required to accomplish that before Christ's return, which he had come to expect within a few years.

One can add another descriptor of his spirituality: *primitive.* In religion as in politics, Americans had liberated themselves from the restraints of history, freeing them to search for the model of Christian belief and action in an uncomplicated, uncorrupted past. Thomas Jefferson looked for these "first things" in the words of Jesus snipped from a Bible, while Thomas and Alexander Campbell and Barton Stone, leaders in the Restoration movement, found them in the apostolic church revealed in the Book of Acts and the letters of the apostles. More revolutionary innovators such as Joseph Smith, the Shakers, and John Humphrey Noyes discovered their authority in new, extra-biblical revelations, but they shared with the others a belief that truth was simple and accessible to faithful seekers.[49] There is no better illustration of primitivism than Miller's poring over Scripture on his own with centuries of accumulated commentary tucked away on the shelf. It was the allure of this demo-

49. See Hatch, *Democratization,* 167-70.

cratic exegesis as much as his millenarian vision of the future that would attract and hold his audiences.

Fitting in with his newfound brothers and sisters, Miller continued to resist setting himself apart from them so radically by preaching the approaching destruction of the world. At the end of the decade, though, a combination of event and circumstance shook him from his lethargy. The event was a wholesale attack on an institution that had figured greatly in his spiritual wrestling: the Masons. At first Freemasonry attracted rationalists, like Miller, who found in it a vehicle for fellowship and developing and demonstrating civic virtue without requiring belief in illogical doctrines or belonging to exclusive sects. But in the years that Miller joined and belonged to the lodge it developed a decidedly Christian ethos, emphasizing the same fraternal and benevolent qualities evangelicals were promoting. At the same time, evangelicalism was adopting the rational rhetoric of republicanism. The rapprochement made Masonry a meeting place where people of all faiths and sects could gather and unite in the cause of charity, leading at least one Mason to forecast "[a] happy Masonic millennial period" that would soon commence "to the inexpressible joy of all the inhabitants of the earth."[50] Miller undoubtedly gained experience in benevolent work through his lodge long before he applied those lessons in the Baptist church, and the fellowship he found there would have pleased his primitive dislike for sectarianism and yearning for common ground where rational men could build righteous community based on virtue.

After his conversion, Masonry offered something more personal, a rational piety that allowed him to move slowly toward a more affective spirituality that required a level of trust in God he had not yet achieved. It was, in short, a safe place where God and angels could mingle with Wisdom and Virtue. As Steven G. Bullock puts it, "For cosmopolitan Americans eager to avoid both a narrow and parochial sectarianism on one hand and an equally dangerous nonbiblical rationalism, Masonry seemed to reinforce an enlightened middle way." This was the mood of a song Miller composed en-

50. Steven C. Bullock, *Revolutionary Brotherhood: Freemasonry and the Transformation of the American Social Order, 1730-1840* (Chapel Hill: University of North Carolina Press, 1996), 173.

titled "A Masonic Dream," an allegory that, in the safety of dream, mixed surviving rationalism with biblicism. A conversation with pious friends had turned to freemasonry, "that wondrous art,/a secret had been kept so long." But they condemned it as diabolical. "They said that Satan had a part/In making of a league so strong." Hurt and confused by their comments, he went to bed. "When [M]orpheus closed my eyes to sleep/A form Divine so bright did shine/And since it is no harm to dream,/With liberty I'll tell you mine."

Like Bunyan's Pilgrim, Miller now followed his guide to "a glorious Temple" where, reflecting Masonic ritual, he knelt at the west gate and received a name, donned a head band and apron, and learned lessons in virtuous living from his guides. "Their implements being laid aside/In vocal concert all combine/The heavens reverberate the song/To praise the architect divine." Then the imagery shifts from masonic to biblical, reflecting Masonry's claims to Moses as their founder. "I am, I am now strengthned me/With vigour to my course pursue/And when my rod a serpent, see/The leprous flesh appeard as new. . . . My shoes I put from off my feet/ while on the holy ground I stood/The burning bush did not consume/Being p[r]eserved by Israels God. Here mystic characters I read/Jehovahs praise was all my theme/The rod I saw and manna bread/I woke and lo, I'd dreamed a dream." It was both as a Mason and a Baptist that he could "praise the architect divine."[51]

The anti-Masonic movement that erupted across the North in the late 1820s deprived him of this comfortable compromise. William Morgan, a western New York Mason, threatened to publish a book divulging secrets of the order. In 1826 he was arrested on fabricated charges and jailed in Canandaigua. A band of men kidnapped him, and he was never seen again. Although no body was ever found and no crimes proved, the public assumed that Masons abducted and murdered him to prevent his publishing the book. When investigations failed to offer a reasonable explanation and courts refused to take action, a firestorm against the Masons erupted across the

51. The song is included in the folder "Poems and Acrostics" in the Miller Papers. Someone has written the date 1847 on it, but the steady handwriting demonstrates Miller could not have written it then, when he suffered from a chronic tremor. It probably dates from the 1820s and 1830s, as did so many other items in the folder.

North. Fueled by antagonism to Masons' elite status and the power they seemed to wield over courts, legislatures, and governors to prevent justice to Morgan, an anti-Masonic movement and political party organized to "recapture" government for the people. At the same time evangelicals increasingly found Masonry to be competitive rather than complementary, and they demanded exclusive fellowship and commitment from their church members. Formalists denounced Masonists as secular and atheist, while antiformal evangelicals suspected them of seeking to take the country backwards to the British model by creating a national church — perhaps Presbyterian or Episcopalian. Charges flew, and by 1832 many Americans had concluded that to be a Mason was to be un-American and un-Christian.[52]

In this heated battle churches fired clergy for being on the wrong side of the issue while congregations and associations divided and even disappeared. Masonry proved one of the most divisive issues among Christians since the War of 1812, sporadically flaring for ten years from 1826 to 1836. Rancor in Miller's Washington Association became so destructive that in 1829 it called a special council to seek a remedy, in the meantime urging churches "to exercise Christian moderation and forbearance, and endeavor to diminish and not to widen the unhappy breaches already too visible among them." To no avail; two years later the Bottskill [Antimasonic] Association seceded, taking with them six congregations (Hampton not among them). "No church who refuse to apply the laws of Christ," it said, "or who do not apply them for the entire removal of Speculative Freemasonry from their fellowship, shall be numbered in the Association." It survived a scant three years but temporarily stopped Baptist growth in the region.[53]

Miller's Masonic connection could not have gone unnoticed. As a longtime Mason and onetime Grand Master, he found himself on the defensive in the church and community. For fifteen years after becoming a Baptist he had remained a Mason, but in September 1831 he wrote a grudging letter of resignation from the local lodge,

52. See Goodman, *Christian Republic.*

53. Goodman, *Christian Republic,* 63; *Washington Association Minutes,* 1829; *Bottskill Association Minutes,* 1831-1833.

not because belonging to the Masons was wrong but "to consilliate the feelings of my Brethren in Christ" and to avoid "fellowship with any practice that may be incompatible with the Word of God amoung masons." Controversy continued. Two years later he complained that the Hampton church granted letters of dismission to three anti-Masons even though they proclaimed "they could not and would not walk with the Ch[urch]." Apparently Miller's Masonic past was still a lightning rod, for he swore, "I never said — nor practiced, anything knowingly to injure my country, the Ch. of Christ — or my fellow creatures." At least he could attend the 1833 annual meeting of the Association in good conscience as the delegates advised churches to treat Freemasonry "as they would any other evil."[54]

Even so, Masonic imagery continued to suffuse Miller's writing. According to his memoir, another dream, very similar to his first, inspired him to begin preaching. Once again, celestial guides led him to an upper room filled with light and pilgrims singing "Hallelujah to the Lamb!" Odd references occur throughout the tale, but he interpreted the dream as God's confirming his faith and course of action. Bliss denied twice that dreams held any particular significance for Miller, but he also remembered Miller's referring to the dream frequently over the years. Seemingly inconsequential events would remind him of details in the dream, as though they had been portents.[55] Caveats notwithstanding, this was not the last time Miller would use dreams to convey messages obliquely. More significant, as we shall see, was his later description of the dream's impact that would signal his drift toward a more romantic, affective spirituality.

It cannot be coincidental that Miller resigned from the Masons less than a month after his first public lecture on the end of the world. Revealed religion now required him to make a choice, and revival sounded that clarion call. During a conference meeting in the

54. September 10, 1831, Miller Farm; Miller to Truman Hendryx, April 10, 1833, Miller Letters.

55. Despite Bliss's denials, but Miller's own comments tended to refute Bliss's assurances. For a discussion of the role dreams have played in innovative religion, see Ann Taves, *Fits, Trances, and Visions: Experiencing Religion and Explaining Experience from Wesley to James* (Princeton, N.J.: Princeton University Press, 1999).

spring of 1828, the Hampton congregation broke into tears "or labouring under solemn conviction for sin." Among them were "2 or 3 young men and a number of young women," including two of his own children, Bellona and William. The refreshing spread through the region, sparking millennial anticipation again and provoking the Washington Baptist Association to pray, "May the Lord hasten it in his time."[56] Miller was a delegate, and whether or not he fanned the excitement, it must have encouraged him. In 1829 he resumed a practice of his youth, jotting down Bible references of sermons, but now he added notes on the preachers' principal points. Messages based on Amos, "prepare to meet thy God," and on Mark, "prepare ye the way for coming of Christ," particularly attracted his attention. "The Millenial or Glorious day will commence on the exert[ion] of the People of God," he noted the preacher saying. Whether or not he was yet prepared to dispute the means, Miller heard something else in the sermon. One prepares for the coming of Christ in part by "exhorting to duty" in all one's connections, especially family and church. The preacher thus verified what he now heard "continually ringing in my ears, 'Go and tell the world of their danger.'"[57]

By 1830 he was moving in that direction. According to his memoir, Miller at some point began sharing his apocalyptic beliefs privately and individually with others to the extent that he achieved "no little celebrity in his denomination in all that region." There is little direct evidence of this. Quite possibly he discussed his millenarian views with others at meetings of his Baptist association or the Vermont Missionary Society. In 1825 he wrote to a sister and brother-in-law in Canada exhorting them to care for their "futurity" and penning a hymn of praise, but there was no mention of an approaching end of the world. Bliss recounted a story of his debating the second coming with a local physician who had proclaimed him a "monomaniac" on the subject, but otherwise Miller never mentioned the incident. As personal memory or family lore, it could have happened at any time before, during, or after the Millerite movement. In the 1840 edition of his published lectures Miller claimed to have written one

56. *Washington Association Minutes*, 1828. Refreshing was noted again in 1831.

57. Miller to N. Kendrick, March 12, 1828, Miller Letters; Sermon Notes, 1829, Miller Papers, Jenks Collection; Bliss, *Memoirs*, 92.

of them "twelve years hence" — in other words, in 1828 — but if so, no draft of it has survived.[58]

It was in 1831 that his views first became public. He hoped to persuade some minister to preach a warning, thereby avoiding the necessity of his doing it, and in February Hampton pastor Leman Andrus received an eight-page demonstration of "a few Evidences of the time of the 2nd coming of Christ" that would happen in "1843 or 1847 at most." There is no record of a response from him; Andrus left the congregation shortly after. Three months later Miller wrote again to sister Anna Atwood and her husband Joseph, now a Universalist, continuing his exhortation but this time adding a dire warning. "You may depend on it my friends, that Jesus will come within 12 years, in the year 1843 or before, in that year the prophecies will be compleated the dead Saints or bodies will rise, those children of God who are alive then, will be changed, and caught up to meet the Lord in the air, where they will be married to him. the World and all the wicked will be burnt up (not anihilated) and then Christ will descend and reign personally with his Saints; and at the end of the 1000 years the wicked will be raised, judged and sent to everlasting punishment (this is the second death)." He threw down the gauntlet, challenging Joseph's Universalist friends to a theological duel, even offering to pay all the expenses if they proved him wrong.[59]

The lamb had to all appearances suddenly become a lion. He had gained "freedom to converse on the subject" and demonstrated his willingness to "defend his own views, and oppose those differing from him." His hopes in Andrus disappointed, Miller looked farther afield. Hampton was seeking a new minister, and someone invited Truman Hendryx, a Baptist preacher in Salem at the southern end of Washington County, to visit with the congregation. A Baptist brother warned Hendryx there was a man in the Hampton church "possessing considerable influence who had many curious notions on doc-

58. Paulina Miller and William Miller to Joseph and Anna Atwood, June 28, 1825, Miller Letters; Bliss, *Memoirs,* 94-97; William Miller, *Evidence From Scripture and History of the Second Coming of Christ About the Year 1843* (Boston: B. B. Mussey, 1840), 300.

59. In the *Apology and Defense,* 16, Miller said he "prayed that some minister might see the truth, and devote himself to its promulgation"; Miller to Anna and Joseph Atwood, May 31, 1831, Miller Letters.

trinal points and on the prophecies, particularly on the latter and also (to use the brother's language) that he was 'hard on ministers who differed with him.'" Reluctantly, Hendryx agreed to pay a visit, and after a week of preaching he had steeled himself sufficiently to pay his respects to Miller "tremblingly, and with the utmost caution." Several other prospects for the pastor's post visited, and, he said, "I found I was not altogether alone" in feeling intimidated. During Hendryx's visit, though, Miller successfully challenged his postmillennialism, using Scripture to demonstrate that Christ himself would purify the world in twelve years. At the end Miller told him that this was his view. "Well," responded Hendryx, "it is mine."[60]

Miller had always been pugnacious, even feisty, and he could be cruel. Emily, who lived with Anna and Joe Atwood, was unmarried, and Miller goaded her. Gossip said a former beau of hers was going to marry an "old maid" housekeeper "about your age, and not half as handsome — see what you have lost for being so nice." Don't you become an old maid, he wrote, "if you can buy a man for love or money — and if there is none that will be sold or given for love, do beg one — old or young, big or little, gentle or simple, drunk or sober. get one and take off the curse."[61] No wonder preachers feared crossing swords with him. Confidence fed determination, and when he was sure of himself Miller could act decisively, though sometimes roughly. In the summer of 1831, he was clear not only about the message — Jesus was coming — but about himself. With no one else beating drums to warn the world of impending destruction, he was ready. He needed only the opportunity.

How he came to preach for the first time is legendary among Adventists. The story mixes verifiable fact, heroics, and apologetics. As Miller recalled late in life, and as family lore has preserved the tale, one Saturday he received a particularly strong urging: "Go and tell it

60. Bliss, *Memoirs,* 93; no pastor for the Hampton Church was listed in the *Washington Association Minutes* in 1831; Hendryx to Joshua V. Himes, April 14, 1850, Miller Letters. Hendryx wrote in response to a request from Himes for letters and personal reminiscences intended for what became Bliss's *Memoirs.* He defended Miller's gruff approach to people, saying it only happened "because he saw or thought he saw a spirit of self-importance," but he did not deny that Miller might have "dealt harshly with a brother for holding an error."

61. Miller to Anna and Joseph Atwood, May 31, 1831, Miller Letters.

to the world." While he had been feeling the compulsion for many years, this was so powerful that he promised God he would go if someone would invite him to speak. Since as yet no one had, Miller felt safe. That same afternoon a nephew arrived with an invitation to preach the next day to Baptists in Dresden, sixteen miles northwest across Lake Champlain. They were without a preacher and wanted to hear what Miller had to say about the end of the world. Caught in a trap of his own devising, he fled to a grove just west of the farmhouse and begged God to release him from the contract, but to no avail. Submitting to God's will, Miller traveled to Dresden that evening with his nephew, preached the following morning, and was so warmly received that he spent the next week with them lecturing on the approaching second coming of Christ.[62]

The date of Miller's first sermon is problematic, and while determining it does not affect the history of the movement it does illustrate Miller's sometimes hazy memory of details. In later memoirs he dated the first sermon on the first Sunday in August, but he gave three different years, 1824, 1832, and 1833. Bliss had the last word and corrected him; it must have happened in 1831, and if it indeed took place in August it must have been no earlier than the second Sunday. The first Sunday was the seventh, and on the ninth he wrote to Truman Hendryx from Low Hampton without mentioning this landmark event in his life.[63] Bliss is correct; in March 1832 Miller reported having "lectured on it in a number of places this winter." As justice of the peace, Miller signed summonses and held justice court at the farm, keeping very careful records of proceedings in a blot book and in hundreds of receipts and duplicates. He signed warrants and summonses on August 8, 9, and 10 of 1831, and

62. Bliss, *Memoirs,* 97-99. A charming rendition of the story adds details from family memory, including the nephew's name (Irving), the church's familiarity with Miller's views, the nephew's crossing Lake Champlain by boat at Brennan's Landing, and the congregation's meeting in a house, with Miller sitting in an armchair to lecture. Arthur Whitefield Spalding, *Pioneer Stories of the Second Advent Message,* rev. ed. (Brushton, N.Y.: TEACH Services, 1995), 40-49.

63. *Midnight Cry* 1, no. 1 (November 17, 1842), 2; Himes, *Views,* 12; Miller, *Apology and Defense,* 17; Bliss, *Memoirs,* 98n. See also Francis D. Nichol, *The Midnight Cry: A Defense of the Character and Conduct of William Miller and the Millerites* (Washington, D.C.: Review and Herald, 1944), 43n.

not another until August 23. The only Sunday that month with a full unobstructed week following it was August 14, making it the most likely date of his first preaching and weeklong series of lectures in Dresden.[64]

Evidence verifies other details of the story. Miller's sister Sylvia had married Silas Guilford and moved to Dresden, where they helped to establish a Baptist church in 1823. It was small and always struggling, like Dresden itself, with no more than forty members at any time and usually with half that number. It frequently lacked a minister and was always hungry for preaching from any who would go there. That was the problem. Every description of the town calls it isolated; an 1850 gazetteer says Dresden "[is] so difficult of access that it is almost impossible to get to it, except by way of the Lakes." The headwaters of Lake Champlain on the east narrow and split to become little more than rivers. It would have been a difficult trip, but with steamboats (operating since 1823) and ferries at various locations it was not impossible to travel by horse in a good day's ride from Low Hampton. Surely he had shared his views with Sylvia and other relatives, as he had with Anna and Joseph, so the congregation was probably primed to hear what he had to say. Revival had been flaring locally for months, stoked by a new technique: four-day, protracted meetings that reaped hundreds of converts. Miller himself tallied newly won souls in Granville, Hartford, Salem, Poultney, Benson, Brandon, Middletown, and Rutland, a sure sign that May of the Lord's "pouring out his Spirit in this region." Fervor had cooled somewhat later in the summer, but the Hampton Baptists (undoubtedly with Miller in the lead) had arranged for their own protracted meeting to begin in early September, with a guest preacher from Georgia.[65] It was a climate fit to breed millennial expectations.

64. Miller to Joseph and Anna Atwood, March 27, 1832, Miller Letters; Justice Record, 1831-1834, Miller Farm. When Adventist Historic Properties purchased the farm and began restoration they found a barrel in the attic containing these documents, cited above in note 40.

65. On the Guilfords' role in founding the congregation see J. B. Lippincott, *History of Washington County, New York* (New York: J. B. Lippincott, 1873), 288; the description of Dresden is from Corey, *Gazetteer*, 249-50. The Vermont Association described the town as "quite remote from other Churches of our denomination, and consequently enjoy[ing] but few privileges" (*Minutes*, 1835, 10). The Washington As-

His pastor at the time, Isaac Fuller, took much credit for midwifing Miller's preaching career. In 1840, not having heard from Miller in a year, Fuller scolded, reminding him, "I have been, as it were, by [your] side from the commencement of [your] life as a writer or a public speaker. I had the honor (as I believe God esteems it) & the shame (as many of my brethren esteem it) of an humble instrumentality in starting [you] out to proclaim the 2d advent near; & I stood by [you] and prayed for [you] at [your] first public lecture."[66] One can imagine Miller's fretfully asking his pastor to accompany him on that terrifying journey and the preacher encouraging him along the way.

This scenario fits the image of a man on his knees in the woods begging God to release him from their agreement. As his dreams reflected Bunyan's allegorical journey of life, this story repeats the self-negation and negotiation of all biblical prophets when called to deliver a difficult message. This doesn't render untrue the more hagiographic version of Adventism's creation myth, an inexperienced messenger setting out alone on a wilderness road to begin a dangerous mission. It rather projects that story in terms both Miller and his readers would readily comprehend, the human capacity both for fearfulness and courage. This was the same man who endured enemy fire in battle while imagining deadly scenarios at home. Assurance and doubt had always pulled at him and would continue to do so. "I sometimes feel as though I can do all things 'through Christ strengthening me,'" he once confessed to Hendryx. "[A]nd sometimes the shaking of a leaf is terror to me."[67]

God comforted, too. Discovering the imminent end of the world

---

sociation noted the refreshing in 1831: "The present is evidently a season of unusual refreshing from the presence of the Lord, to many portions of his moral vineyard. It may with the utmost propriety be said there is the sound of an abundance of rain. And we rejoice to say it has begun to descend upon some of the churches in this association" (*Minutes,* 1831, 8. See also Miller to Hendryx, May 31 and August 9, 1831, Miller Letters.

66. Fuller to Miller, December 10, 1840, Miller Letters. Fuller was so upset at Miller's not writing to him that he used the third person in referring to the addressee. I have substituted the second person for clarity. This scene also raises the likelihood that Fuller played a significant role as counselor, mentor, and teacher during those long years that Miller studied his Bible and honed his apocalyptic views.

67. Miller to Hendryx, August 27, 1835, Miller Letters.

had been God's personal gift to him, reward for returning to his roots and for working arduously to defend God's word. In all this God had shown himself, unlike humans, to be constant, full of grace and provision even for him who was unworthy, disobedient, unlovable. God's omnipotence was acceptable to Miller because while conversion made relationship with that God possible, exegesis made it reasonable. So long as the gift remained private, personal, its reconciling effect was all the proof Miller needed of its truth.

Going public would raise the stakes. Predicting the end of the world would make Miller the godfather of untold hopes and dreams, not just his own and his family's. Unfortunately, the world that awaited his portentous news had already gone far to reshape Miller's archaic vision of a transcendent God approachable only by God's fiat. An increasingly market-driven, democratic culture understood relationship with God more easily as *contract* than as *covenant,* a set of mutually agreed-upon rights and obligations, causes and effects, potentialities and boundaries. Promise of future bliss might provide immediate benefits and inspire arduous labors and uncountable sacrifices in its interest, but, unlike Miller, they would ultimately need more than good feelings to justify all that. God would have to keep the promise; Jesus would have to show up. Miller may have gone far to authenticate his fatherhood close to home, but soon he would become responsible for the spiritual fate of dependents in the thousands. It remained to be seen what his paternity, and God's, might have wrought.

CHAPTER FIVE

Go and Tell It to the World

According to William Miller, Isaac Sawyer, his pastor early in 1832, agreed with his view of the Millennium and would preach it if he were not so "affraid of being a Millerite."[1] Already, a scant five months after lecturing in Dresden, Miller was using a label that would become notorious and test the response to his message. Considering his own fourteen-year refusal to speak publicly, he might have been more patient with others' reluctance. That he was not indicates something more important than public reputation, more personal, was at stake.

When Miller promised to tell it to the world, he had family, church, and locality in mind, the only world he knew. Miller was preaching to his family, lecturing among fellow Baptists, seeking confirmation from his pastor. The week after lecturing in Dresden, Eli B. Smith invited him to speak on the end of the world to his Baptist congregation in Poultney,[2] again, to those who had long known him as friend, neighbor, and civic leader. Reluctance to believe and

1. Miller to Truman Hendryx, January 25, 1832, Miller Letters, Jenks Memorial Collection of Adventual Materials, Aurora University, Aurora, Illinois [hereafter cited as Miller Letters].

2. Sylvester Bliss, *Memoirs of William Miller: Generally Known as a Lecturer on the Prophecies, and the Second Coming of Christ* (Boston: Joshua V. Himes, 1853), 99. Beginning in 1834 Miller kept a log of his itinerary noting where he preached and the Scripture texts of his sermons, but in the first three years the narrative depends entirely on Miller's memory of events from 1842 and 1845. As we have seen, his recollection was not always sound.

commit to action from any of these people became a personal rejection that sparked fear for their salvation and worry that he was failing in his "parental duties" as a father and community leader. Worse, their doubt fed his own. Chronology and history supported his theory, he said to Hendryx, but the smallest error in either left all afloat. "I wish I could know my adoption as strong," he admitted, "as I believe my calculation is right."[3]

Despite his own private doubts, the approval of his network pulled him forward. This intimate world bound by blood and mutual obligation had long nurtured Miller's spiritual growth, and now it midwifed the Millerite movement. Excitement and revival followed in the wake of his lectures. Miller became a lay leader of the Dresden church, and in 1832 it witnessed twenty baptisms, the best report the tiny congregation ever enjoyed.[4] Refreshing had been warming the Poultney church for nearly a year under Smith's stewardship, and the congregation gave his views a warm welcome.[5] Then Miller lectured in Pawlet and other unspecified towns in western Vermont, and he asked sister Anna to arrange an invitation for him to preach in and around Bolton, Lower Canada, which eventually he received.[6] That summer he attended several protracted meetings, and though there is no evidence of his preaching or lecturing at any of them, word of his views must have circulated. Everywhere he lectured, Miller said, "I have had large assemblies. [T]here is an increasing anxiety on the subject in this

3. Miller to Hendryx, October 23, 1834, Miller Letters.

4. *Vermont Baptist Association Minutes,* 1833. Miller was a delegate from the congregation at the annual meeting and also a messenger from the Washington Association. J. B. Lippicott's *History of Washington County, New York* (New York: J. B. Lippincott, 1873), 288, records a revival that by 1833 had boosted total membership to sixty and lists Miller and Elder Isaac Fuller as preachers.

5. J. Joslin, B. Frisbie, and F. Ruggles, *A History of the Town of Poultney, Vermont, From its Settlement to the Year 1875, with Family and Biographical Sketches and Incidents* (Poultney, Vt.: J. Joslin, B. Frisbie, F. Ruggles, 1875), 112.

6. On Millerism in Canada see J. I. Little, "Millennial Invasion: Millerism in the Eastern Townships of Lower Canada," in *Anglo-American Millennialism, from Milton to the Millerites,* ed. Richard Connors and Andrew Golin Gow, Studies in the History of the Christian Tradition 13 (Leiden: E. J. Brill Press, 2004), 177-204, and Denis Fortin, "'The World Turned Upside Down': Millerism in the Eastern Townships, 1830-1845," *Journal of Eastern Townships Studies* 11 (Fall 1997): 39-53.

quarter."[7] His reputation grew in the Baptist world in which he was already regionally known. Truman Hendryx was not the only preacher to show up at the farm to "talk Bible" with Miller. In March 1832 a licensed preacher "from Hamilton" (a seminarian) visited "to learn these strange notions of 'crazy Miller'" and asked to board there for several months to "study Bible" with him.[8]

Popularity surprised and delighted him. He regaled Hendryx with reports of invitations flowing to the farm, refreshings following in his wake, and hardened skeptics falling to their knees. A gang of ten "blackguards" in Beekmantown threatened that if he did not "clear out of the State" they would "put me where the dogs would never find me." But God "poured out his spirit" and blessed his work. Lest he succumb to pride, Miller asked his old friend to pray for him "that I may always see my need, feel my weakness, & be kept humble & that I may always declare the truth. Do Pray."[9] A prodding to humility may explain his frequent self-deprecation, referring to himself commonly as the "old man," an "old dry stick," an "old stammering man," a "great wicked sinner." When Isaac Sawyer moved he left the congregation with no preacher, wrote Miller, "except the old man with his concordance. [A]nd he is so shunned with his cold, dull & lifeless performance, that I have strong doubts whether he will attempt again." The tone suggests parroting of his critics, a sardonic weapon he often used against opponents. But he was capable of false humility, taking pleasure in being so humble. Ambition always snuggled with diffidence just under the surface of his personality. "I wish I had the tongue of an Appollos & the powers of mind of a Paul," he confided, "what a field might I not explore what powerfull arguments might not be brought to prove the authenticity of the scriptures, but I want one thing, more than either the spirit of Christ and of God. for he is able to take worms and thrash mountains."[10]

In reality, Miller was an effective speaker. One commentator de-

7. Bliss, *Memoirs,* 99; Miller to Anna and Joseph Atwood, September 16, 1832; Miller to Hendryx, October 1, 1832, Miller Letters.

8. Miller to Truman Hendryx, March 26 and May 20, 1832, Miller Letters. Miller completed the letter two months after beginning it.

9. Miller to Hendryx, October 23, 1834, Miller Letters. Four months later, in his letter of February 11, Miller repeated the request almost word for word.

10. Miller to Hendryx, April 10, 1833, Miller Letters.

scribed his voice as "strong and mellow," and though his style was "not remarkable either for grace or eloquence,"[11] simplicity was a virtue. He was certainly unprepossessing in appearance — short and heavyset with a ruddy, round face — but listeners could see something of themselves in this man whose limited schooling, plain clothes, and lack of pretense matched their own. To all appearances he was just like them, and he reaped the benefit of a democratic culture that valued commonness. Age was no handicap either. In his early fifties, Miller may have been ten years beyond the average life expectancy, but survivorship lent his words gravity and wisdom. Jackson-era Americans did not so glorify youth that they had forgotten the respect owed to the fathers.[12]

Furthermore, what he had to say made sense. Miller's message mixed rational argument with compelling imagery that not only persuaded the mind but piqued the senses. Patterned on the schedule of a protracted meeting, his course of lectures on the second coming of Christ gathered people for as many days as they requested, as often as three times a day, lasting into evening candle time. He would pray, line out a hymn or two the audience would sing, and then present a tightly framed argument that progressed from one lecture to the next, setting forth his expectation of Jesus' imminent return and the reasons he believed in it. The syllabus changed over time in response to circumstance and public response, but, as his earliest publication illustrates, initially it conveyed three messages.

The first was expository. Jesus is coming, and simple arithmetic applied to prophetic chronology showed when. Daniel received a vision of four kingdoms (Daniel 2:39-45) that would endure for 2300 years. Exegetes had long believed it foretold the duration of earthly time after the reoccupation of Jerusalem following the Babylonian captivity. Miller and exegetes commonly dated this to a decree of Artaxeres in 457 B.C. Applying the day = year formula, subtracting

11. Quoted in Francis D. Nichol, *The Midnight Cry: A Defense of the Character and Conduct of William Miller and the Millerites* (Washington, D.C.: Review and Herald, 1944), 122, 123.

12. An interesting example is the popular adulation of George Robert Twelve Hewes, last survivor of the Boston Tea Party. See Alfred Young, *The Shoemaker and the Tea Party: Memory and the American Revolution* (Boston: Beacon Press, 1999).

457 from 2300 took listeners to the end of the vision, 1843. But there were other confirming elements to the prophecy.

> 2300 years from 457 years before Christ, Daniel's vision will end. 490 years from the same 457 B.C. Christ was crucified and the 70 weeks ended. The fourth kingdom and the last of all earthly kingdoms, was divided into two parts, the first began 158 years B.C. and lasted 666 years to the end of the pagan daily sacrifice abomination, which was 508 A.D. The last number given in Daniel (viz) 1335 carries us down to the resurrection and will end A.D. 1843. In this last number is included the reign of Antichrist, 1260 years begining [sic] in A.D. 538 and ending A.D. 1798; also the 1290 beginning A.D. 598, and ending A.D. 1798. The remaining 45 years are for the spread of the gospel; the resurrection of the two witnesses; the church to come out of the wilderness; the troublous times; the last great battle; and the second coming of Christ, to raise his people; and reign with them personally the thousand years following.[13]

Careful listening over several sessions was required for people to grasp his complicated chronology, but sensory metaphor helped. One fanciful image after another marched before them as Miller led audiences through prophetic time as Daniel's vision projected it, explaining how history had fulfilled each one represented by images like the segmented "man" of gold, silver, brass, and iron and clay; the four-faced beast (lion, sheep, man, eagle); the ram, the goat, the big horn and the little horn. Thus was prophecy rendered concrete; the work of God across salvation history came back to life in the here and now.

Beyond exposition, his lectures conveyed a second, apologetic, purpose. Illustrating the fulfillment of prophecy proved the authenticity of Scripture and the authority of the God who gave it to the world. The end is coming, he told Hendryx, and as evil grows in the

13. Miller, *Evidences from Scripture & History of the Second Coming of Christ about the year A.D. 1843, and of his Personal Reign of 1000 Years* (Brandon, Vt.: Telegraph Office, 1833), 31. This pamphlet is a compilation from articles that appeared in the *Vermont Telegraph,* discussed below. Only two of those pamphlets have survived, though their manuscripts are contained in the Miller Papers at Aurora University.

last days the power of Satan to confuse and distract will make it increasingly difficult to convert people. So preachers must lead listeners "by slow and sure steps to Jesus Christ."

> I say slow because I expect they are not strong enough to run yet. sure because the Bible is a sure word and where your hearers are not well doctrinated, you must preach Bible you must prove all things by Bible you must talk bible. You must exhort bible, you must pray Bible, and Love Bible, and do all in your power to make others Love Bible too.[14]

Using nothing but a Bible and concordance when lecturing, Miller kept listeners focused on that essential point. "Profane history," as he called it, was an important tool to demonstrate the reliability of prophecy, but it only played a supporting role to Scripture. "It is an argument to convince the men of the world, that the Bible is true," he wrote, "for they are always ready to admit profane history but not the Bible."[15]

The third message was homiletic. Proving the authenticity of the Bible through the fulfillment of prophecy must prompt faith in and commitment to God. Evidence could convince the mind, but moving people to act required something more dramatic. Now old poetic proclivities came to hand, helping Miller paint vivid pictures of the impending cataclysm. Using phrases that almost certainly came from his preaching, Miller described for Hendryx approaching horrors as the horsemen of the Apocalypse were unleashed.

> [S]oon, very soon, God will arise in his anger and the vine of the earth will be reaped. See, see, the angel with his sharp sickle, is about to take the field. see younder, trembling victims fall before his pestilential breath. high and low rich and poor trembling, falling before the appalling grave, the dreadfull "Cholera." Hark, hear those dreadfull bellowings of the angry nations. It is the presage of horrid and terrific war. Look! Look again! see crowns, and kings, and kingdoms, tumbling to the dust. see Lords, and Nobles, captains, and mighty men all arming for the bloody

14. Miller to Hendryx, January 25, 1832, Miller Letters.
15. Miller to Hendryx, November 28, 1834, Miller Letters.

> deamon fight. see the carnivorous fowls fly screeming through the air. see, see these signs.

Then nature itself will become the instrument of death:

> behold the heavens grow black with clouds the sun has vailed himself, the moon pale and forsaken hangs in middle air, the hails descend the seven thunders utter loud their voices. the lightnings send their vivid stream of sulphros flames abroad and the great City of the nations falls to rise no more forever, and forever.

Now, having evoked terror, Miller carefully offered hope and comfort:

> At this dread moment. Look, Look. Oh! look and see, what means that ray of light. the clouds have bust assunder. the heavens appear the great white throne's in sight. Amazement fills the universe with awe — he comes — he comes. behold the savior comes, lift up your heads ye saints he comes! — he comes!! — he comes!!![16]

Sitting for hours in the glimmer of candles hearing stories of kingdoms rising and falling, monstrous animals prowling through history, and angels delivering visions must have been enormously entertaining. No wonder his audience came back night after night anticipating the next piece of the end-time puzzle, wondering what secret might be revealed next. If some walked away convinced that Miller was right, many others went home at least wondering if he *might* be right. Even an occasional hardened skeptic was able to change his mind. An Elder Mattison, who attended Miller's course of lectures in Shaftesbury, "got up at the close of my last discourse, and in a most solemn and impressive manner told the congregation that he 'had been convicted, confounded, & converted,' and confessed, he had wrote and said things, against the speaker of which he was now ashamed; he had called him 'the end of the world man,' and 'the old visionary,' 'dreamer,' 'fanatic,' etc."[17]

Effective as it was, if Miller's preaching had remained the only medium to propagate his message, Millerism would have generated

16. Miller to Hendryx, March 26 and May 20, 1832, Miller Letters.

17. Miller to Hendryx, February 21, 1837, Miller Letters.

nothing more than regional excitement. But in the spring of 1832 his views appeared in print for the first time, changing the movement's life and his. The *Vermont Telegraph* published in Brandon was the official organ for the state's Baptists. It championed all the popular denominational causes — missions, temperance, seminaries, sabbath schools, the American Colonization Society, and anti-Masonry (though it never endorsed it). Millennial themes were prominent. In 1829 it reprinted a prophetic chronology (not from Miller) demonstrating that the destruction of the Turks would be complete by 1843, speculated on the condition of the Christian church as one of the signs of the times, publicized various views on allegorical interpretations of Scripture, and showed interest in the conversion of the Jews and the ten lost tribes of Israel.[18] It was the logical vehicle for disseminating Miller's views to a wide audience. Eli Smith's letters occasionally appeared in the paper, and he lent his name to a plan to publicize Miller's views. Smith would pose questions about the second coming of Christ to Miller, and Miller would reply in writing, giving Smith "liberty to publish."[19] The *Telegraph* often printed serialized commentaries on topics of interest to Baptists and responses to them. Miller's exciting topic was timely and sure to attract readers, and since he had already been lecturing, people probably had heard something about him already. By May the articles were appearing, and Miller was confident "it will start some queries if nothing more."[20]

Like the story of his first preaching, there are oddities in this one. Miller said in his account that he tried to remain anonymous to the editor, signing his manuscripts only with his initials, "W. M." But when the editor refused to print his work unless the writer identified himself, Miller complied.[21] Having taken a public stand on behalf of his beliefs, why was he reluctant to claim them in print? Miller may have conflated this story with that of the Fourth of July

18. The *Telegraph* was printed weekly from September 1828 until October 1843, when it went out of production. The Vermont Department of Libraries has microfilmed the issues that have survived.

19. Miller to Hendryx, January 25, 1832, Miller Letters.

20. Miller to Hendryx, March 26, 1832, Miller Letters.

21. William Miller, *Apology and Defense* (Boston: Joshua V. Himes, 1845), 16; Bliss, *Memoirs*, 99-100.

ode that propelled his political career in Poultney, both attempting to project an aura of innocent humility. If it actually happened this way, the peculiarity of his views may not have been the reason for his attempt to remain anonymous. Anti-Masonry was running hottest in the region and denomination then, and the *Telegraph*'s willingness to publicize anti-Masonry might have caused Miller to suspect they would not print his work if they knew who had written it despite his resignation from the lodge.

Also, exactly what was published is not clear. Historians beginning with Bliss have all assumed these were the same lectures the *Telegraph* published in 1833 in pamphlet form as the first printing of Miller's essential text, *Evidences from Scripture and History of the Second Coming of Christ About the Year* A.D. *1843, and of His Personal Reign of 1000 Years.* Not enough issues of the paper have survived to answer the riddle, but those that do show the first of these lectures appeared much later, on October 30, with the sixteen-article series continuing into March 1833. Manuscripts of *Telegraph* articles appearing in the Miller Papers at Aurora University show some of them to have been lectures, while others were responses to critics. All are addressed to the *Telegraph* editor, none to Elder Smith. Unless the paper reprinted the series in the fall, the spring articles could not have been lectures.[22] Miller probably began with a series of letters that gradually built interest, so that in the first printed lecture in October he could claim to be presenting them "[a]t the earnest solicitation of some of your readers."[23]

Regardless, as early as February 1833 Miller was planning to have the *Telegraph* print a compilation of the articles in pamphlet form, using his friends to distribute it,[24] and later that year the pamphlet appeared. The printed word had the impact Miller predicted. His views now spread more rapidly throughout the region, attracting notice and interest. Henry Jones, a colporteur (itinerant salesman of religious and reform literature), read his articles and found his interpretations "both reasonable and scriptural," particularly Miller's

22. Unfortunately, no issues have survived from December 28, 1830, to September 25, 1831.

23. *Vermont Telegraph,* October 30, 1832.

24. Miller asked Hendryx how many copies he could distribute. Miller to Hendryx, February 8, 1833, Miller Letters.

view of the personal rather than spiritual reign of Christ. Miller tried to enlist him as a student and fellow preacher on the second coming,[25] but Jones would prove to be at best a frustrating disciple. Moral reform, at first temperance and then antislavery, captured his commitment, and while he eventually preached premillennialism he remained aloof from the meat of Miller's message. Still, he added Miller's publications to his list of available literature and in that way helped popularize his views. Undoubtedly it was at Jones's suggestion that Miller sent several copies of his pamphlet lectures to the *Emancipator,* a New York City antislavery paper, for distribution.[26]

The pamphlet's success inspired Isaac Wescott, Baptist preacher in Stillwater, New York, to republish the lectures as a book, using a Troy printer to do the work. If Miller would buy five hundred copies, Wescott offered, he could order a run of fifteen hundred for $135. He chose to do this without consulting Miller, simply informing him of the plan, but he allowed the author the chance to revise the pamphlet if he wished.[27] Accordingly, Miller revised, reorganized, augmented the lectures, and adjusted the title slightly. *Evidence From Scripture and History of the Second Coming of Christ, About the Year 1843; Exhibited in a Course of Lectures* thus appeared in 1836 with Wescott recorded as copyright holder. Distribution, by sale and gift, was so extensive that he produced a second edition two years later, using a different printer, with two other editions following (under different auspices) in 1840 and 1842.

Publicity and public activity required an official Baptist response. Their democratic polity that encouraged each believer to discern truth and to act on it sometimes bore bitter fruit. Some, like Miller's grandfather Phelps, were inspired to preach innovative

25. Jones to Miller, February 21 and May 13, 1833, Miller Letters.

26. Charles W. Denison to Miller, March 25, 1834, Miller Letters. Jones had tried to enlist Miller as an agent for the *Emancipator* in Washington County, and accepting the pamphlets may have been part of a deal. Denison was diplomatic in responding to Miller's views, offering compliments but also pointing out several difficulties.

27. Isaac Wescott to Miller, March 6, 1835, Miller Letters. Francis Nichol credits Wescott with producing the 1833 pamphlet (*Midnight Cry,* 57). While he offers no evidence to support this, it may explain Wescott's presumption. Later events suggest interest in Millerism or aiding the cause was not his principal motive.

ideas, even heresies, and charlatans posing as preachers duped people out of money, property, and other men's wives. In 1831 the Washington Baptist Association warned their congregations to discourage from preaching any man "who is not well known, without satisfactory recommendation of recent date." With Miller itinerating more frequently, the warning could be applied to him. As early as February, Hampton Baptists had talked of affording him a license to preach, but it was not until September 14 that they provided it.[28] Miller was typically both excited and self-effacing about it. Only two days later he wrote to sister Anna, "My Brethren have given me a license unworthy, and old, and disobedient as I am. 'Oh to grace how great a debtor.'"[29]

He was no longer merely William Miller, *Esquire,* but *Reverend* Miller. The first, earned by his election and service as justice of the peace, posed no problems for him, but this new honorific troubled his Baptist sensibilities. Isaac Sawyer had criticized Miller for referring to him as *Rev.* and when Hendryx applied the title to him Miller copied Sawyer's words verbatim. "I wish you would look into your bible & see if you can find the word Rev. applyed to a sinful mortal as myself and govern yourself accordingly."[30] Regardless, he carried the license with him so long, folded and creased, that a fresh copy was required. Other endorsements followed from Baptists, restorationist Christian Connexion preachers, and Methodists, some with dozens of signatures attached. The language varied. Hampton Baptists were "satisfyed Br. Miller has a gift to improve in Publick and are willing he should. . . ." Another, dated March 19, 1835, was equally innocuous, but some who had heard his lectures added their own, more enthusiastic endorsement: "Having heard [Miller's] Lectures, I see no way to avoid the conclusion that the

28. *Washington Baptist Association Minutes,* 1831; License, September 14, 1833, Miller Letters.

29. Miller to Anna and Joseph Atwood, September 16, 1833, Miller Letters.

30. Sawyer to Miller, March 5, 1834, and Miller to Hendryx, March 22, 1834, Miller Letters. Sawyer had referred to himself as a "sinful creature"; otherwise, the wording is identical. Miller mentioned discussion of licensing him to Hendryx on February 8. That it took seven months for it to happen may have resulted from opposition to his views in his congregation, but it could also have resulted from Miller's self-effacement.

Coming of Christ will be as soon as 1843." Ten preachers agreed, among them S. Dillaway, then of West Granville, who would play a central role in his later expulsion from the Baptist church.[31] Thus these endorsements became an early means for allowing believers to commit themselves not just to the general idea of a premillennial advent but to Miller's views specifically.

The endorsement of longtime Baptist colleagues along with the printed word opened doors for preaching. In 1834 the pace quickened and, while seasonal and sporadic, essentially did not subside for ten years. Isaac Sawyer, now preaching in Jay, New York, arranged for him a projected month-long lecture tour of northern towns including Westport, Jay, and Keeseville. Isaac Fuller, a longtime missionary in the Vermont Association who had filled pulpits in Dresden and Poultney, was preaching Miller's views in Chautauqua County in western New York, spreading interest and planting early seeds in that region. Miller counted at least seven other ministers doing the same.[32] Invitations to deliver lectures and preach at protracted meetings arrived regularly. In October Miller began noting the date, place, and Bible texts of every sermon he preached in "text books," mapping his location virtually every day for nearly ten years.[33] From 1835 through 1837 he preached an average of sixty-eight times a year to audiences at home or in his home region of Washington County, New York, and Rutland County, Vermont. Often the call was for a single sermon, but occasionally he would deliver an entire course of lectures, which kept him occupied for a week or longer. In 1835 an invitation finally took him to Lower Canada (Quebec) across the border from New York for nineteen days, followed by preaching in Vermont for two weeks on the way back home. There were but a handful of appointments in 1836 until mid-September, but then another tour of northern New York towns kept him on the road until the end of October.

With the new year the pace quickened. More often Vermont and New York preachers requested an entire course of lectures, keeping

31. These documents are located in the folder "Certificates of Endorsement" in the Jenks Collection.

32. Miller to Hendryx, February 8, 1833, Miller Letters.

33. Text books, October 1, 1834–June 23, 1844, Jenks Collection.

Miller away from home for weeks at a time. He had learned how to make the most effective use of his labor, scheduling appearances regionally rather than individually — in Shaftesbury, Rupert, and Wells at the end of January; Shrewsbury, Andover, Weston, and Mount Holly in March; North Springfield, Haddon, and back to Mount Holly in June; Ludlow and Plymouth in November. Truman Hendryx wanted him to travel west to Cayuga County, where he was pastoring a church in Locke, but the prospect didn't please Miller. Hendryx would have to judge, after reading Miller's list of all the places to which he had been invited, "whether I ought to spend my time & means to labour in your Chh . . . as I know not that I should have an other place in those parts."[34]

Though this sounded crass, Miller was being realistic. Time was short, for the world and for himself. Aging through his sixth decade, the once-robust farmer found travel exhausting and debilitating. Journeying by sleigh in winter months was comfortable compared to the coaches required when there was no snow, wooden boxes held up by leather straps that allowed the passengers to swing and sway along the route. Outlying towns that had no stage service required him to ride in by horse over often terrible roads that floods sometimes rendered impassable. Having arrived at his destination, quarters could vary from hotels in larger towns to taverns where travelers shared beds to makeshift "guest quarters" in sponsors' houses and tents at camp meetings. Not surprisingly, periods of illness punctuated the itinerary. A "severe cold" laid him up in April 1835, and the following year a "bilious complaint" forced him to cut short an appearance in Lansingburgh and return home, where he remained bedridden for three weeks. In 1837 he received the first diagnosis of the congestive heart failure that would ultimately claim his life, revealing to son George, "[T]he Doct. Thinks I am tending to the dropsy."[35] All this sapped his strength as the need for action was becoming more urgent. Ever aware of his mortality, Miller realized time had become precious.

34. Miller to Hendryx, February 11, 1835, Miller Letters.

35. Miller to George W. Miller, February 27, 1837, Miller Papers, Center for Adventist Research, Andrews University, Berrien Springs, Michigan [hereafter cited as Miller Letters AndU].

Truthfully, Miller and his message were commodities, and he was learning how to market them, not for money but for conversions. By the mid-1830s modern evangelism had assumed the psychology, if not the rhetoric, of consumer capitalism to market the Word. Charles Grandison Finney's human-centered view of conversion rejected the old-school understanding that the power of God changed the lives of those whom God chose, making people the fortunate but passive recipients of grace. Finney's New Measure revivalism assumed that people choose to grow into the salvation that God offers to all by submitting their will and accepting the redemption God freely offers to repentant sinners. Making right choices required marketing correct options — in other words, persuasion — and his human-focused measures did that. Hellfire-and-brimstone preaching positing Heaven against Hell, direct personal exhorting one-on-one, and testimonials to Jesus' power to save sinners from sure destruction moved listeners to conviction of their sinful condition, desire for salvation, and decision to trust God's grace and follow Jesus. Using the proper means, a skilled preacher could work up a revival and reap the profits in sinners baptized, pews filled, and lives changed. Demand for them was high, and the supply of skilled itinerants swelled to meet it. From 1824 to 1832 the flames of the Second Great Awakening scorched the land from New England to Michigan, establishing public conversion and the methods that produced it as *the* standard of evangelism among Protestants.

Miller began preaching on the end of the world just as this awakening was flickering. His apocalyptic message stoked the fire and fed his reputation as a skilled itinerant able to produce great results. Like others in the field, he quickly learned marketing strategy to gain the widest possible dissemination of his views and achieve the greatest potential impact. Scheduling his visits more effectively was one lesson. Picking the best towns and sites was another: places on stage routes that were easy not only for him but audiences to reach; population centers with newspapers that could advertise his appearance; meeting halls that could seat large numbers, preferably with stoves in the winter. Picking the right time was as important. There should be no distractions from his visit, like quarterly meetings or harvests or evening work. Some support from local clergy was imperative, if for no other reason than to assure a meeting hall, and while he was a good Baptist he gladly accepted calls from Methodists, Presbyterians, Congregationalists, and Christian Connexion preachers, making his audiences increasingly interdenominational.

As his popularity increased, Miller was not above making demands. He promised Truman Lamb that he would go to Granville, Vermont, if the church would build a new meetinghouse. They did, keeping him frequently apprised of its progress until its completion, when they called on him to keep his promise.[36]

With refreshing following in his wake, and as publicity spread, Miller became a prize to be won. Prospective hosts competed for him, offering large halls (Elder Fleming's in Portland "will contain two thousand hearers"), intense interest that promised big audiences ("he will have a large congregation to listen to him"), and rising prospects because of local revivals ("the field is white ready to harvest"). Allen Sprague in East Montpelier, Vermont, was not above emotional manipulation. Miller would come and lecture there if he "loved me and the souls of men in this place."[37] Financial inducements were common. Miller did not charge a fee, but prospective hosts frequently offered to cover his costs, and some offered an honorarium. Jehiel Claflin said his audience in West Brookfield would "freely pay all your expenses & more," Truman Lamb offered to pay Miller to come to Granville, and Jonathan Woods's invitation to lecture asked for Miller's "terms for the same." N. W. Smith knew Miller did not charge for lecturing, but "we shall feel willing to do something." At Middlesex "the prospect of getting money here to reward you for your labour is very small at present but how the people will feel when they come to hear I cannot tell." If they could not offer cash, some projected brisk sales of Miller's lectures, and Anthony Lane thought his appearing in New York City "would probably lead to enabling you to publishing another edition of your book."[38]

36. Truman Lamb to Miller, September 30 and December 13, 1839, Miller Letters.

37. Thomas F. Barry to Miller, December 25, 1839; N. W. Smith to Miller, June 12, 1837; E. B. Crandall to Miller, November 23, 1837; Allen Sprague to William S. Miller, March 15, 1839; Plano to William S. Miller, November 3, 1839, Miller Letters.

38. Claflin to Miller, July 10, 1838; Lamb to Miller, September 30, 1839; Woods to Miller, February 20, 1839; Smith to Miller, June 12, 1837; Joseph Chase to Miller, December 8, 1838; Anthony Lane to Miller, April 4, 1838, Miller Letters.

While Miller never discussed fundraising in the movement,[39] financial support was essential. Promulgating the message cost money, and while Miller was far from poor, cash was not always readily at hand. Stage tickets, rooms in hotels, and meals required immediate payment, and while some hosts could supply his needs, others could not (the people in Cobleskill were "too poor to promise anything but a welcome reception").[40] Producing the two editions of his book was expensive, and it was from sales that Miller reimbursed printers and binders. Money never came back to them fast enough to meet their needs, particularly during the economic depression of 1837-39, when cash was universally scarce. Frantic pleas to pay his bills and threats to sue added urgency to the pace of sales. Before stamps entered into wide use in the 1840s, recipients of letters paid the postage, so, though welcome, invitations flooding in to the farm proved a mixed blessing. Reimbursements and spontaneous donations from listeners helped defray some of these expenses, and Miller probably used his political connections to handle the rising cost of mail.

Before the mid-1830s Hampton residents had to pick up letters in Fairhaven or Whitehall, but by 1834 Hampton received its own postmaster, William S. Miller, who operated a post office at his own farm and tavern a mile west of his father's. With the office came franking privileges, the right to receive and send mail free of charge, and William S. now put that to use assisting his father's career. More than that, he became Miller's managing secretary, forwarding letters that arrived at the farm while Miller was gone, keeping him abreast of local news and politics, brokering arrangements between Miller and local hosts when they could not reach him directly, and keeping him in contact with the family while he was lecturing.[41]

39. Later on, charges that Miller was making money off the movement would make all the Adventist leaders reluctant to discuss money matters at all.

40. D. Collins to Miller, April 15, 1837, Miller Letters.

41. Letters from the early 1830s show names for the town varying from Hampton, to North Hampton, and finally Low Hampton as the post office searched for a formal name for the mail station. On May 5, 1834, William S. wrote to his father, who was lecturing at Keeseville, New York, and for the first time franked the letter "FREE Wm. S. Miller PM." Henry Jones tried to take advantage of this, asking William S. to write to him more often "as my present means, are not such as to be at

With Millerism pulling its messenger into a bigger world, the eldest son kept him anchored as much as possible.

Even so, in Miller's physical and emotional absence, the family did not thrive. Death claimed sister-in-law Electa and sister Paulina in 1832, and in July 1835 his "good old mother" Paulina suffered a stroke and died. Sister Anna and daughter Bellona, as yet unmarried as she turned thirty, both suffered from chronic back pain, and recovery seemed to him unlikely (though Bellona did improve over time).[42] William S. had already married and established his own household, and in 1835 it was Langdon's turn. But Miller was on the road, lecturing in Cornwall, so Langdon wrote of his intention and of his intended bride, "a girl of good caricter and a pious Mind." Miller did not know the girl and cautioned in his reply that "passions of the human heart are like the weather, sometimes boisterous as March winds, then like April showers, and again like the cold snows of December or warm sun of July." With ghosts of past precocity haunting the page, he advised his son that if the couple would root their common lives in Christ they could build a home that would "serve as a check to the mind, that may otherwise rove into the giddy maze of the world — to find pleasures in novelty, noisy revelry, or vain and wicked employments." So he gave his blessing and arrived home to be present and probably officiate at the wedding the following week.[43]

If Langdon's news aroused sober reflection, George caused his father real pain. For years Millers and Phelpses had joined the flood of migrants to the western territories as they opened for settlement. The "Genesee fever" drew Silas Guilford to western New York, and in 1834 cousin Benjamin Phelps wrote to the family from Auburn, Michigan, describing in glowing terms the lush landscape, bounti-

---

much cash expense for postage." Jones to William S. Miller, November 4, 1834, Miller Letters.

42. Phelps, Miller Family Genealogy; Miller noted his mother's death at the end of a letter to Truman Hendryx, August 29, 1835; Miller to Joseph Atwood, February 28, 1835, Miller Letters.

43. Langdon Miller to Miller, January 11, 1835, Miller Letters; Miller to Langdon Miller, January 13, 1835, Miller Letters AndU. Apparently Robbins delivered Langdon's letter to Miller and returned with a reply, thus explaining the rapid correspondence.

ful harvests, and booming opportunities there.[44] Reports like these spread throughout New England and eastern New York, producing a second land craze. Son George, now coming of age, already owned a farm, probably deeded by his father, but he traveled west with one of the Millard boys. He liked the country and decided to sell his Hampton farm and stay — without his parents' blessing and contrary to his father's wishes. Once a source of youthful rebellion, Miller was now its victim. In 1837 a period of silence ended when George wrote home to arrange for his farm's sale but also to express regret for his disobedience. Father, brothers William and John, and sister Lucy Ann all wrote in reply, begging him to come home, as his oldest brother put it, in reply to "a Father's Prayers" and "a Mother's tears." Father was more blunt, remembering "when you took your own government into your hands." He readily forgave George for the offense against him, but God would have to forgive him, too, and that was not so certain. "I have given you to God," wrote Miller, and "he has released me from any further obligation towards you, for you are beyond my watchcare."[45] George would eventually reconcile with the family,[46] but not before much damage had been done.

Relations with Lucy also became strained. Crusading affected their marriage much as had his service in the War of 1812, putting emotional as well as physical distance between them. His absence was frequent enough in the first few years, but in the fall of 1838 Miller was away from home most of October and November. In 1839 lecturing in Vermont claimed the entire month of January, and a campaign in Massachusetts and Vermont occupied him from April

44. Benjamin Phelps to Miller, May 10, 1834, Miller Letters.

45. William S. Miller to George Miller, March 7, and Miller to George Miller, February 27, 1837, Miller Letters AndU. Both letters, along with notes from John ("I have grown to anormous size") and Lucy Ann ("Mother has knit you some new socks"), were included in the packet.

46. Miller informed Henry Jones on September 9, 1839 (Miller Letters), that he had been lecturing in Michigan, but that was not the reason for the trip. A merchant had accepted cloth and other items from Langdon Miller to sell on consignment and had not forwarded proceeds from their sale. Miller went to Marshall to confront the man on behalf of his son. Whether George was involved in the situation or Miller visited George is unknown. See Hanson Goodrich (Marshall, Michigan) to Langdon Miller, October 7, 1839, Miller Letters.

19 to July 1. That fall he left Hampton in mid-October and did not return home until late March of the following year, a full five months later. Lucy and one or more of the children sometimes accompanied Miller to appointments closer to home, but not as frequently as he liked. His absence left her in charge of the farm and the children. William wanted her to meet him on the road, but there were chores to be done and people to manage, so it was hard to get away. Besides, traveling exhausted her. As William S. once put it to his impatient father, "she cant stand it so well as what you can it appears."[47] Also, Lucy may have felt uncomfortable in the socially sophisticated circles in which her husband was increasingly moving.

For his part, Miller was tired, often ill, lonely, and cranky. When he asked her to join him Lucy often demurred, so Miller enlisted William S. to coax her. Increasingly, the eldest son found himself caught in the middle between the two parents. "Mother said she cannot come down," he once reported, but she "wanted I should write and tell you to write as often as you could untill you come home." In November 1839 Miller was almost desperate for Lucy to join him in Massachusetts for at least part of the long campaign there, but William S. could offer no hope of it. So Miller asked Eliza Sprague, wife of his Lowell, Massachusetts, host, to intercede on his behalf. She wrote dutifully to Lucy that William would not be home before March, so "we thought you had better meet him here . . . he is very anxious to see you and I think it will cheer up his spirits a great deal." To no avail. William S. wrote back, "I hardly think Mother can come" though "we all feel enxious and willing that she should go." It would not be good for her health to be traveling, he said, though if it had been earlier in the season she might have attempted the journey. By the end of the month Lucy felt better and thought she might set out for Boston, once hog butchering was over, though, as William relayed the message, she "thinks she is not justly intitled to those remarks you made to her." But in December her mother fell ill and Lucy could not leave her. Exasperated, Miller wrote his son in a tone reminiscent of his Plattsburgh days, "If [your Mother] does not come next week, I shall know she has no affection left."[48]

47. William S. Miller to William Miller, July 1, 1839, Miller Letters.

48. William S. Miller to Miller, May 5, 1834; Eliza Sprague to Lucy Miller, No-

Miller's views produced as much tension in the family as his absences. Mother Paulina never accepted his prediction,[49] and his children, save for William S., were at best lukewarm to religion. Their spiritual lethargy frightened Miller both as a preacher and a father. His congregation, too, was now divided. Isaac Sawyer had supported him, but in 1835 his successor, Brother Halping, came out "violently" against Miller's literal interpretation of Jesus' reign during the Millennium. Miller launched a counterattack: "If he is worth a few shot of powder & ball God helping me . . . [t]he Bible, grace & spirit of God will conquor him." Two years later Halping was gone, but the congregation was deeply divided, and it did not seem to improve. "How often I think of Hampton," he lamented, "of the people, of my children. Why will they not believe? Why will they not hear? Why not be wise? O God do awaken the people of God in Hampton & those who are sleeping over the vulcano of Gods wrath. do my father convert my children!"[50]

Careful tending, not just by their father, did seem to have an effect. Brother Solomon, still living in the original homestead by the river, converted at the end of 1839 and, according to William S., was "going the whole load in Gospel prophecies . . . he eats like a hungry dog the crumbs that fall from his masters table." Solomon's excitement infected the whole family: "[W]e hope that Robbins Bellona and . . . Saterlee will convert for I was up there to your house a few nights ago and Mother Miller was there[.] we got a talking on the signs of the times and it was a sober time[.] Satterlee said it seemed to him that it was his Duty to speak in a conference meeting, he feels soon [,] in view of what is a coming."[51] The good news was timely, for at the end of the decade troubles were accumulating, and Miller needed family support more than ever.

By any standard — numbers of invitations to lecture, converts due to his preaching, months on the road, glowing reports of revival

---

vember 4, 1839; William S. Miller to Miller, November 12, November 18, November 30, December 11; Miller to William S. Miller, December 12, 1839, Miller Letters.

49. According to Bliss, Miller's mother "did not receive his views, but always told him to preach the whole truth, as he believed it, and do his duty" (*Memoirs,* 123).

50. Miller to William S. Miller, November 17, 1838, Miller Letters.

51. Miller to Hendryx, April 28, 1835, and February 21, 1837; Miller to William S. Miller, November 17, 1838, and December 11, 1839, Miller Letters.

from local preachers — Miller could have claimed success for his crusade. Endorsements from a variety of preachers attested to his rationality and effectiveness and to the interdenominational appeal of his message.[52] Revivals flaring from that campaign prepared him for an extensive, and arduous, five-month tour of Massachusetts in 1839 and 1840. No longer limited to small towns and farmer audiences, 1838 campaigns in Lansingburgh and industrializing Troy, New York, added an urban context to his work and new circumstances to consider. He must come to lecture in Lowell on March 20, wrote Timothy Cole, "as that is the time that our factory people are liberated from their evening labour and can better attend the Meetings evenings &c."[53] In the rapidly changing American society, "taking it to the world" had assumed new meaning.

But success brought problems Miller could never have foreseen. Up to 1837 Millerism was its founder's personal "property": he created it, disseminated it, defined it. Publicity and popularity, largely the result of his book, thrust Miller into a more sophisticated world for which his farmer life had not prepared him. Increasingly the movement called on him to seek the aid of others, and that inevitably weakened his personal control. The Lansingburgh revivals provided him with a circle of creative and energetic colleagues — Charles Cole, Isaac Wescott, and others — who shared great potential for active leadership. It was Cole who first suggested printing a Millerite newspaper as "the most effectual way to enlighten and save souls . . . all most any number of subscribers might be obtained."[54] The idea never reached fruition, perhaps for lack of money in those depression times. And it was Wescott who decided on his own to publish Miller's lectures as a book, including its author in the discussion only after already arranging with a printer and binder to produce the work. Though the effects were powerful, his action's

52. March 12, 1835, signed by forty-two Regular Baptists; November 22, 1838 signed by twelve Christian Connexion preachers including Joshua V. Himes, L. Delos Fleming, and Timothy Cole, soon to be principal leaders in the movement; January 23, 1839, signed by four Freewill Baptists; January 26, 1839, signed by three Methodists including Josiah Litch; Miller Letters.

53. Timothy Cole to Miller, February 7, 1839, Miller Letters.

54. Cole to Miller, March 27, 1837, Miller Letters. Interestingly, the next month, when Cole raised the question again, it had become Miller's idea (April 5, 1837).

propriety was questionable, suggesting the fragility of Miller's personal control of the movement.

Indeed, the nascent triumvirate soon collapsed in rancor. In April 1838 Wescott and another colleague, Thomas Brand of Troy, arranged for a second edition of *Evidence.* As before, Wescott informed Miller of it in July almost as an afterthought and suggested to the author through his son that "if he has any alterations he wishes to make I wish him to write what they are and send them to me without delay." Charles Cole had already warned Miller what was coming. He had agreed to supply a chronological chart for the new edition, apparently assuming that Miller was directing the project. But Wescott informed him peremptorily that he and not Miller owned the copyright, which so upset Cole that he withdrew from the project. In May Cole warned Miller, again through William S., that Wescott and Brand "have not the glory of God in view," and he was worried that if the second edition were to appear as planned Miller "will suffer an irrepairable loss of nearly all his teaching and writing." It is not clear if the loss he projected was financial or literary, but he feared "that all is not right."[55] Miller obviously disregarded the warning, because he provided three new lectures for the second edition, and Wescott's name again appeared as owner of the copyright. He probably was. When plans were afoot in 1839 for yet a third edition of the book by a new publisher, Joshua V. Himes of Boston, Wescott wrote to William S., threatening to "prosecute any person who sells a copy of that work" because "I can prove, by at least two witnesses that your father disposed of the copy right to me. Besides I have his own letter on the subject."[56] Regardless, Miller's new Boston friends knew how to handle the situation and spared him the effects of his naiveté. The third edition appeared in 1840, with Miller named as copyright owner.

While publicity enabled the rapid growth of Millerism after 1837, it also inspired rumors about him that proved durable and demoralizing. In March 1839 news that Miller had died produced a

55. Wescott to William S. Miller, July 1, 1838; Cole to William S. Miller, May 9, 1838, Miller Letters.

56. Wescott to William S. Miller, April 28, 1840, Miller Letters; Himes to Miller, May 4, 1840, Joshua V. Himes Papers, Massachusetts Historical Society, Boston, Massachusetts.

flurry of letters to William S. from worried family and Millerite connections. Joseph Chase in Middlesex, Vermont, "was told for a fact that Mr. Miller was not living . . . that he went to Rochester [and] Woodstock was taken sick returned home and soon died." George Hacket in Cambridge heard that fever had stricken the entire family. Phelps cousins had heard from two sources that Miller had dropped dead in the pulpit while preaching, one "a young Lady in Panton Vt . . . stating she had the news from a Baptist minister who came to the place," and the other "a young gentleman from the west who states that he saw a letter sent to Hampton giving an account of his death."[57] Thus did rumors easily spread.

More malicious was the story that began circulating in the winter of 1838 that Miller had confessed to a hundred-year error in his chronology. Supporters who had invested their hopes and personal reputations in his prediction were desperate for Miller to explain the error or refute it. Timothy Cole didn't believe it, but Miller needed to tell him immediately if it was true "for our enemies are [putting] in circulation the report that you have acknowledged your mistake." Andrew P. White in western New York had heard the story and told Miller of "quite an anxiety in this vicinity to ascertain the truth of this report . . . to stop the mouths of some who are inclined to ridicule every thing serious." William Storrs had been preaching Millerism in Broome County, New York, and was desperate to know if the error placed the second coming a century earlier or later, in 1743 or 1943. He demanded, "I shall look for a reply immediately, and without fail."[58]

Public criticism of Miller's views from ministers and those in authority, especially Baptists, proved more worrisome. Early on, pastors occasionally closed their pulpits and meetinghouses to his preaching, and there were those who wished to silence him. One writer to the *Vermont Telegraph* suggested that "if his doctrine is *new*,

57. Joseph Chase to William S. Miller, March 13, 1839; George Hackett to William S. Miller, March 18, 1839; Lucinda S. Phelps to William S. Miller, April 18, 1839, Miller Letters. Why this should have happened in the spring of 1839 is not clear. In 1836 and 1838 Miller had indeed been quite ill, but his health had returned, and he was engaged in an energetic campaign throughout the state.

58. Timothy Cole to Miller, July 25, 1839; Andrew P. White to Miller, November 20, 1839; William Storrs to Miller, September 2, 1839, Miller Letters.

or if it be *another gospel* [recalling Joseph Smith's claims for the *Book of Mormon*] which is brought unto us, he ought not to be received into the churches, nor bid God speed." The editor, who had been the first to publish Miller's views, rejected the recommendation out of hand with the (traditionally Baptist) admonition, "Free discussion, brother — free discussion."[59] Miller expected harassment from bullies and infidels, but opposition from preachers angered him and provoked his well-honed sarcasm. The *Telegraph* printed some anonymous letters to the editor giving him and his views some hard knocks, but Miller told Hendryx not to be concerned: "I have heard Lions roar, & jackasses bray, & I am yet alive." Later, in Massachusetts "two dogs" were following him from town to town refuting his views, but he had taken on all his detractors. "The lion is subdued, the two wolves are silenced, and the foxes have fled to their holes."[60]

Inevitably, Millerism's peculiar message and its growing popularity provoked a response from orthodox Baptists. When it came, Miller interpreted it as a conspiracy concocted by his own Vermont Baptist Missionary Society. He may have been right; the critique seems to have been arranged the same way he had arranged for his own views to be publicized using the same organ, the *Vermont Telegraph*. In October 1837 a Darius Squire requested the paper to give Miller's views a public airing. The editor, Orson Murray, responded that such a review would have been forthcoming already, but the man who had agreed to provide it, Aaron Angier, an articulate pastor and rising light in the Vermont Baptist church,[61] had been suffering from near blindness. But Angier recovered, and on November 15 he took up the gauntlet to keep "promises made to my friends."[62]

Debates in the paper typically took the form of a dialogue, and that may have been the intent in this case, but it did not happen that way. In his first article Angier detailed six specific objections to

59. *Vermont Telegraph*, November 15, 1837.

60. Miller to Hendryx, February 28, 1833; Miller to William S. Miller, May 17, 1839, Miller Letters.

61. Henry Crocker identifies him as a onetime pastor in Orwell who became active in the cause of seminary education for preachers, serving as a trustee of the Derby Literary and Theological Institute. Crocker, *History of the Baptists in Vermont* (Bellows Falls, Vt.: P. H. Gobie Press, 1931), 134-35, 263, 460, 543.

62. *Vermont Telegraph*, November 15, 1837.

Miller's thesis. Some of them raised doubts about his exegesis: the seventy weeks in Daniel's vision did not end with the death of Christ; there is no biblical justification for the day/year formula in prophecy; Miller was inconsistent in his use of Scripture, thus violating his own rules of interpretation. More substantially, said Angier, neither Daniel nor the apostles knew the time of the end because God did not reveal it to anyone, not even to Jesus. Miller's thinking was wrong; the divine promise he taught (that God would reveal the times of the end) did not exist, nor apparently did his "rational" God who would not promise judgment without giving us final days to prepare for it. Furthermore, wrote Angier, his ideas would arm infidels with weapons to use against the gospel should his predictions fail. Having said, and implied, all that, Angier assured Miller, "I do not come now as your *antagonist,* but as an *enquirer after truth.*" He pleaded for a sober exploration. "When convinced on any point, I hope to have the candor to acknowledge it, and misjudge greatly, if I may not expect from you the same." The editor, too, prayed for "Christian courtesy" in the discussion, and to readers he pleaded, "[D]ivest yourself of prejudice, examine, and then decide."

Miller would have none of it. He had long confronted the very difficulties Angier raised, including the possibility of his prediction failing and thereby harming the cause of Christ. Angier had said, "If you are wrong I doubt not you wish to know it. If right, we all should believe it." In his 1833 pamphlet Miller had said the same thing, using remarkably similar words: "The time is at hand that will try my views on this point, and if it should prove different from what I expect, and from what I do now most sincerely believe; then will I, if my life is preserved be willing, I hope, to confess my folly to all who may read these pages; I have had great distrust of myself; but the word of God will be accomplished, not one jot or tittle of his word will fail."

Three years later, his mood had completely changed. In the 1836 edition Miller stated that after fourteen years of Bible study "I have come to the following conclusions, and do now commit myself into the hands of God as my Judge."[63] No longer ambivalent, he was

63. Miller, *Evidences,* 6; *Evidence from Scripture and History of the Second Coming of Christ, about the year 1843: Exhibited in a Course of Lectures* (Troy, N.Y.: Kenble & Hooper, 1836), 10.

combative. "I wish to say to brother Angier, time is precious, — and certainly if I am correct." The fate of souls is in the balance. "Therefore we ought to be very careful that the blood of souls are not found on our skirts." When Angier warned that failure of the prediction would arm infidels, Miller replied, "I cannot for a moment suffer a thought in my mind, that it is worthy of a christian discussion," since Noah, Lot, and the other prophets faced the same challenge. "The amount of it is, 'What will the world say?'" Finally, "If brother Angier has no better arguments then this (only one) in his first communication, I do beg of him for the love of truth, to withhold altogether." Editor Murray felt called to clarify that Angier was simply asking a reasonable question about the potential effects of Miller's views, not raising an argument against them. Given Miller's tenor, any thoughts of a dialogue vanished. Angier published an additional seven articles critiquing Miller's views, and then Miller published six in rejoinder.[64]

Simple explanations come to mind for Miller's hardened resolve — increasing popularity, frequent repetition of the vision, a growing though geographically scattered community of support, strengthening apologia in the face of self-doubt, the need to justify his career, rising inability to consider the possibility of failure as sacrifices for the cause mounted. All no doubt contributed to it. But more than response to external stimuli shaped Millerism. The movement was a projection and product of its founder's inner wrestling with God. What did it really mean "to be good," to be obedient as a dutiful son, to steward God's gifts as a faithful father? Increasingly Miller came to accept Millerism — the message and the movement — as a special gift from God through which he would achieve all that. As a child of God, he would "tell it to the world," despite his fears, in obedience to the divine call, and as a father, now of thousands, he would steward God's promise as Christians came to explore the nature of that promise in their lives.

To accept the prediction was to trust God; to promulgate it was to witness to God. Through Millerism he was heeding the Great Commandment — love one another — and the Great Commission

64. *Vermont Telegraph,* November 27, 1837; the series ran through March 21, 1838.

— go! And in the light of this intimacy with God, both the commandment and the commission took on new meaning. How do Christians love one another, and to whom was he being sent? Answers led him to what was for him new and profound understanding about the church in the last days, teaching lessons that would set him apart from, and at odds with, other evangelicals. For now, though, his growing "family" was proof of God's trustworthiness and God's blessing on Miller, a blessing that others increasingly recognized. He may have reluctantly accepted the label *Reverend,* but in 1837 Charles Cole became the first person in the existing record to ascribe to Miller the endearing and enduring title that confirmed all: "Father in Christ."[65]

65. Cole to Miller, April 5, 1837, Miller Letters.

The Great Chart, Millerism's most powerful instructional aid. Prepared by Charles Fitch and Apollos Hale and printed by Thayer & Co. in 1842

Joshua V. Himes, Miller's "son in the spirit."

Lucy Miller, from an oil portrait by W. M. Prior about 1841. The painting and Prior's portrait of William Miller now hang in the Miller farm.

Lucy late in life, from a daguerreotype taken about 1853 shortly before her death. William Miller Farm.

Carte-de-visite portrait of Miller said to be from a daguerreotype, probably produced in the early 1840s. Below the portrait is printed his greeting and autograph, "I remain yours affectionately. Wm Miller"

Another carte-de-visite. The greeting suggests it comes from late in the movement, perhaps after one of the significant disconfirmations, but before his handwriting deteriorated.

E. W. Thayer of Boston produced this lithograph of Miller in1841, not long after printing the Great Chart for Himes.

DAGUERREOTYPE VIEW OF MR. MILLER'S LATE RESIDENCE.

Miller house in the Federal style as it appeared in Bliss's *Memoirs* in 1853, four years after his death. Probably after Lucy's death in 1854 it was "modernized" in the Greek Revival style as it appears today.

Miniature portrait, identified on the back as "W. Miller." Definitely not the Advent founder but possibly William S. Miller.

N. Currier portrait of Miller, 1843, "approved by his friends," derived from E. W. Thayer's lithograph.

CHAPTER SIX

My Heart Inclines More towards Them

Given his sardonic sense of humor, Miller might have seen the irony in his becoming spiritual father to thousands while having discredited himself as a father to his own children because of youthful disobedience. If we are to take protestations of humility (prideful as they were) at face value, earnest disciples found in him qualities invisible to himself — wisdom, experience, gravity. Most important, his method of studying and interpreting Scripture shed light on the Bible that opened to them a new, living relationship with God. Gifts like these described one who was a parent more than a preacher, and grateful "children" were now responding not just with acceptance of his views but with genuine affection for him.

The strength of Millerite subjectivism comes as a surprise. All descriptions of the movement, positive and negative, have emphasized its speculative qualities — rational or irrational, orthodox or heterodox. It thus seems out of sync with the sentimentality of American secular and religious romanticism in the 1830s that redefined relationships of all sorts, above all the bonds connecting humanity, nature, and God. In reality, the crusade to awaken the world and prepare for the imminent *personal* return of Christ was rooted in this very impulse. Throughout the movement's life the influence of sentiment in Miller's ministry strengthened progressively. Two very different accounts of his 1816 conversion illustrate that growth. Miller's first memoir, in 1842, recalled its impact as essentially intellectual. "I saw Jesus as a friend, and my only help, and the word of God as the *perfect rule* of duty . . . and the Scriptures, which before were dark and contradictory, now became the lamp to my feet and light to my path. My mind became settled and satisfied." Three years later, the demise of his predictions required an apology and an explanation of why he had believed that Christ would come in 1843, then 1844. Miller now remembered that earlier conversion very differently: "It seemed that there might be a Being so good and compassionate as to himself atone for our transgressions, and thereby save us from suffering the penalty of sin. I immediately felt how lovely such a Being must be; and imagined that I could cast myself into the arms of, and trust in the mercy of, such an One . . . and in Jesus I found a friend."[1]

To be sure, distinct public agendas help to account for the shift toward the affective. In 1842, while Millerism was evangelizing an admittedly peculiar idea, it was helpful to project a powerful God who had conveyed a clear and consistent message, thus implying that Miller and his ideas were authoritative and rational. In 1845 and after, as the movement shattered, comforting the disappointed called for a compassionate God who would take care of His people. Apologetics notwithstanding, Miller's piety was genuine. Conversion is by definition subjective, since it is one's relationship with God that "turns" from abstraction to reification; God ceases to be a principle and becomes a living reality. So it was with Miller. The God who had been a transcendent force of power and judgment became present, and through the person of Jesus he was tangible and approachable, not only through the mind but in the heart.

Nothing demonstrates that in Miller's life better than his millenarian belief, the product of this new relationship, that this Jesus "will come again in his glory & person"[2] to take away sin. The God who loved him had given him clear knowledge about the event on which "the ardent faith and pious hope of the tried and tempted child of God centers." Just as Jesus' first coming "was literally according to the prophecies," so we "may safely infer will be his second appearing, according to the scriptures." It was a highly personal vision, not derived from intellectual or theological tradition but

1. Joshua V. Himes, *Views of the Prophecies and Prophetic Chronology, Selected From Manuscripts of William Miller With a Memoir of His Life* (Boston: Joshua V. Himes, 1842), 11; William Miller, *Apology and Defense* (Boston: Joshua V. Himes, 1845), 5.

2. Articles of Faith, written in a manuscript Sheriff's Book, Jenks Memorial Collection of Adventual Materials, Aurora University, Aurora, Illinois.

from his experience of a God whose Word was accessible in Scripture, whose effects were visible in nature, and whose flesh was preparing to return in glory and power. Neither was the promise merely abstract — a millennium of peace, happiness, and justice. The effects of parousia were material. For he comes to "gather his elect, raise the dead . . . chain satan a thousand years, destroy the wicked, who destroy the earth, glorify his people, with his own glory, cleanse and purify his church, present her to the Father without spot or wrinkle, live and reign with his people, on the 'new heavens, and new earth,' which he will create."[3]

It was the hope of seeing all this realized that made chronology so compelling. The year 1843 was more than a predicted date. Decades of prophetic interpretation, comparison with historical events, complicated chronologies, and now preaching had made it a focus of expectation and intense yearning that he expressed to others through poetry sustained by Scripture. Beyond the terrors of destruction lay the promise of reunion with "our dear Redeemer" and with a God who is faithful. Within nine years, he wrote to Hendryx in 1834, "if we are what we profess 'Look for a new heavens & a new earth wherein dwelleth righteousness.'

And the dark orb shall from its ashes rise	Isa 65:17
While the new heaven, descending from the skies	Rev. 21:10
The bride adorned in robes of righteousness	" 2
Shall with the bridegroom enter into rest	He. 4:9
Then Oh my soul, will you permitted view?	Psalm 130:5-8
The word fulfilled, "created all things new"	Rev. 21:5
And all the banished, trials, sins and fears	" 4
To live and reign with Christ a thousand years	" 20:6[4]

It was a vision calculated to evoke strong emotions — love and hope — that have more to do with the heart than with the mind.

3. William Miller, *Evidences from Scripture & History of the Second Coming of Christ about the year* A.D. *1843, and of his Personal Reign of 1000 Years* (Brandon, Vt.: Telegraph Office, 1833), 4, 5.

4. Miller to Hendryx, August 17, 1834, Miller Letters.

Anger was also steering Miller. As we have seen, popularity of his views attracted opponents who attacked him in the same media he used so artfully — newspapers, pamphlets, and books. Some commentators were measured, taking Miller's views seriously while rejecting his conclusions, but many others were scornful. Indeed, small presses developed a cottage industry printing anti-Millerite pamphlets, much like today's tabloids, with titles like *The Theory of William Miller, Utterly Exploded* and *The End of the World Not Yet.* An anonymous Boston writer compared Millerism to the "pestiferous breath of the Simoon"; a Vermont pamphleteer averred, "Were Satan permitted to delude the people with an error in the garb of religion, it is believed he would adopt *Millerism*"; Kittredge Haven in *The World Reprieved* popularized the growing rumor that Miller was amassing a fortune from sales of his book.[5]

No shrinking lily himself, Miller was capable of responding in kind. But he did not reserve his ire just for scoffers; even mannered critics like Angier received broadsides. And as criticism of his views mounted, so did the anger of his response. The feisty tone revealed in his 1836 revised lectures now shaped a new interpretation of his critics. "I know the world are taunting us with the inquiry 'Where is the promise of his coming?'" Such people simply fulfill the prophets' warning that "there should be mockers in the last time, who should walk after their own ungodly lusts." The "trials, pains[,] afflictions, persecutions, poverty and distress, which the people of God suffer in this world" could lead one to despair. "But no, we will not complain, for to suffer the short period of three score years and ten at most, will only give a greater zest to the glory which shall fol-

5. Otis A. Skinner, *The Theory of William Miller Concerning the End of the World in 1843, Utterly Exploded* (Boston: Thomas Whittemore, 1840); L. F. Dimmick, *The End of the World Not Yet: A Discourse Delivered in the North Church, Newburyport* (Newburyport, Mass.: Charles Whipple, 1842); *An Appeal to the Common Sense of the People, or the Miller Delusion!!!* (Boston: I. R. Butts, 1843); A. S. Barton, *Millerism Refuted by History, in a Series of Letters to a Friend* (Windsor, Vt.: Joseph Fairbanks, 1842); Kittredge Haven, *The World Reprieved: Being a Critical Examination of William Miller's Theory* (Woodstock, Vt.: Haskell and Palmer, 1839). The quotations above appear in Francis D. Nichol, *The Midnight Cry: A Defense of the Character and Conduct of William Miller and the Millerites* (Washington, D.C.: Review and Herald, 1944), 529.

low at the appearing of our Lord and Saviour the great God and Jesus Christ." He peppered lectures with unflattering descriptions of "D D's," doctors of divinity, as "Latin book-worms" and Greek scholars "trying to be wise above what was written [for they] have lost their balance and [fallen] into absurdities too ridiculous to mention."[6]

Unfair treatment by the popular and religious press added to his growing anger. In the Miller Papers appears a manuscript apparently written in 1838, a reply to a Vermont editor who had published a piece titled "Mathias, Miller, and Smith." Though the reply was anonymous, Miller almost certainly wrote it. The handwriting is his, and the tone bears his unmistakable penchant for sarcasm and hyperbole. The author describes himself as "a farmer by occupation" who had "been acquainted with this Mr. Miller" for nineteen years. The article's headline placed Miller's name between the others, like Jesus crucified between two thieves, the writer noted — an effective, if self-serving, allusion. The editor could find nothing laudable to say about the prophet; the writer retorted, "It was said of another in the scripture, 'there is no form nor comeliness in him that men should desire him, he appeared as a root out of dry ground.'" Contemplating the editor's note of alarm at the preaching of such false prophets as Miller and his forecast of disaster to flow from it, the writer asked, "What will you do sir?" There is no option other than "to pull this Imposter down." He did not expect that to happen "under a republican form of government," but he was aware that "one of the disciples suffered as did his Lord and master."[7] Given the character of opposition to him and the fate of other religious innovators in his day, he fully expected to meet with violence.

A certain paranoia always lay just under the surface of Miller's personality, and by 1839, with enemies on all sides, desire for justification added urgency to the predicted date.

> I meet with no opposition to my face, all opposition is stabs in the dark, Lying & sarcastic publications in our religious papers is the

6. *Evidence from Scripture and History of the Second Coming of Christ, about the year 1843: Exhibited in a Course of Lectures* (Troy, N.Y.: Kemble & Hooper, 1836), 12, 54.

7. Anonymous to the editor of the Vergennes *Vermonter,* located following a letter from Justus Dalee to Miller, January 31, 1838, Miller Letters.

> principle [sic] opposition. My enemies are, all of the Editors of our religious periodicals. All of our [Doctors of Divinity], nearly all of our scholastic divines, many of our ministers who try to imitate the great men, & who follow in the wake of the popular, all the proud Revs, all bigots, all Universal Ministers, all rum drinkers, all tavern loungers, all gamblers, all political demago[gues] — all who love the present evil world more than they love God.[8]

Along with visions of redemption for the saved on the last day Miller contemplated the fate of his enemies. It would be dreadful.

When from the great white throne indignant ire	Rev. 20:11
Shoots forth its blaze and sets the world on fire:	Mal 4:1
Then all the wicked, all the proud could boast	"
"Shall be as stubble, saith the Lord of hosts"	"
Then Kings & Captains, tyrants mighty men	Rev. 19:18
Are the last supper for the fowls of heaven.	" 17
And kingdoms, thrones & powers, dominions riven	Dan 2
Like chaff before the Angry whirlwind driven.	" :35
The dragon papal beast, The great arch foe	Rev/ 19:20
Shall sink to endless night eternal woe.	" 20:10[9]

So prevalent was the hostility surrounding him that he almost despaired of seeing faithful souls at the end. "Where, oh my brother, where is there any Christian? few, few can be saved. I feel some alarmed, but not as much as I might seeing the day draweth near when every mans work will be tried and so as by fire. Yes, my Br as sure, as God lives, & his word stands, the day, the great day is near, very near even at the door. I am more and more convinced that we live on the threshold of eternity."[10]

With both confidence and impatience strengthening him, Miller

8. Miller to Henry Jones, September 9, 1839, Miller Letters. He was fond of describing opponents unflatteringly as dogs and jackals, once referring to newspaper publishers as "little yelping editors." J. Sawyer to Miller, November 23, 1838, Miller Collection, Andrews University, Berrien Springs, Michigan.

9. Miller to Hendryx, August 17, 1834, Miller Letters.

10. Miller to Hendryx, March 6, 1835, Miller Letters.

crossed the border between messenger and prophet. As the decade progressed landmarks became clearer to him. The 1260 days/years of the Church's captivity came to an end in 1798, when Napoleon captured the pope. It also fulfilled the Church's wandering in the wilderness, prophesied in the sixth chapter of Revelation. That left, according to Daniel's vision, forty-five years to the end. In Miller's reckoning, therefore, few signs remained. The sixth trumpet began to blow when the Turks sent an army to attack Constantinople in 1448, and Muslim power was to reign for 391 days/years. So the period of Turkish/Ottoman reign would come to an end in 1839. Shortly after, the seventh trumpet would sound, the third woe be let loose on the world, and the seventh vial poured out, all simultaneously "about the year 1840, if my former calculations are correct."[11] The completion of the prophecies would take place, as calculated, sometime in 1843, when Daniel's vision would terminate with Jesus' second coming and the resurrection of the righteous dead.

Miller first predicted the fall of Turkey in 1831 and added supportive evidence and greater detail as the decade progressed. The year 1840 would bring wars, a great revolution, "divisions among all sects, societies and associations of men upon earth." The papacy would be "divided into three parties, to show her dissolution."[12] To Truman Hendryx he sent special warning: "[A]fter 1839 there is to be voices, thunders, lightnings, & great earthquake, great Babylon is to be divided & fall, all the kingdoms of the earth to be removed & a great hail, is four years too long, some object because it is too short, but I cannot please you all, must follow bible."[13]

When war broke out between Egypt and Turkey in 1838, it seemed that the prophecy was coming true, particularly after the Ottoman fleet was summarily defeated at the Battle of Nizip in June 1839. Millerites were excited. Josiah Litch, a New England Methodist minister who adopted Miller's views in 1838, equated the fall of the Ottoman Empire with the termination of the sixth trumpet

11. *Evidence,* 1836, 187.

12. See Miller's "A few Evidences" from 1831, Jenks Memorial Collection of Adventual Materials, Aurora University, Aurora, Illinois, 8; *Evidences,* 1833, 42; *Evidence,* 1836, 187, 219.

13. Miller to Hendryx, November 28, 1834, Miller Letters. In a similar vein see Miller's letter to his sister, Anna Atwood, February 28, 1835, Miller Letters.

blast, echoing Miller and others. But he went further, predicting it would happen in August 1840 — more precisely, August 11. Stories about the situation in the Middle East appeared in the maiden issue of the Adventists' first newspaper, the *Signs of the Times,* and then throughout the year. Charles Cole in Lansingburgh "was as strong as ever in the Faith seeing the terminations of the Eastern nations" and "the drying up of the Turkish Empir[e]." Miller's son William S. cheered over the news: "I rejoice to see the entire fulfillment of the prophecies as that we may be delivered from this state of bondage of sin and corruption." Isaac Sawyer asked, "But what do you think of the war between Egypt and Turkey?" It was an event "of great moment" signifying that Ottoman power was "utterly crippled & the Sultan dead. What do you think of this, bro M?"[14]

Though he said little about the predicted event publicly, Miller privately thought the war and its outcome confirmed his writing. Henry Jones had never accepted the revealed time, but now he had proof that the times really were revealed. "See my br. in my printed lectures 1st Edition [1836] Page 97 or 2d Edition [1838] Page 121. Compare with the news of the Ottoman kingdom, and then deny if you can the fulfillment."[15]

Euphoria, however, was short-lived. European powers sided with Turkey to limit the Egyptian victory, and the end of the war in 1840 resulted in stalemate rather than the destruction of the Ottoman Empire. The failure marked the first significant disappointment for the movement, and it was Miller's name, not Litch's, that the public attached to it. "The eleventh of August has passed," wrote O. A. Skinner. "What say brethren, do you still cling to Millerism?" But Millerite hopes rebounded, forecasting the pattern of future disappointments. Miller could say truthfully that the prediction was

14. On Litch's role see Eric Anderson, "The Millerite Use of Prophecy: A Case Study of a 'Striking Fulfilment,'" in Ronald L. Numbers and Jonathan M. Butler, eds., *The Disappointed: Millerism and Millenarianism in the Nineteenth Century* (Knoxville: University of Tennessee Press, 1993), 78-91; William S. Miller to Miller, January 24 and November 18, 1839; Sawyer to Miller, September 17, 1839, Miller Letters.

15. Miller to Jones, September 9, 1839, Miller Letters. The 1838 edition was essentially a reprinting of the 1836 edition save for the reordering of some of the chapters; see *Evidence from Scripture and History of the Second Coming of Christ, about the year 1843: Exhibited in a Course of Lectures* (Troy, N.Y.: Elias Gates, 1838).

not his, and that while he had hoped for a fulfillment he never preached the date *"without qualification"* but had always addressed it "as a matter of opinion."[16]

Though technically correct, Miller's response was disingenuous. As we have seen, he had long spoken in letters and print about the impending demise of Turkish power in 1839 and was publicly linked to the prophecy, if not to Litch's specific date. On the stump, he tended to be more loquacious. Isaac Fuller, Miller's longtime mentor and defender of his views, took him to task for emphasizing the importance of 1840 and for being so specific before audiences. "I have been not a little sorry for one thing you have often said in your lectures — that you were of the opinion that no sinners wod be renewd after the 11th of August. You recollect that I told you when you were in my house, that I was afraid that your confidence in expressing yourself might injure the effect of the whole subject. I know you stated that there might possibly be a variation of a few months from the specific time; but this exception is wholly overlookd, & so, in many minds, the falshood of your whole system is already provd by your failure in this particular." Having prophesied that there would be no conversions after August 11, it is also possible that he claimed, as critics charged, that any so-called conversions after August 11 "would be of Satan & such as were to be damned!!" Other predictions credited to him were that after 1840 there would be no more rain, or births, or marriages.[17]

Just as Miller could adjust stories in his memoir to meet his mission's current needs, he changed details of his message depending on his assessment of an idea's public utility. For instance, early in the life of the movement he pointed to signs in the heavens as proof of the prophecies' literal fulfillment. A spectacular shower of stars on November 13, 1833, fulfilled the prediction in the "Little Apocalypse" in Mark's Gospel that "the stars of heaven shall fall & the powers that are in heaven shall be shaken." In undated notes for a lecture, he included among twenty signs of the times pointing to

16. *Signs of the Times,* vol. 1, no. 14 (October 15, 1840), 112; vol. 1, no. 12 (September 15, 1840), 92.

17. Fuller to Miller, December 10, 1840; Joseph B. Smead to Miller, April 9, 1841, Miller Letters.

Christ's approach "the falling of the stars or me[teor]s."[18] But the shower of stars did not appear as evidence in any of his book's editions, and in the 1840s he and other Adventist leaders would take pains to distance themselves from "superstitious" interpretations of astronomical events.

He was not being intentionally dishonest. While the approaching deadline strengthened his commitment to the *idea* of the imminent apocalypse, ironically it also made empirical elements of his vision, like chronology, less significant to him. Deducing when prophetic visions began and ended, adding and subtracting the duration of kingdoms, and comparing prophetic *types* with "profane" historical events were all fraught with potential human error. God's promises were not, and faith that God would keep God's promises in whatever way God chose, regardless of human expectations, made the failure of human predictions, even his own, bearable. The details could shift readily because the hope was infallible.

Charles Grandison Finney took note of this odd, imperturbable quality in Miller. In 1842 while in Boston he attended a couple of Miller's lectures, and at the end of one of them Finney met with him privately to "convince him that he was in error." He might have expected a debate, but the conversation went in a surprising direction. Finney raised objections to Miller's interpretation of Scripture and, as he put it, "showed him that he was entirely mistaken." Miller's reply was noncommittal: "He replied, that I had adopted a course of investigation that would detect his errors if he had any." So far as Finney was concerned, he had already done that! Again, he questioned Miller's interpretation of a figure in Daniel's vision, supplying a postmillennial understanding of the biblical allusions that precluded Miller's millenarian views. Astonishingly, Miller agreed with everything he said. In spite of that, he clung to his views, leading Finney to conclude, "[I]t was vain to reason with him." The meeting ended with Miller giving him an autographed

18. Draft article for the *Vermont Telegraph,* Miller Letters. While he did not date the manuscript, he referred in the first line to the "remarkable phenomenon of Nov. 13th" without including the date, indicating that he was writing that year or shortly after. Because copies of the paper are not extant for these months, we do not know if the *Telegraph* printed it. The reference in his list of signs appears in notes, again undated, contained in the folder "Draft Sermons," Jenks Collection.

copy of his book, assuming that careful study would lead Finney to accept his conclusions.[19]

It was more likely emotion than logic that drove Miller to misinterpret the results of Ottoman collapse and to make further predictions whose failure earned him ridicule and scorn. The sixth trumpet's blast was to bring more than just the end of Turkish power. According to the parable of the ten virgins in the twenty-fifth chapter of Matthew, a bridegroom comes to his wedding feast to find that five wise virgins have faithfully kept their lamps lit looking for him while five foolish virgins have not. He invites the faithful watchers into the wedding feast but shuts the door against the five who were unprepared, leaving them in darkness. Miller commented on this parable for the first time in the 1836 edition of *Evidence.* The wise virgins were "believers in God" and the foolish virgins represented "the unbelieving class of mankind." The bridegroom is Christ, and his shutting the door against unbelievers "implies the closing up of the mediatorial kingdom, and finishing the gospel period." In other words, before Jesus comes into the wedding feast (returns to the world) he will judge humanity, separate the wicked from the faithful, and shut the door of mercy on their sins. At this point, salvation will no longer be possible, their damnation assured.[20]

By 1834 Miller had decided that the end of probation would happen simultaneously with the completion of the sixth trumpet blast. After that, sinners would receive no pardon. In November he forecast to Truman Hendryx, "This 3½ years will be the time the foolish virgins will come and knock & say Lord, Lord open unto us, but he will say depart I know you not, it is my oppinion the door of mercy will be shut in the year 1839" after which "there will be no rain (of grace) but trouble, anguish, wrath, mallice, hattred & distress will fill every part of those who are out of [Christ]."[21] Over the next two years his views clarified and his feelings strengthened. It was in this period that he augmented his lectures for the new edition, adding

19. Charles Grandison Finney, *Memoirs of Rev. Charles G. Finney, Written by Himself* (New York: Fleming H. Revell, 1876), 370-71. None of the Millerite sources records this meeting, though George R. Knight mentions it in *Millennial Fever and the End of the World* (Boise: Pacific Press Publishing Association, 1993), 139.

20. *Evidence* (1836), 190-92.

21. Miller to Hendryx, November 28, 1834, Miller Letters.

among others the chapter on Matthew 25. At the end of 1836 he concluded that "the sealing time is about closing up" even earlier than he had expected. "I did not think that the door of mercy would be closed untill about 1839," but very soon, he added, "he that is filthy will remain so." At the end of 1839 Miller warned his children, "The door is not yet shut. o children, my children, do pray for yourselves. soon the door will be closed, what then will my children do[?]"[22]

It was not chronology but sentiment that caused Miller to focus on probation's terminating. At the end of 1836 his mood was remarkably similar to his depressed state while encamped at Plattsburgh twenty years before. Then, Lucy's ignoring his letters moved him to contemplations of death. Now, Christians' apathy provoked the same gloom. "I find but few christians in all my travels that have any spirit of prayer for sinners," he wrote to Hendryx. "[A]nd all with whom I have conversed tell me the same story." Once the door of mercy shuts "there will be no use . . . for me to warn people of their danger. I shall then I think cease preaching." Indeed, having once forecasted violence against him, Miller now foresaw death, even martyrdom. "I have a presentiment that I shall be taken away, perhaps seal my faith by my blood. You say this is visionary or hypo. perhaps it is so. I cannot account for my feelings any better way myself."[23]

Of course, as Miller's predictions and judgmental preaching became more specific, their failure provoked intensified ridicule. When the 1839 deadline passed, O. A. Skinner attacked: "[A]ccording to Miller's predictions, the day of grace has closed, and the work of regeneration has ceased for ever!! As nothing can be done for the conversion of souls, we suppose Brs. Himes and Burnham, Mr. Miller's coadjutors of this city [Boston], will suspend their labors." He had heard that Miller said there would be no marriages after Litch's predicted date of August 11. "We have however married three or four couples since then. How is this? Was Mr. Miller wrong in his calculations, or are these some of the obstinate that are determined to stand out to the last?"[24] Of course, Skinner and criticisms like his

22. Miller to Hendryx, December 23, 1836; Miller to William S. Miller, December 12, 1839, Miller Letters.

23. Miller to Hendryx, December 23, 1836, Miller Letters.

24. *Signs of the Times,* vol. 1, no. 14 (October 15, 1840).

simply confirmed for Miller his character. "I am fully satisfied," he wrote to Hendryx, "that the true servants of God must expect for the remainder of the time which they may have in the world, persecution and scorn."[25] Thus the warfare blazed.

Hostility from the secular world was not surprising, but Miller expected support from Christians. He was often disappointed. In 1832, at the movement's inception, Miller had detected "a taking sides, a mustering of the troops for the battle, the church is strengthening her stakes."[26] The age-old warfare against infidelity was rousing Christian spirits, and Miller played his part by defending God and Scripture from deists and mockers. As the decade progressed he became increasingly distressed to find among his opponents many who claimed to be Christians but who distracted potential recruits or lulled them into sleep.

Worst among these were the Universalists. As formulated by John Murray, William Ellery Channing, and Hosea Ballou, Universalism preached that Jesus' death bought the salvation of all sinners (general atonement) rather than the sins of the elect alone (particular atonement). God's love was such that he would not bear to inflict eternal suffering on anyone; it was that love rather than the fear of damnation that should draw converts to him. As one historian puts it, "Universalism effectively set aside the traditional psychological foci of religious belief — sin, guilt, repentance, and judgment — that absorbed and channeled human anxiety. A sovereign God, a common humanity, and universal regeneration at death were its major reference points."[27] Rationalist and democratic, Universalism attracted a wide following and vied with the Baptists and Methodists, particularly in newly settling areas. In the 1830s it enjoyed its greatest growth. This came as no surprise to Miller, for as the end approached he expected to see "all denominations but the true Chh of Christ join the Universalists," for they will deceive many. All but the "true Elect will be universalists within 6 or 8 years," he predicted.[28]

It horrified Miller to discover that his brother-in-law, Joseph

25. Miller to Hendryx, April 28, 1835, Miller Letters.

26. Miller to Hendryx, November 17, 1832, Miller Letters.

27. Ann Lee Bressler, *The Universalist Movement in America, 1770-1880* (Oxford: Oxford University Press, 2001), 41-42.

28. Miller to Anna Atwood, September 16, 1833, Miller Letters.

Atwood, and perhaps his sister Anna had converted to Universalism. They became the object of Miller's first forays as an evangelist. Don't be deceived, he wrote Joseph, "for the time is shortly coming that will try every mans work whether it be good or evil, and if you love the Lord Jesus show your love by believing his word." He implored, "Repent oh my brother repent. The tears of a Mother will appear against you. The groans of your dearest friends will be swift witnesses against you in a coming day." Miller's warnings ignited a heated quarrel. Joseph called Miller a pharisee who was trying to "cram down" his throat a dogma of "endless misery," "priestcraft," and "Hell fire." Miller denied it, charging Joseph with aping his Universalist friends. Why don't you "throw by your slang about '<u>creeds, Pharisee, Rattle snake skin, scorpion's sting, venoms of asp</u>,'" he responded. "[G]ive me the simple plain language of your own heart," wrote Miller, rather than "the borrowed gear of <u>Wolves</u> in sheeps clothing."[29]

The dispute allowed Miller to develop a brief against Universalism that sharpened his own soteriology. Universalism was un-Christian, he wrote, because it ran contrary to the Bible: "[N]o person can believe in universal Salvation without discarding a part of that precious book." Depend on it, "just as sure as the word of God is true, Universal salvation is not true." It denied God's merciful nature, for without damnation there is no reformation or cause to seek it. "When & where may we see a Universalist congregation fervent in prayer and supplication for the conversion of sinners?" If all are elected to salvation then there can be no justice, and God becomes a liar. "All your sophistry, will not, cannot destroy the justice of God." He continued,

> I believe in Election without which no rebel can be saved, or in other words will be saved, and I believe in the word of God, in his justice as well as grace, in his unchangeable nature as well as love, in Jesus Christ as a Savior as well as Judge. I believe in God

29. Miller to Joseph and Anna Atwood, March 27, 1832, September 16, 1833, May 14, 1835, Miller Letters. Atwood's reputation generally was suspect. He may well have moved to Upper Canada to avoid prosecution; there he was jailed briefly for an unknown offense, probably for indebtedness. Anna suffered chronic back pains, as did Miller's daughter Bellona, and there is some suggestion that she was defrauded. Eventually she returned to New York, perhaps living with William and his family, before her death.

> [made] manifest in the flesh. I believe he has appointed a day in which he will judge the world in righteousness when all those who are born in Christ whether in Earth or heaven will be gathered in him to eternal life and the wicked will be sent away into everlasting punishment.[30]

Just as the growing popularity of Universalism was a sure sign of the approaching end of the world, stories of Universalists' dramatic conversion to orthodoxy under the influence of Millerite preaching signaled the truth of their message and God's blessing on their crusade.

More heterodox than Universalists and equally condemned were the day's self-proclaimed prophets, chief among them Joseph Smith. Scanning the religious landscape, Miller placed the Mormons at the bottom of the hill of popularity, where they had to "dig for golden revelations, and if they find, it must be more tangible than the former, or their golden book will arrive to the New Jerusalem before its voteries." Another, the prophet Matthias in New York, who claimed authority from God to judge the world, had established a cultic following that attracted wide publicity.[31] Joseph Smith attracted relatively few followers, and Matthias even fewer, so they did not compete with Millerism. But they all fed from the same well of popular apocalyptic and millennial expectation that accompanied the Second Great Awakening. As we have seen, the public reasonably connected Miller's predictions of the end of the world with the antics of both Smith and Matthias. After all, Smith first published the Book of Mormon the same year Miller began preaching about the end of the world, and both published major works over the next several years.[32] The alliteration of Mormons, Matthias, and Millerites was too tempting to editors, so Miller found himself having to de-

30. These quotes appear in Miller's letters to Joseph and Anna Atwood cited above. The long exposition of his testimony is in the letter of September 16, 1833. It was this passage that undoubtedly provoked Atwood's criticism of his dogmatism.

31. Miller to Hendryx, March 22, 1834, Miller Letters. On the career of the prophet Matthias, see Paul E. Johnson and Sean Wilentz, *The Kingdom of Matthias: The Story of Sex and Salvation in Nineteenth-Century America* (New York: Oxford University Press, 1994).

32. Richard Lyman Bushman has published the most recent biography of the Mormon founder, *Joseph Smith: Rough Stone Rolling* (New York: Alfred A. Knopf, 2005).

fend his reputation from this popular association and to deny any claims to being a prophet himself, let alone a messiah.

Universalists and homegrown seers were targets for all orthodox Protestants, not just Miller. Fighting their heresy in tandem with Baptists, Methodists, Congregationalists, and Presbyterians, when he left the hilltop farm in Hampton and marched onto the plain Miller reasonably expected orthodox Protestants would join his battle to prepare the world for Jesus' second coming. Instead, he found those who should have been leading the army were fighting each other and, worse, often against him, on the Enemy's side. In the 1830s "the church" was riven, fighting over what it meant to be Christian, their civil war taking precedence in the battle against "the world." Far from becoming recruits, often they became signs of the times, too, and Miller reserved for them the sharpest arrows in his quiver. Rather than allies, they were traitors to the cause of Christ.

Jacksonian America was a land of choices. The same spirit that empowered political, economic, and social decision making for increasing numbers also proffered multiple paths to faithful life in this world and salvation in the next. All kinds of innovators, not just the heterodox, offered new insight into the nature of God (theology) and explored new ways to organize Christian life (ecclesiology) and paths to salvation (soteriology). The cacophony was confusing. Old Calvinist landmarks were transforming into visions of God and church made in the image of a democratic, capitalist culture. Those invested in the new ways saw signs of the Millennium dawning, but many from the old school were convinced the sun was setting on the church and the world.[33] There is no evidence that Miller concerned himself with any of these deep questions before initiating his apocalyptic movement. After his conversion, he led the Hampton congregation much the same way as had his father, and while he expanded his leadership to the regional denomination, unlike the elder Miller, he did so without contemplating or commenting on the nature of church, other than raising some questions in the 1820s about the proper exercise of church discipline. He and the Hampton Baptists

33. See particularly Mark A. Noll, *America's God: From Jonathan Edwards to Abraham Lincoln* (New York: Oxford University Press, 2002) and Nathan Hatch, *The Democratization of American Christianity* (New Haven: Yale University Press, 1989).

supported missions, Sunday schools, seminaries, temperance, and undoubtedly other new means of communicating the good news.

But in the 1830s, Miller*ism* demanded engagement with these central issues. Postmillennialism impels action, the work of purifying the world in preparation for Jesus' second coming, essentially making it possible for the parousia to take place. Premillennialism compels action, preparing oneself for judgment by living faithful lives here and now. By anticipating the end of the world and final judgment, one effectually places a foot in the next world; being faithful to God requires a believer to live here the way he or she would live there, under the direct rule of Jesus. Thus the old earth takes on qualities of the New Earth, and that requires a clear understanding of how God acts and how Christians should live. The millenarian imperative now pushed Miller to develop a theology, an ecclesiology, and a soteriology, forcing him to confront the many conflicting options of the day. It was tempting to leave these issues in the hands of Jesus, who would solve all disputes on the last day, but if the door of mercy to sinners was closing they needed to know what God expected of them here and now.

In 1834, surveying the denominational field, Miller found little to commend any of the churches (a sentiment shared, ironically, by Joseph Smith). Methodism was "becoming verry proud"; Episcopalians "remain status quo as the only legitimate clergy without any pretense to more piety than her neighbours, yet claims an ascendancy for her well educated ministry & Bishops"; Quakers, divided between the orthodox and the pro-revival Hickisites, demonstrate "that two families in one house, is one too many"; Baptists, growing rapidly in numbers, "are determined on climbing the hill 'Popular oppinion,'" but they "begin to grow dizzy in their height, and fragments are falling off on either hand, Cambellites, Culverites, (& perhaps you [Hendryx] will say Millerites), at any rate the whole hill 'popular oppinion,' will crumble to pieces."[34]

Division was symptomatic of foundational changes taking place in evangelical theology and culture, shaping the medium in which Millerism grew. In the 1830s evangelicalism was redefining the Great Commission, reaching beyond the relatively narrow con-

34. Miller to Hendryx, March 22, 1834, Miller Letters.

straints of family and community in answer to its own apostolic call, like Miller's, to "tell it to the world." Early in its life, Millerism and the new evangelicalism marched together, each supporting the other, mutually fueling their growth. Initially neither could hear the clash of beats their respective drummers were sounding. Miller's spirituality was becoming less rational and more affective, and this led him to a new understanding of the Millennium, the church, and his mission. Passion in Miller brought him closer to people, defining his mission in terms of intimate, concrete relationships. The new evangelicals, on the other hand, while growing more sentimental were ironically also becoming more abstract — instrumental and institutional. Concentrating on effects often subverted the power of affect. The budding partnership between Millerism and the new revivalism initially brought sweet victories for both, but it would dissolve in mutual recrimination.

Miller never described himself as an evangelical; he had no need for distinguishing labels. In the world of his childhood and youth, save for differences in worship style, all Christians he encountered were essentially alike. They believed in a sovereign, omnipotent, omnipresent God, accepted the Bible as God's word, knew Jesus to be Son of God and Savior, and leaned on him for assurance of salvation. That came about through a process of transformation, or conversion, of one's heart that God undertook in the lives of his chosen. Evidence of such substantial change was required for baptism and/or membership in any of the Christian denominations in his midst — notably Presbyterian, Congregational, Baptist, and Methodist. That two particularly, the Baptists and Methodists, were adding new qualities to Christian church life probably escaped his notice; since his family was solidly Baptist he took their way of being Christian for granted. The Baptists were growing explosively in numbers in newly settled regions because they preached simplicity in church order (the priesthood of all believers, radically democratic polity, a standard christological creed) and piety (personal relationship with God through Jesus, devotionalism, rejection of vice, charity toward one's neighbors).[35]

35. A helpful summary is Mark A. Noll, *The Work We Have to Do: A History of Protestants in America* (New York: Oxford University Press, 2002), particularly chapters three and four.

But at the beginning of the nineteenth century the evangelical personality was splitting. The American Revolution's emphasis on personal choice and the experience of peripatetic revivalism on the frontier from 1798 to 1820 softened the theocentric assumption that God alone could transform a human heart. One notes Miller's youthful conviction that he had to do *something* to earn God's love and acceptance, expressing a common proto-homocentrism in evangelical practice (if not thinking) that grew quietly under the surface. That he later ascribed his conversion solely to the compassion of a benevolent God illustrates Calvinism's endurance, but largely as convention. Subsequently joining the Baptists, contributing to missions, and taking his place in the governing of the church were looked-for signs of a changed life and his status as a rural squire. Bible study was a standard pietistic response to the God who had saved him, and he ascribed the discovery of Christ's imminent return that it produced to clarity that comes from God's grace, a light that was available to anyone. The millenarian notion that Jesus would personally and physically return to prepare the world for his thousand-year reign by purifying it with fire was unconventional, and he knew that. But he never claimed to have received a special revelation. Anybody who studied the Scriptures in the same manner as he had would reach the same conclusions. Nothing in these events caused Miller to question accepted views of the nature of the church or how the faithful believer was to act in the world.

By the mid-1830s he was questioning both, which brought him to critical decisions, and to an ecclesiology and soteriology that emerged from his heart rather than his head. In 1826 Charles Grandison Finney launched the final phase of the Second Great Awakening in a series of revivals that swept New York State and spread into New England and the Old Northwest, earning for western New York a reputation as "the burned-over district" (a title he coined) and for himself the title "father of modern revivalism."[36] Finney accomplished this by initiating a series of "new measures" to

36. The classic account of these events is Whitney Rogers Cross, *The Burned-over District: The Social and Intellectual History of Enthusiastic Religion in Western New York, 1800-1850* (Ithaca, N.Y.: Cornell University Press, 1950). See also Charles E. Hambrick-Stowe, *Charles G. Finney and the Spirit of American Evangelicalism* (Grand Rapids: Eerdmans, 1996).

inculcate penitence and then to move penitents to conversion. Among these new techniques were anxious benches where proto-penitents could get special attention from exhorters whose job was to keep them struggling until victory was assured; praying for people by name; protracted meetings that seated men and women together "promiscuously." Proper means, said Finney, could achieve the desired ends.

Accompanying the new measures was a theology of conversion that Finney systematized. Like Universalists, Finney rejected Calvinistic limited atonement in favor of the general atonement. Unlike Universalists, Finney preached that one needed to accept the salvation Christ's death purchased and grow into its benefits by subordinating one's will to the will of the Father, using the gifts of the Holy Spirit to make right choices. By practicing self-restraint one could even achieve perfect sanctification in this world. It was theology perfectly suited for a culture shaped by the market economy and democratic politics. Wealth, power, now even salvation it seemed, rested in one's own hands, and as the phrase "go ahead" became the national cheer, the manifest destination appeared to be nothing less than heaven itself.

The orthodox were stunned. To critics it appeared that the new measures were substituting human technique for divine prerogative, homocentrism for theocentrism, Arminianism for determinism. To them, if America was going anywhere it was heading straight to hell. By the mid-1830s what was then known as the New School was quickly achieving the status of orthodoxy among evangelicals, while their critics, suffering under the label *Old School,* seemed hopelessly reactionary, archaic, elitist. At stake in the dispute were core questions about the nature of the church, of mission, and of salvation. For whom was the Great Commission intended? To whom was the good news to be carried? What role, if any, did humans play in their salvation?

This was not a new debate. Nineteenth-century American evangelicals were experiencing in their own context a tension that had always existed in the church between two sets of answers to these core questions. To builders of the early church in Jerusalem, particularly Peter, James, and John, God's call was to carry the good news back to the people they knew, their network of family and neighborhood.

Thus they lived out the literal meaning of the word *evangel,* to be sent with a message. The product of their work was what historian Raymond Brown called Johannine churches: small, intimate congregations that defended themselves against corruption by the outside world.[37] On the other hand, missionaries like Paul and Silas heard the call very differently. They were apostles, the word literally meaning to be sent *out,*[38] in this case not only out of Jerusalem but out of Judaism, to gentiles and pagans scattered across the Mediterranean world. The apostolic church would be global, even imperial. Evangels and apostles, seemingly fulfilling the same role in spreading the gospel, in reality created two very different kinds of communities, one intimate and inner-directed, the other abstract and extroverted. The split between Old School and New School evangelicals fit the same pattern. New School revivalists created an apostolic personality that sought to reach beyond the narrow confines of family, congregation, and neighborhood to build an army of converted souls who would march into the world, claiming everything and everyone for the Lord. The combination of practical technique and perfectionist theology produced a benevolent empire of seminaries, associations, newspapers, and denominations that over time so successfully consumed the evangelicals' sense of mission that the conservative opposition receded to the deepest corners of historical memory.

But opposition did remain. The Old School was only one sign of a more widespread demurring from popular revivalism. Primitive Christianity in general refused to yield the field. The quest to restore the "apostolic" church ironically resulted in creating communities that more nearly fit the Johannine, evangelical model — small,

37. See particularly *The Community of the Beloved Disciple* (Mahwah, N.J.: Paulist Press, 1979) and *The Churches the Apostles Left Behind* (New York: Paulist Press, 1984).

38. Etymology of these words appears in Gerhard Kittel, ed., *Theological Dictionary of the New Testament,* 9 vols., trans. Geoffrey W. Bromiley (Grand Rapids: Eerdmans, 1964-1974). For the etymology of *evangel* see volume 2, 707-8. According to Kittel, the evangel is "the herald who precedes the people on its return from Babylon to [Z]ion," thus leading the Jews back home from exile. For his treatment of *apostle* see volume 1, particularly 407, where he describes the word in early usage as applying to "a group of men sent out for a particular purpose."

close-knit Churches of Christ, Disciples of Christ, and independent Christian congregations. Independent and self-sustaining, they eschewed educated clergy in favor of homegrown preachers and focused energies on reviving their own spouses and children rather than exporting Christianity outside their relatively narrow bounds.

Baptists were by nature primitive in polity, but the movement toward cooperating in regional associations, an increase in the number of Baptists seeking seminary training, and the creation of missionary societies evinced an apostolic proclivity. It sparked a hostile reaction. In the 1820s an anti-mission or primitive Baptist movement erupted in eastern New York. In 1832 Gilbert Beebe began publishing a newspaper in New Vernon, not far from Hampton, called the *Signs of the Times,* the same title that would adorn the Millerites' first newspaper in 1840.[39] To him seminaries, associations, missionary conventions, and reform organizations were products of human arrogance. Evangelists were not to invite into the church people whom God had not selected for salvation, like guests inviting strangers into a host's home, but should reach out only to those whom God places in their path. All this crusading activity had not improved the world since the days of the church's founding. While he was not millenarian in the same sense as the Millerites, Beebe's preaching did reflect the primitive church's eager anticipation of Jesus' return.

Judging from Miller's support of missions, abolition, and apparently Christian education in the 1820s, his ministry developed initially on the apostolic side of the Baptist personality. His 1822 "Statement of Beliefs" hinted at a limited atonement; "all those for whom Christ intervened" could find salvation, he wrote. But article seven

39. The principal contemporary history of the Primitive Baptists is Cushing Biggs Hassell and Sylvester Hassell, *The Church of God, from the Creation to A.D. 1885; including especially the history of the kehukee primitive baptist association* (Middletown, N.Y.: Gilbert Beebe's Sons, 1886). He cites two anti-mission associations in New York, but only one dates from this period, the Lexington Association, founded in 1825 (page 905). The movement was much more popular in the South, so Beebe moved his paper to Alexandria, Virginia, in December 1836. But he returned to New Vernon three years later ("Autobiography of Gilbert S. Beebe," *Church of God,* 934-36). The best scholarly history is Byron Cecil Lambert, *The Rise of the Anti-Mission Baptists; Sources and Leaders, 1800-1840* (New York: Arno Press, 1980).

was decidedly Arminian: "I believe that Jesus Christ is an offering of God to sinners for their redemption from sin, and that those who believe in his name may take him by faith and go to God and find mercy and such will in no wise be rejected."[40] But by the 1830s, after years of Bible study and millenarian preaching, he was strongly determinist, as his argument with Joseph Atwood against Universalism clearly shows. Those who try to "shun the restricted atonement" get stuck, he said. "The only way for the general folks, is, to say nothing, and think less." By 1838 he was moaning that Arminians had won the day: "[O]ur churches as well as ministers have all departed from the Calvinistic creed, and to mention 'Election' would in a public congregation produce about as much effect as an electrical battery with the whole congregation hold of the conductor."[41]

The church had betrayed its orthodox heritage, and Scripture explained the reason. Revelation 12:6 describes a woman who flees into the wilderness to a "place prepared of God, that they should feed her there a thousand two hundred and threescore days." To Miller the woman was the true church, exiled into wilderness when the Roman Catholic Church secured its authority in 538. When Napoleon captured the pope in 1798, the true church returned from exile.[42] At first, this appeared to Miller to be good news. In March it seemed to him that the "Church was never in a higher state of cultivation on earth than at the present day & for thirty seven years past" as the "four winds of opposition to it" had been restrained — "Kingcraft, Priestcraft, [Mohammadanism], & deism or infidelity." By the end of the year he changed his mind. When Christianity assumed temporal power, kings and emperors fed the church and it became corrupted, transformed into "the man of sin." All the while a faithful remnant, the real church, suffered in secret (in the wilderness) where "God nursed & fed the dear [church] with the true doctrine of the gospel." As soon as Napoleon "destroyed the civil power of the man of sin," the church lost its wilderness virtue. The world "began to pay their compliments and court to the Lady in the wilderness, great men, rich men, & nobles became her admirers, and the poor

40. Miller, Statement of Belief, September 5, 1822, Jenks Collection.
41. Miller to Hendryx, April 10, 1833 and September 8, 1838, Miller Letters.
42. *Evidence* (1836), 178.

dear silly maiden, was so overjoyed with her royal, rich, noble, suiters that she removed her residence into the 'city' and became fashionable, courted, and I fear a harlot."[43]

The New School and new measures were proof. In 1834 increasing popularity of the new theology led him to conclude that "8 or 9 years hence there will be few, very few, who will preach the doctrines of grace or salvation by grace." Hendryx agreed, telling Miller of the "inside heart trouble" to see "those who profess to be saved by grace claim the honor of doing the work themselves." A year later Miller wrote: "Our great Divines, are actually mad, mad with the mania of popular applause. The great success with which their ambitious schemes have been crowned for a few years past, have actually produced a phrenzie in their imagination, so that the means are more to be worshiped, preached & proclaimed than the great First Cause." Where once the church leaned on her God to walk, now she has "been to a dancing school, and one that [knows] all the new measure steps" to teach her "to walk deceitfully, and not honestly as in old wilderness times." This, he said, "is one of the clear signs of the last day."[44]

A corrupt church nurtured a polluted clergy. "What a great change in our ministry within 30 years. The present are no more like the past, than a dandy is like an old farmer in a striped shirt, a wollen frock. . . . Oh! How many are ignorant of the first principles of the word." Their preaching is no more than "Priest Craft, to keep people ignorant of the bible, and make a trade of it. They make merchandise of the blessed word of [G]od" to make themselves popular rather than seeking the "rich treasure" of the gospel. His complaint struck a chord with other Calvinists. Wrote Seth Ransom of Benson, Vermont:

> My Father was a Congregational Minister, who left this world for a better in 1829. He often mourned the degeneracy of the order he belonged to in both doctrine & practice. He often spoke of it so with tears. A desire for honour, profit & pleasure were some of the items which gave him pain to see. I well remember when a candi-

43. Miller to Hendryx, July 21 and December 23, 1836, Miller Letters.

44. Miller to Hendryx, February 25, 1834; Hendryx to Miller, March 8, 1834; April 28, 1835; December 23, 1836, Miller Letters.

> date for the ministry was talked of. The first inquiry was "has he a call from God?" Now, will you become a missionary and go to the heathen? The qualifications required in Paul's epistle to Tim[othy], are seldom mentioned & I fear seldom possessed. It is a lamentable truth, as much as I regret it, the Congregational order is almost extinct. The name is almost all that is left in this region. Now we hear from the pulpit "the new way" & "the old way of getting religion," talked out boldly. Conviction ridiculed & the agency of the spirit denied in conversion. Lord how long? how long shall this mania raign over these deluded mortals? It should be stamped on the heart of every preacher of the gospel. Paul may plant & Apollos water, but, God giveth the increase.[45]

Apostolic means to convert the world was the inevitable result of human ambition. Missionary, tract, and Bible societies proliferated, and undoubtedly they had some good effect in scattering knowledge abroad, one of the signs of the end days. But the effect excited human pride rather than praise for the work of God. Hearing of one preacher's call to send 60,000 ministers to convert 600,000,000 heathen, Miller was scornful: "Now me thinks, if it stands thus we had better get up a contribution, and send all of our present stock [of ministers] off. I will give my quota of expense. I mean the learned ones. We can raise up & qualify more soon. And I think the churches would enjoy a little season of rest. But did he tell how many heathen had been converted by the 1000 missionaries which have gone within 50 years past[?] By this means we might make a very close calculation and act accordingly." No, the scheme made too much of human capacity. "'Jesus Christ and him crucified,' is but little thought of, and certainly but little talked of at the present day, by our publick proclaimers. . . . Instead of prayers, exhortations and sermons, in our publick meetings as formerly, we have reports, resolutions, and speaches. Instead of union, division. Instead of being separate from the world, we amalgamate. Instead of religion, money — instead of humilliation, pride, in the room of persecution, we have flattery. and popularity in the room of shame and contempt."[46]

45. Miller to Hendryx, October 26, 1837; Seth Ransom to Miller, March 19, 1838, Miller Letters.

46. *Evidence* (1836); Miller to Hendryx, July 27, 1838.

If more proof of the futility of human means were needed, abolitionists provided it. To what extent Miller took action to end slavery before preaching Millerism is unknown, but he made his radical views on the subject clear to Truman Hendryx in 1834. Apparently Hendryx had written criticizing the American Anti-slavery Society's radical call for immediate, unconditional abolition, preferring the voluntary, gradualist approach of the American Colonization Society. In his habitually ironic manner Miller scorned Hendryx's passivity. "These Abolitionists, Emancipators, Liberators must be put down," he teased.

> What[,] emancipate 2,000,000 of brutes, unless we call molatoes half brutes only, then say 1,000,000 brutes & 1,000,000 half brutes. No, no this would flood our country with beasts surely. . . . [God made them black] and so we may beat them, bruise them, sell them, buy them, not teach them, not give them Bibles, not preach to them, shoot them, and cut their throats if they should try to get free. . . . I think Br. Hendryx that the Abolitionists who say that the Negroes are to be free aught in justice to have their throats [cut] from e[a]r to ear for saying these things. What think you Br. Hendryx? . . . the great, the good benevolent Colonisation Society transports and banishes them to Liber[i]a where one half die from starvation and the "seasoning" as they call it. Now we know they would not do it if they were men because it would be murder. That Society are Christians, & they murder [?], no. For "as much as ye have done it unto the least of these ye have done it unto me" says Christ.[47]

But while he agreed with William Lloyd Garrison, Miller found the radicals' actions to be less than effective. In 1840 Miller attended a session of the American Anti-slavery Society's meeting in New York and watched as they argued over principles and procedures. "They are in trouble, divided, split in two, scattered, and weakened by their uneasy designing and master spirits," he reported. "It teaches us that all earthly things are passing away, all the combinations of men however pure may be their principles in the abstract, are perverted by wicked and designing characters." So "the

47. Miller to Hendryx, February 25, 1834, Miller Letters.

year of Jubilee to the poor slave is not near if man is the cause. But God can & will release the captive. And to him alone we must look for redress."[48]

That did not render him passive. Regardless of his opinion of abolitionist societies, his reputation as a friend of slaves inspired a conductor on the Underground Railroad to send a runaway to him for help. In 1844 a man appeared at the farm with a note introducing him as "a fugative from the iron hand of slavery." He was "of considerable consequence to his claimant" and federal marshals were "in hot pursuit," so the writer sent him to Miller, since no one in the vicinity would be more ready "to feed the hungry & direct a stranger fleeing to a city of refuge than yourself." The Champlain Valley was a principal escape route to Canada for people fleeing from Southern slavery and Northern slave catchers. Just north of Miller's farm in Ferrisburg, Vermont, Thomas and Jemima Robinson operated one of the most active stations, and while there is no evidence of Miller's satisfying this specific request, it is likely that he did.[49]

Surveying the extent of human ambition and corruption, it was no wonder to Miller that the world was full of "Antis & isms." Some of the sects were hospitable to Miller's ideas, the Old School Baptists most of all. "Yes," he said, "and my heart inclines more towards them." But all the sects were "now more or less partaking of the Babalonish cup" and were out of the wilderness, catering to worldly powers and ambition, "except O[ld] school Baptist"[50] who shared Miller's contempt for agencies of human means. "Come then Lord Jesus, for vain is the help of man. He will never, no never, nor ever or ever mend himself." There can be no impediment between the believer and the actuating God. "I have finally come to this conclusion," Miller wrote, "that I must read the bible for myself, try all that in me lies to divest myself of prejudice, judge with candor, get rid of self, preach what I believe to be truth, try to please God more than man." The result had been rich blessing. "Hitherto the Lord hath helped

48. Miller to William S. Miller, May 16, 1840, Miller Letters.

49. Philander Barbour to Miller, November 8, 1844, Miller Letters. A brief description of the Robinsons' activities at their farm, Rokeby, appears on the National Park Service's web page *Aboard the Underground Railroad,* http://www.cr.nps.gov/nr/travel/underground/vt1.htm.

50. Miller to Hendryx, April 2, 1836, Miller Letters.

me. . . . I have been absent from home more than ¾ of my time. & truly God has been with me. I have heard sinners cry out. I have seen many infidels yield the point to truth: but I have no mechanical operation, no [mercy] seats, no converting power in man. It is all God & blessed be his name, he proves it so in this case certainly. For the old trembling man, illiterate and rough, he can do nothing."[51]

He had come far since the days of his rational, Masonic spirituality. The change is clear in comparing Miller's 1820s musical paean to Masonry and the 1831 dream, published twenty-two years later, that spurred him to public preaching. Impressing Miller in his allegorical journey were the design of the temple ("every part/Was well proportioned just and true") and the song of praise it evoked from the inhabitants to its builder, "the architect divine." In his dream, so similar in imagery, Miller was not moved by the principles or the scenes he encountered so much as by the spirit of those he met. "Here was a communion indeed," he said, not rooted in virtue or principle but flowing from "the love they had one for another. I thought I felt its flame — its pure, unadulterated love." Through preaching Millerism, Masonic visions of fraternity's uniting all in rational brotherhood gave way to yearning for the primitive church that would join together "persons of all denominations of Christians, yet all distinctions were taken away."[52] All would be accomplished not by human action but by God.

That work was clearly progressing. By the end of the decade Miller had taken his message of warning and hope to thousands, almost single-handedly creating what the public now universally called the Millerite movement. While he was personally primitive and Old School, ironically it was the revivalism flowing from the new measures that best accounts for his success. As I have argued elsewhere, it was the message's capacity to provoke conversion that enticed preachers to invite his lectures into their meetinghouses and camp meetings even when they disagreed with him, the effects of his ideas often meaning more to them than their content. He

51. Miller to Hendryx, July 27, 1838, Miller Letters.

52. Miller, "A masonic Dream," Jenks Collection; Sylvester Bliss, *Memoirs of William Miller: Generally Known as a Lecturer on the Prophecies, and the Second Coming of Christ* (Boston: Joshua V. Himes, 1853), 90.

might privately bemoan the new measures, but in the public mind predicting a date for the end of the world was one of them, simply an inventive means to inculcate conversion.[53] For his part, Miller also was content with the strange marriage. Details of ecclesiology were of no more importance to him than the fine points of prophecy. A critic who thinks he has the whole truth and then "bends all the scripture to his point" doesn't see the whole picture, he once said. "And who knows but that old br Miller has the same fault?" No matter — he could "leave all in the hands of my divine Master, and wait for his decision."[54]

Others were not so patient. Throughout the campaign Miller had been praying for God to send workers for the harvest, and as the new decade dawned, God responded. The Massachusetts crusade in 1839 introduced Miller to workers who created a system for carrying his message to the world more broadly than he had ever imagined possible. Young, energetic veterans in the war against Satan and vice, these new apostles assembled an army for the Lord and marched out to Armageddon, setting a pace that the aging Miller could not match. As an evangelist he had faithfully shared his message with those whom God had placed in his path, and while that path strayed ever farther from hearth and home, he had maintained the intimacy that came from personal contact and direct control. Now, means that exceeded the new measures in innovation transformed Millerism into Adventism,[55] the regional crusade into a mass movement, and *Father* Miller increasingly into a remote, abstract father figure.

53. David L. Rowe, *Thunder and Trumpets: The Millerites and Apocalyptic Thought in Upstate New York, 1800-1850* (Chico, Calif.: Scholars Press, 1985), 24-26.

54. Miller to Hendryx, July 27, 1838, Miller Letters.

55. George R. Knight first proposed this helpful distinction between the Millerite movement of the 1830s and the Adventist movement of the 1840s in *Millennial Fever.*

CHAPTER SEVEN

I Am Coming On . . .

While preaching at Vermont conferences in 1838 and 1839, Miller met the men who would transform Millerism into Adventism — Josiah Litch at a Methodist conference in Bethel and, at a Christian Connexion conference in Calais, L. D. Fleming of Portland, Maine, Timothy Cole of Lowell, and Joshua Vaughan Himes, pastor of the Chardon Street Chapel in Boston.[1] Coming to the movement from different traditions, they all found the idea of a personal second advent appealing. Methodists liked its capacity to provoke conversions and spark revivals, and Connexionists, products of the restoration movement, were drawn to its biblicism, empiricism, and promise of a return to the purity of the primitive church.[2] Chief among them, Himes would be the architect and manager of Millerism's conversion from a popular crusade to a mass movement. For nearly a year after Himes met Miller in Calais there seems to have been no contact between the two, but in October 1839 Himes got word from David Cambell (who would soon become a principal critic) that Miller was lecturing in Groton, Massachusetts. Seizing the opportunity, Himes invited him to preach on

1. Affidavit and endorsement, Bethel, Vermont, January 26, 1839 and Calais, Vermont, November 22, 1838, Miller Papers, Jenks Collection of Adventual Materials, Aurora University, Aurora, Illinois.

2. Shortened labels for members of this group are all awkward; I use the term *Connexionists* sparingly and only when syntax requires it. Himes penned the entry on the Christian Connexion for *The Encyclopedia of Religious Knowledge,* ed. J. Newton Brown (Brattleboro, Vt.: Brattleboro Typographic Company, 1838), 363-64.

the second coming in his chapel.[3] Miller did not respond, but when the two met at another Christian Connexion conference at Exeter, New Hampshire, Himes again extended the invitation. This time Miller agreed and in December undertook a series of lectures in Boston, introducing the city to his views and himself to a new and enthusiastic supporter.[4]

Hearing Miller preach the first time had piqued Himes's interest, but this full course of lectures convinced him. "I found myself in a new position," he recalled. "I could not believe or preach as I had done [about the spiritual reign of Christ]." In what would become a characteristic fashion, Himes quizzed Miller: Do you really believe this? If so, what are you doing to spread the message? Why is it so few people have heard anything about it? Miller's response was also characteristic. Rather than taking umbrage at this slight to the enormous labor he had already expended, he became defensive. "What can an old farmer do?" he asked. "I was never used to public speaking; I stand quite alone, and, though I have labored much, and seen many converted to God and the truth, yet *no one,* as yet seems to enter into the *object* and *spirit of my mission,* so as to render me much aid. They like to have me preach and build up their churches; and there it ends, with most of the ministers, as yet. I have been looking for help — I want help!" Himes then said, "[W]ill you go with me where doors are opened?" Miller replied, "Yes, I am ready to go anywhere. . . ." Recalled Himes, "Here I began to 'help' Father Miller."[5]

The recollection could have been self-serving, but the story rings true both in Himes's commanding spirit and Miller's self-effacement. The Low Hampton farmer was not the first innovator Himes championed. In 1832 he introduced Bostonians to Alexander Campbell, a principal founder of the restorationist movement, by sponsoring publication of his critique of Joseph Smith and Mormonism, even contributing a preface to the book. Ironically, using language that would become all too familiar to the Millerites, Himes

3. Joshua V. Himes to Miller, October 18, 1839, Joshua V. Himes Papers, Massachusetts Historical Society, Boston, Massachusetts (hereafter cited as Himes Papers).

4. Sylvester Bliss, *Memoirs of William Miller: Generally Known as a Lecturer on the Prophecies, and the Second Coming of Christ* (Boston: Joshua V. Himes, 1853), 139.

5. Bliss, *Memoirs,* 140-141.

sympathized with friends in Boston who had been "grieved and afflicted in consequence of the [Mormon] delusion," and he warned others not to be "swindled out of their property" by becoming "miserable subjects and dupes of these singular fanatics."[6] In the bare ten years he had been in Boston, Himes had earned a reputation as an effective agitator in moral reform generally — antislavery, nonresistance (pacifism), and women's rights — and he had become friends with William Lloyd Garrison, after whom he named a son. He was as effective a model of the professional reformist as Charles Grandison Finney was of the modern revivalist. Counted as colleagues were Ralph Waldo Emerson, Theodore Parker, and James Russell Lowell. Himes was much later described as a "radical and an enthusiast by temperament," searching constantly for the perfect solution to moral dis-ease, and as a man who was single-mindedly committed to the "*success* of the apostolic gospel."[7]

Initially, it is surprising that the insular, Old School farmer could have developed an intimate working relationship with this urban and urbane man of such apostolic proclivities. But the partnership was a natural fit for both. On the one hand, Himes offered Miller the sophisticated clerical support for which he had always yearned, and with it affirmation and a certain legitimacy in his own eyes. On the other hand, the second coming of Christ promised Himes the total apostolic victory he sought, global regeneration immediately and imminently. He had become restive with human means that proved fallible, slow, and divisive. Single-minded focusing on reform had caused his Connexion congregation in Boston to remove him as their pastor, so he and several supporters had founded the Second Christian Church that met in the Chardon Street Chapel.[8] Now he had found the certain agent of global regeneration, God's purifying fire. Just as Miller long ago had promised to take his message to the world, Himes too was determined that "the

6. Alexander Campbell, *Delusions, An Analysis of the Book of Mormon with an Examination of its internal and external Pretences to Divine Authority* (Boston: Benjamin H. Greene, 1832), 5.

7. David T. Arthur, "Joshua V. Himes and the Cause of Adventism," in *The Disappointed: Millerism and Millenarianism in the Nineteenth Century,* ed. Ronald L. Numbers and Jonathan M. Butler (Knoxville: University of Tennessee Press, 1993), 38-39.

8. Arthur, "Himes," 38.

warning should go to the ends of the earth."[9] Differing in much, they shared the same mission and commission.

Himes took charge immediately. "I am coming on," he warned, "and when I come — look out. All my soul will be in it."[10] Indeed, applying his immense energy and using his many connections, Himes applied himself as feverishly to the millenarian task of warning the world as once he had worked for the postmillennial goal of purifying it. A skilled entrepreneur, he took Millerism from the outstretched hands of its crafter and marketed it as a commodity in the public square, giving it mass appeal and stamping it with the character by which it has been known ever since.

Himes accomplished this by mobilizing three resources. The most important was publication. In the first year he arranged for a new edition of Miller's lectures and compiled material from Miller's writings for a new work, *Views of the Prophecies and Prophetic Chronology,* including the first memoir Miller wrote explaining how he had come to discover the near approach of Jesus. Working with William Lloyd Garrison's publisher, Dow and Jackson, Himes produced and edited the movement's first newspaper, *The Signs of the Times,* which began semi-monthly publication (within two years it became weekly) a scant three months after Miller's first lectures in the city. There followed printed chronologies, pamphlets, an entire Second Advent Library, hymnals, portraits of Miller, a second newspaper, *The Midnight Cry* in New York and then, shorter-lived, the *Philadelphia Alarm, The Western Midnight Cry, The Southern Midnight Cry, The Advent Shield and Review,* and the *Advent Message to the Daughters of Zion* — this last publication edited by and marketed to women. In the short span of four years, his efforts produced millions of documents distributed by sale and, just as often, free of charge to the public.[11]

Second, Himes attracted skillful workers and mobilized supporters for action. The Methodist and Connexion practice of meeting in regional conferences was the model for what became a series of sixteen Second Advent General Conferences held in major cities

9. Arthur, "Himes," 141.

10. Himes to Miller, January 17, 1840, Himes Papers.

11. Arthur, "Himes," *passim,* and George R. Knight, *Millennial Fever and the End of the World* (Boise: Pacific Press Publishing Association, 1993), 76-84.

and strategically located Adventist centers across the North, including Boston, New York, Portland, Lowell, and Low Hampton. Conferences provided a platform for new lecturers to try out their skills and to create their own followings: Henry Jones, Henry Dana Ward, Josiah Litch, George Storrs, Charles Fitch, Reuben Starkweather, Joseph Bates. Each conference produced a printed report that added to the literature available for distribution. In these ways they served to educate the public, affirm converts, establish policies for the movement, and organize regional cohorts of leaders who could maintain momentum once the conference closed, through study cells and prayer groups. Thus, while reaching out to large numbers they provided the same intimate, small group contact in large cities that gave longevity to the movement in small, rural congregations. There, where Millerism had slowly grown for seven years, conferences were of little use, so the New York session of the general conference in May 1842 recommended camp meetings as a more efficient means to rouse the countryside and to unite rural Millerites with urban Adventists. By now an old-fashioned revival technique, Adventists gave it a New Measure twist by creating the largest canopy in the world, which could seat an audience of six thousand. The Great Tent always sparked curiosity and drew large crowds wherever Himes raised it — Albany, Buffalo, Cleveland, or Boston — and it became something of a logo for cartoonists who wanted to lampoon Adventist speakers and their audiences.[12]

Third, since publication and publicity required money, Himes effectively systematized financing for Adventism's many ventures. His own money launched the *Signs of the Times* and undoubtedly other publications early on. Passing the hat at conferences generally covered the costs of printing their reports, and while we do not know their full extent, personal donations generally were significant. A man named Flanel signed over a piece of New York property, and its proceeds paid for an edition of the *Midnight Cry.*[13] Rental fees for halls that were large and strategically located were steep, and the Ohio tour of 1843 cost over $2000, though it raised a thousand dollars on the

12. Knight, *Millennial Fever,* 102.

13. Nathaniel Southard to William S. Miller, January 12, 1843, Miller Letters, Jenks Memorial Collection of Adventual Materials (hereafter cited as Miller Letters).

road. So Himes organized an auxiliary of workers and contributors in Boston called the Berean Hall Association and called upon them to raise money for special campaigns. A lecture series in New York, he wrote them, would leave a deficit of $200. "I know how much the brethren in Boston have done — and are willing to do," but he asked them "to look at the case, and do what seems to them to be right."[14] On at least three occasions Himes mentioned printing tickets and the possibility of charging admission,[15] and while there is no evidence this was done commonly it probably happened from time to time.

One of his most significant plans was to help Miller financially so he could focus attention single-mindedly on the movement and not be distracted by material concerns. Miller was not wealthy, and the crusade was not covering his expenses. So to guarantee his ability to go on tour, Himes proposed giving Miller an allowance of $100 a month "during the present Fall, and winter, if you will come on and spend one, two, or three Months, and lecture in the places I have in view, where you would have audiences of 1500, & 2000 people." He was not proposing this out of "a mercenary character," but he thought "if you leave home, and all its enjoyments I think you should be fully remunerated. 'The Laborer is worthy of his hire.'" Even so, he stated emphatically — with a sketch of pointing fingers — "This proposition is a profound secret between us."[16] There is no indication that Miller accepted the offer or that Himes followed through on it. As we shall see, it came at a critical moment, when Himes undoubtedly feared Miller would never again leave Low Hampton unless he had assistance. Certainly, given the numerous public rumors that Millerism was nothing but a money-making scheme (the new financing measures undoubtedly feeding them), discretion was called for.

In the process of marketing Millerism, Miller himself became a commodity to be peddled to admiring supporters. A Boston artist, W. M. Prior, had painted Himes's portrait, and Himes arranged to

14. Himes to Prescott Dickerson of the Berean Hall Association, April 27, 1842, Himes Papers.

15. Himes to Miller, January 2, 1840 and March 25, 1841, Himes Papers. Renting space in the "Oppollo buildings" in New York, he told Miller, would be so reasonable "we can meet the expense without, an admission fee — Lectures free, and without difficulty." Himes to Miller, April 13, 1842, Himes Papers.

16. Himes to Miller, November 3 and October 21, 1840, Himes Papers.

have him do Miller's. Miller boarded with him during his first Boston tour, and Prior did a sketch "in simple dress" that he used as a model for the oil portrait. E. W. Thayer then produced a lithograph based on the portrait that was printed as a frontispiece in Himes's *Views of the Prophecies* and also in a bound second volume of the *Signs of the Times.* Copies were sold to the public for twenty-five cents apiece, one quarter of that going to the Adventist cause, and at least one admirer framed the picture and hung it next to Himes's. In 1843 Nathaniel Currier produced a commissioned portrait showing Miller, one hand raised in preaching and the other resting on the Bible, undoubtedly used as a fundraiser. Still another souvenir was a carte-de-visite complete with autograph and greeting: "I remain as ever looking for the Lord Jesus Christ unto eternal life."[17] Pithy scriptures from his lectures appeared on paper seals that believers could purchase by the sheet, cut out, and attach to letters and envelopes as quick and easy warnings to others and personal witnesses to their faith in Miller's prediction.

Himes's exhaustive efforts enabled Adventism to reach people who had never heard of the approaching apocalypse — in western New York, Ohio, and Michigan, south to Baltimore and Washington, and across the Atlantic to England.[18] Despite Miller's eight-year,

17. Himes to Miller, October 21 and November 19, 1840, Himes Papers; Nathaniel Southard to Miller, January 12, 1843, and Delilah LeCompte to Miller, April 22, 1844, Miller Letters. When Miller died there were so many unsold copies of the lithograph that Himes used them as scrapbook sheets on which he glued copies of Miller's obituaries sent in from around the country (Obituaries, Miller Papers, Jenks Collection). The family was eager for Prior to come and "take the portrats of them all" (William S. Miller to Miller, November 27, 1841, Miller Letters). Undoubtedly it was he who painted Lucy's portrait, either at the farm or when she visited her husband in Boston. Both paintings now hang in the Miller Farm. There is also a miniature portrait identified as William Miller in the Miller Farm museum that is most likely of William S. Miller. Again, the artist is unknown. A copy of the Currier print can also be seen at the Miller Farm museum. A photograph of the carte-de-visite appears as the frontispiece to Clara Endicott Sears's *Days of Delusion: A Strange Bit of History* (Boston: Houghton Mifflin, 1924). Lucy lived long enough to have a daguerreotype taken; a print of that also can be seen in the Miller Farm museum.

18. One of Himes's disappointments was the inability to take Miller to England. He had suggested such a tour to Miller and even had a tour planned when the fervor over the final predicted date for the end of the world, in October 1844, diverted their attention.

nearly solo crusade, the large majority of his followers undoubtedly came into the movement under Himes's stewardship. And the short deadline, a scant three years to the predicted end, encouraged a high level of commitment and energy and sustained it for the duration. Historians have commented on the quality of relationship between these two unlikely partners. Wayne R. Judd suggested that the Bostonian's ambition compensated for Miller's felt and often-expressed inadequacies and made of him "a welcome convert." David Arthur noted their "mutual respect and trust," and while describing a leadership style that could be "flamboyant" cites contemporaries' description of Himes as unassuming, noting that he never sought "personal position." Managing the movement rather was the product of his "commitment to a cause larger than himself." George Knight sees him as "overbearing at times" but a man with "a firm conviction of his place in prophetic history" that "enabled him to put his considerable talents behind Miller and his cause."[19]

All these descriptions capture the essential quality of partnership between the two, but the relationship was complicated. A creative tension kept it dynamic. Miller's habitual self-doubt grated against Himes's commitment, energy, and awareness that time was fleeting. True, Miller remained the messenger, and Himes never forgot that, but the cause was as much his as its founder's. Himes set out to help Miller, but sometimes it was Miller who was called upon to assist him. Himes once thanked God that he would "have his aid in the battle yet to be fought with the 'Beast and False Prophet.'" In publishing the *Signs of the Times,* he said, "[I] must still depend upon you as my main stay, while your health will permit you to render me aid." He was aware of the exhausting pace of the work, and he wished he could "help Father Miller, or do some of his work for him." But "as it is, I have to draw upon him, & lean more than I really ought — yet the cause is depending, and what else can I do?"[20]

19. Wayne Judd, "William Miller, Disappointed Prophet," in *The Disappointed: Millerism and Millenarianism in the Nineteenth Century,* ed. Ronald L. Numbers and Jonathan M. Butler (Knoxville: University of Tennessee Press, 1993), 27; Arthur, "Himes," *Disappointed,* 42; Knight, *Millennial Fever,* 92.

20. Himes to William S. Miller, October 10, 1840; Himes to Miller, November 3, 1840; Himes to William S. Miller, October 9, 1840, Himes Papers.

Accountability to the cause enabled both of them to overcome the tensions that inevitably erupted. Himes was demanding, even imperious. Letters conveyed impatience and urgency with single or double underlinings, sets of exclamation marks, crudely drawn fists with finger pointing and stereotypical phrases — "without fail," "I want you to . . . ," "I am determined," "you must," "no ifs nor ands," "send send send without fail!!!" Time was short, and there were articles to be written, lecture tours to be planned, critics to be "done up," chronologies to be checked. Miller found it exhausting to march to Himes's pace, and he complained about it publicly. In the *Signs of the Times* he said, "I have more business on hand than two men like me could perform." He was lecturing twice a day, fielding questions, answering letters "from all points of the compass," facing critics, reading "all the 'slang' of the drunken and the sober; and since [referring to the William Henry Harrison campaign] 'hard cider' has become so popular, *these publications are not few.*" On top of that "Brother Himes has claims, — Dea. Piersons has his, — Bro. Cambell must be righted etc." The letter continues like this for fourteen more lines.[21] The gripe smacked of braggadocio, but it scolded, too.

For his part, Himes had cause for impatience. Miller was not an easy man to manage. Letters from Himes went unanswered, making it impossible to know if he was writing the required articles or if he would show up at scheduled lectures. To be sure, given the slow pace of the mails and Miller's rapidly changing schedule, it was difficult for letters to catch up with him. That is why Himes and others sometimes wrote duplicate letters, one directly to Miller and one to William S., who could forward it to his father. Too, the advent of Himes's leadership initially resulted in two movements, the older Millerism and the new Adventism, and it took time to coordinate them. Miller still made his own appointments while Himes made promises for him as well, and they sometimes conflicted. Himes expected Miller to lecture in Boston while he was gone touring in the West. "[B]ut when I see that the breth-

21. "Miller's Letters — No. 8," vol. 1, no. 11 (September 1, 1840), 81. Miller had responded in a similar vein to Hendryx's complaint about his not writing. See Miller to Hendryx, May 19, 1841, Miller Letters.

ren draged [sic] you off everywhere else, and poor Boston — and the Tabernacle had to be desolated! I said to myself I'll have pay for that, (if time continue.)"[22] The tone was intended to be jocular, but the impatience was real.

Circumstances notwithstanding, Miller was indecisive and undependable. Regarding plans for tours to Salem and England, for example, Himes had to keep prodding: "What about Salem? What about England? Let me have a letter soon." The critically important General Conference scheduled for October 1840 in Boston required Miller's presence. Himes took it upon himself to include Miller's name on the flyer advertising it, assuming, "By all means you will act with us" in it. Not hearing from him, Himes repeated both his apology for using his name without permission and his request: "I do so hope for your full approbation. Do let me hear from you soon." A month before the event he asked again, "Please write me about this. Let me know whether you will, or can come. . . ."[23] Isaac N. Walter complained regarding arrangements for a meeting in New York. He had suggested May 7 and asked Miller for an alternative if that did not suit him. "But instead of this you only said, 'I shall be in New York in one or two days of the time specified in your letter.' Now what calculations could be made from the face of your letter?" Himes had written assuring them that Miller would be there on May 12, but they had already advertised Miller's being present May 10. Rather than create any more confusion they withdrew their invitation for the present, "and then we shall wait till we receive something definite from you and something that we can rely on that the people will not be disappointed and dissatisfied."[24]

Worse, Miller sometimes did not appear at scheduled appointments. "I have now been in [New York] 3 days waiting for you," wrote Himes, "but as yet we see or hear nothing of Brother Miller. I hardly know what. . . . Please let me hear soon; and oblige me and relieve my feelings." John Andrews in Claremont, New Hampshire, complained about Miller disappointing them: "We have made our calcu-

22. Himes to Miller, November 14, 1843, Himes Letters.

23. Himes to Miller, September 28, 1842, two letters without date written on the back of a printed flyer advertising the General Conference located in the collection after a letter dated August 3, 1840, Himes Letters.

24. Walters to Miller, April 28, 1840, Miller Letters.

lations to have you come to this place on the strength of your promise. But as you have ingaged in another place we shall expect you here as soon as you git through in that place."[25]

In addition, as we have seen, Miller had an extroverted tendency to say things out loud he would later regret, whether in the excitement of the occasion, as when he was lecturing, or because he wanted to please people. Later he might not remember what he said. This created the aforementioned crisis over Himes's new edition of *Evidence*. Isaac Wescott, whose name appears as copyright holder for the 1838 edition, and Miller engaged in a long dispute over payments to the printers and the number of copies owed to Miller and received by him. Still, in January 1840, possibly because he had gotten wind of a new edition under way, Wescott offered to settle the "old affair" and to republish with Miller. In April, now fully aware of Himes's activities, he threatened to sue "any person who sells a copy of that work unless arrangements are made with me" claiming proof "by at least two witnesses" and Miller's "own letter upon the subject" that he had "disposed of the copy right to me." On May 13 he wrote in a more conciliatory tone, offering to cover the remaining debt to the printers, Tuttle and Belcher, if Miller would agree to repay him. "I am poor, and no money," he wrote, "and a large family on my hands." At the same time he refused to "relinquish any of my claim as I have stated above unless the affair is amicably settled."[26]

Lack of sophistication in matters like this rather than duplicity undoubtedly explains Miller's difficulty. He may indeed have unwittingly given copyright to Wescott in some fashion orally, and perhaps even in writing. But Wescott's role and motives are not above suspicion. It's hard to imagine why, with a dispute raging, he would offer to work with Miller on another edition unless it promised profits. Certainly Himes was clear about who was to blame. In 1893 he noted on the back of the May 4, 1840, letter from Wescott that he "proved *false* — and had neither *faith* or honor." Regardless, one of

25. Himes to Miller, May 14, 1840, Himes Letters; Andrews to Miller, June 2, 1841, Miller Letters.

26. Wescott to William S. Miller, April 28 and May 13, 1840, Miller Letters. See also Wescott to Miller, September 16, 1839, and January 9, 1840, Miller Letters.

Himes's first experiences working with Miller was to be confronted with a mess that he had to clean up. He did that with characteristic dispatch. "I will see you in N.Y. & arrange the matter," he wrote. "Be prepared in some way to meet it and dispose of it." So Miller did, in whatever fashion. To avoid any complications with his own edition Himes offered to pay Miller "for the right, what is right" by giving him a discounted purchase price for one hundred copies, and he purchased the book's plates from the printer to ensure that it would be "under my control."[27]

Beyond matters of personality, Miller's deteriorating health frustrated plans and itineraries. In February 1842 he turned sixty, and an exhausting pace of travel and work took its toll. He was away from home from mid-October 1839 to the last week in March the following year and gone again most of May, then from February to mid-April 1841 and for weeks at a time that fall and winter. The same pattern held true until mid-March 1843. On the road he frequently complained of coughs and soreness and usually came home exhausted. Now serious disease became chronic. Dropsy had been diagnosed several years before, and erysipelas, a painful skin condition that caused rash and boils, recurred so frequently the family called it "the old complaint." Early in October 1840 Miller finally informed Himes he would attend the Boston session of the General Conference and set out, but he got no farther than Fairhaven, just two miles from home, when typhoid fever struck him down and his children had to fetch him. He sent a letter to the conferees, but his absence forced Himes to give the lectures originally assigned to Miller. Illness kept Miller from attending the second session of the conference at Lowell in June 1841 as well, leaving well-wishers concerned that he might already have died.[28] Then on March 15, 1843, after preaching at Ballston Spa and traveling home, an attack of erysipelas laid him low at Rock City outside Saratoga Springs. A Deacon Dubois gave him shelter, and Lucy nursed him there for at least two weeks until they could carry him home in a bed on a wagon. In April he described himself "very weak in body."[29]

27. Himes to Miller, May 4 and November 3, 1840, Himes Letters.

28. J. K. Wright to Miller, July 20, 1841, Miller Letters.

29. Text Book notations for March and September, 1843, Jenks Collection; "Bro

The *Signs of the Times* kept readers apprised of his condition. In June his health was "in the same feeble state" and "it is feared his labors are almost over." A visitor that month found him "very low for the last two weeks" with boils and a cold and fever that "greatly enraged his other complaints" and "brought him to death's door." Still, "though very low, we think there is a fair prospect of his recovery. . . . His trembling has greatly decreased, his sores are healing and his symptoms are all good. The rest of the family are all enjoying a good degree of health, considering their great anxiety and labors." After another downturn in July, his health gradually improved to the point that in September he could once again accept speaking engagements. With son George accompanying him, Miller set out for Springfield, Vermont. Wrote William S., "He is quite low, yet he is anxious to be out in the field once more before the final gathering takes place, which we all think will be soon."[30] By the middle of October 1843, he took up a regular speaking schedule once again.

Chronic and prolonged illness radically altered Miller's relationship to the movement. Initially his writings appeared frequently in the *Signs of the Times;* in the first issues, the bulk of the material was his. In 1841 it was clear that his capacity for work was limited. The paper advised readers in February that his speaking schedule was full and that *"other arrangements are made conditionally, as his health is in a precarious state."* In August he reported, "I have not been able to write a line before this in five weeks; and even now I am in great pain."[31] Himes was solicitous, driven by concern for the movement but also for Miller, for whom he had genuine affection. He wrote consolingly regarding Miller's absence from the Boston conference, "My attachment to you, and the views you have given to

---

Miller — His Sickness!!" *Signs of the Times,* vol. 5, no. 100 (March 29, 1843), 29; "Letter from Wm. Miller," *Signs of the Times* 5, no. 104 (April 26, 1843), 57. William S. graphically described the boil on his right shoulder: "It has eight heads, and he was wasted considerably under it."

30. *Signs of the Times,* "Notice," vol. 5, no. 110 (June 7, 1843), 109; "Letter from Low Hampton," vol. 5, no. 111 (June 14, 1843), 117; "Notice," vol. 5, no. 167 (July 26, 1843), 167; "Mr. Miller," vol. 6, no. 124 (September 13, 1843), 25.

31. "Mr. Miller's Future Labors," vol. 1, no. 22 (February 15, 1841), 174; "Letter from Mr. Miller," vol. 2, no. 34 (August 15, 1841), 73.

us, are evident and stronger than any earthly considerations. I feel that I can live with you in Gloom or Glory — I look to you, as to a Father for support, and counsel — and aid to carry forward the work of God, in giving the Midnight Cry." His demands had helped weaken Miller's health, and he was apologetic. "You do not know, my feellings [sic], when I am obliged to call upon you so often, and so much for help. I think of your age, and your infirmity &c and could I only help you, or do anything to lighten your care; how gladly I would do it." But, he added, the cause always foremost, "you see how it is — and how I am placed, and will make allowance for me." Sentiments following the attack of erysipelas in 1843 were identical: "you must have your rest on your return. Just consult the Bishop if you please!! So I indulge in my Himesisms. But the fact is I can't give you up. I must have my claim."[32] Ever solicitous he may have been, but his "Himesisms" did not cease.

Even had Miller wished to participate more fully in leading Adventism, his body would not allow it. On the contrary, after many prayers for others more capable than himself to assist, and knowing his own limitations, this new arrangement must have suited him. It is possible that, consciously or otherwise, illness became a convenient reason for withdrawing to the safety of his farm. A certain hypochondria was not unknown among people finding themselves thrust into public notice. George Pickering refers to it as "the usefulness of illness," evidence of which he found in the lives of personalities as diverse as Charles Dickens, Florence Nightingale, Sigmund Freud, and Elizabeth Barrett Browning. Most of the religious innovators of the day — Mother Ann Lee, the Universal Publick Friend, Ellen G. White, Mary Baker Eddy — suffered from chronic pain, and while scholars have noted that it most often happened in women, men could exhibit the tendency as easily.[33] Erysipelas is uncomfortable and sometimes painful but does not usually threaten death.

32. Himes to Miller, November 26, 1840, and November 24, 1843, Himes Papers.

33. George Pickering, *Creative Malady: Illness in the Lives and Minds of Charles Darwin, Florence Nightingale, Mary Baker Eddy, Sigmund Freud, Marcel Proust, Elizabeth Barrett Browning* (New York: Oxford University Press, 1974), 7. See also Ronald L. Numbers, *Prophetess of Health: A Study of Ellen G. White* (Grand Rapids: Eerdmans, 1008) and Julius Silberger, *Mary Baker Eddy: An Interpretive Biography of the Founder of Christian Science* (Boston: Little Brown, 1980).

Unless other undiagnosed diseases were troubling him, it is difficult to understand why it proved so debilitating.

Regardless, being in Low Hampton for months on end, removed from day-to-day operations, had its advantages. For one, Millerism now became fully a family activity. The Millers loved music. His childhood lessons in the singing school came to fruition with his own children, who played instruments and sang often, and William S. pushed Himes to publish more hymns in the *Signs of the Times*.[34] With Advent hymns a common fare in these soirees, Miller's personal presence was to a great extent responsible for the refreshing that would soon lead his children to conversion. More important for him, family members became his travel companions. Lucy had been reluctant to join him, and the children were either too young or occupied with their own lives. Now someone from the family almost always accompanied him — even Lucy — to assist and nurse him on the road.

Detachment provided an additional benefit for Miller. Leaving the daily operation of the movement to others enabled him to assume the role of patriarch. Like Moses in his old age, he could allow his Joshua to organize the troops while he provided moral guidance and a fatherly wisdom that comes only with age and experience. Himes may have found it difficult to work with him, but he also discovered that Miller was indispensable. Along with imperatives sprinkled in Himes's letters were frequent phrases acknowledging this: "the whole enterprise demands the influence and help you can give it"; "Great dependence is placed upon you. There will be no getting along without you"; "all dependence is on Father Miller"; "it will be a failure without you." Regarding the prospects of Miller's visiting Cambridge, Himes wrote, "You can have no idea of the thrill of joy it produced, when I told them you would come to see them if they desired." Such expressions could have been attempts to persuade or cajole him, but the public's expectation and Himes's realization of Miller's importance were genuine. When Miller's 1843 attack of erysipelas forced him to miss a course of lectures scheduled for Albany Himes tried to go on in his place, but "the people all desiring to hear Bro. Miller" did not come and he had to cancel the series. The very

34. William S. Miller to Himes, March 28, 1841, Miller Letters.

real possibility of Miller's dying distressed Himes terribly: "I hardly know what I should do if God were to take you from me."[35]

The fact was, Miller's lecturing was truly effective. Every description of his speaking, whether from Adventists or popular papers, described him as lucid, erudite, and effective in conveying his views. Indeed, surprise at finding these qualities in the squat, antique-appearing old farmer first opened the door to people's hearing his message, whether they accepted it or not. Elder Timothy Cole of Lowell arranged for Miller to speak in his church, and when he met Miller for the first time he saw "an old man, shaking with the palsy" and immediately regretted the invitation. Escorting him to the church, Cole refused to sit with him beside the pulpit, expecting the worst. But Miller began slowly, praying and lining out hymns that the people then sang. He "presented the Scriptures in a manner that did honor to the occasion, like a workman who needeth not to be ashamed." So Cole went to the platform and took his seat beside his preaching guest.[36] A reporter for the *Maine Wesleyan Journal* who attended a lecture in Portland similarly described him as "a plain farmer" who when speaking was "self possessed and ready; distinct in his utterance, and frequently quaint in his expressions." During his nearly two-hour lecture he "succeed[ed] in chaining the attention of his auditory," evincing "much tact, holding frequent colloquies with the objector and enquirer, supplying the questions and answers himself in a very natural manner; and although grave himself sometimes producing a smile, from a portion of his auditors." Miller's lectures were "making a decided impression on many minds, favorable to his theory."[37]

As formulator of the message and its principal lecturer, Miller was, as Himes stated, essential to the cause. But Himes's words reveal genuine affection, and others shared it. The specter of Miller's dying frightened many, and they responded to his illnesses as they might to their own father's. Strangers from across the region wrote to Miller during his long 1843 convalescence sending prayers and pleadings

35. Himes to Miller, January 1, 1841; May 29, 1841; January 22, 1843; June 25, 1844; November 13, 1841; Himes to Nathaniel Southard, March 25, 1843; Himes to Miller, March 24, 1843, Himes Papers.

36. Bliss, *Memoirs,* 135-36.

37. *Maine Wesleyan Journal,* March 20, 1840.

that God might spare him. Many contributed homegrown cures for boils, ranging from plasters to restorative teas, and shared stories of their own experiences with the disease, and physicians and others offered to come and nurse him back to health. Apparently Miller did not think much of herbal remedies. Jesse Thompson, well-known Adventist leader and doctor, regretted that his faith was "so small in the use of Botanic medicine," so he offered to take him to his house, where he would give him special baths every day, "together with the shower bath." It was the least he could do; "I feel that I am under the strongest obligations to you for what you have done for me and my family."[38]

As Miller became a patriarch to supporters, his farm transformed into a shrine. Old friend Leman Andrus's visit while Miller was on the road made Andrus nostalgic: "[T]hat east room of yours where you and I have sat up until mid-night to solve Bible questions looks lonesome to me because Br Miller is not there." Another visitor waxed poetic as he sat in "the very room" where Miller first discovered the truth of Christ's imminent return. "Here is the old fashioned desk, and the 'old family Bible,' and the concordance. . . . How many prayers have here been put up, how many tears shed. . . . The feelings of another world seem to steal over me. . . ." The family took on an air of sanctity, too: "There is a heavenly atmosphere here. . . . They make a band of singers that would charm you. Throughout the family filial and reciprocal confidence and love appear to reign. . . . [O]ne must be here to realize and feel its force."[39]

It was to this sanctuary that Miller returned, perhaps even fled, from his encounter with the wider world. Millerism in the 1830s had drawn Miller out from his home, but its being rooted in extended family and relationships allowed him to remain attached to it. Himes, on the other hand, took him away from home and commissioned him as a warrior in a world of cities — Boston, New York, Portland, Buffalo, Philadelphia, Baltimore, Washington. On the one hand, cities could be fascinating, opening to him the newest fads. In Boston he anonymously visited an anti-Millerite phrenologist to see if by examining the shape and "geography" of his head the man could detect any fa-

38. Jesse Thompson to Miller, June 13, 1841, Miller Letters.

39. Andrus to Miller, November 27, 1841, Miller Letters; "Extract from Bro. Jones Letter," *Signs of the Times*, vol. 6, no. 133 (November 15, 1843), 107.

naticism in his client. The phrenologist found none — and then was shocked to discover whose head he had been squeezing.[40]

In general, though, Miller was never comfortable in cities. On a return trip to New York in 1840 he found it bigger than he remembered, "a world of itself." Two years later this "emporium of the new world" was much more disagreeable: "Nature is almost driven out of the city, nothing appears natural, all is artificial, the earth is changed, now we see no mountains, hills nor dales, no brooks, nor water falls." He could see nothing "but the works of man." The clergy were as thick as grasshoppers "and about as useful, for the same purpose, to feed turkies on." Rum sellers ("Death's pallaces"), bankers ("the shark with a red rag in his mouth"), wealthy nabobs who shut out the pleas of widows and orphans, merchants — all fit Revelation's description of the wicked world. All in all he would "choose the state prision [sic] as I would this city for a place of residence." At the end of such an experience, he wrote, "I feel a severe head ache to day."[41] No wonder he always returned home exhausted and ill, ready to "take comfort," as the old Yankee expression went, surrounded by family and familiarities.

Being at home insulated Miller from much of the controversy that churned Adventism in the 1840s. He could play the "good cop" toward internal dissenters while Himes, Litch, and others were the disciplinarians. Some inventive Millerites added their own scriptural "light" to the movement's message, confusing Adventists and the public alike. George Storrs preached the annihilation of the soul rather than the second resurrection unto eternal damnation and attracted disciples to his views, notably Charles Fitch. In England Millerites developed the belief that Jews had to return to a renewed state of Israel before the second coming, and this "English theory" became popular among Millerites in America as well. Advent leaders condemned the literalism of this "fundamentalist principle" while espousing the literal, physical second coming of Christ. "Bastard Jews,"[42] as Miller called one splinter group, split the

40. Bliss, *Memoirs,* 98-99.

41. Miller to William S. Miller, May 16, 1840, and April 25, 1842, Miller Letters.

42. Henry Jones to Miller, October 8, 1841; Miller to Himes, April 5, 1842, Miller Letters.

Millerites in New York City and formed a commune on Long Island, where they lived according to orthodox Jewish ritual and law. (It's possible that the clothes they donned gave rise to or encouraged stories of ascension robes among the Adventists.) John Starkweather in Himes's own congregation insisted that physical manifestations were the test of divine blessing and divided the people with his proto-Pentecostalism. Perfectionists of all sorts in the movement gained wide publicity for spiritual wifery, visions, prophecies, claims of healing, and attempts to raise the dead. All these would be embarrassing should they show up at the general conferences and camp meetings. It was Himes who took pains to exclude them from the conferences, prevented them from using the Adventist organs, and then received the blame for being high-handed.

Distance also gave Miller "plausible deniability" when it came to policies that proved embarrassing. Setting a time even as relatively vague as 1843 for the apocalypse "*if* there were no mistake in my calculation" was divisive. Some of the strongest leaders in the movement, including Himes, did not preach it, and Henry Dana Ward urged Miller not to emphasize the date because its effects were so harmful to the cause.[43] On the other hand, Silas Hawley was preaching an entirely different year, 1847,[44] and rumors continued to circulate that Miller was refining his prediction ever more narrowly, even to a specific day.

Despite its difficulties, revealed time gradually became a standard in the movement, particularly after the Boston conference in May 1842 strongly endorsed both the idea of a revealed time and its realization in 1843. In November that year, Miller for the first time refined his prophetic expectation to the period extending from March 21, 1843 to March 21, 1844. Later he would claim that this was in response to pressure from brethren who had censured him "for putting in an IF."[45] We have already seen Miller try to distance himself from the aftermath of the August 1840 debacle, a prediction he seems to have advocated more strongly than he cared to admit publicly. His defensive comment in this case bears the same stamp.

43. Ward to Miller, October 25, 1841, Miller Letters.

44. Himes to Miller, November 24 and December 8, 1843, Himes Papers.

45. William Miller, *Apology and Defense* (Boston: Joshua V. Himes, 1845), 24.

George Knight relates that Josiah Litch and Isaac Wellcome heard Miller pronounce as early as 1839 that "Christ would come between the spring of 1843 and March 21, 1844."[46]

If predicting a set time for the second coming earned the public's ridicule, Adventist calls to separate from the churches made it hostile. For years lecturers had criticized the churches for rejecting Miller's message, often in response to the treatment pastors and denominational journals dealt out to them. Increasingly Miller's correspondents described their clergy in unflattering terms: cold, lifeless, blind, unwilling to preach sound doctrine (i.e., Millerism). Separation had been going on quietly for years before 1843, whether by forced exclusion of Millerite zealots or by voluntary removal. Adventist prayer cells had been meeting separately from their non-believing brothers and sisters, and some in the larger cities had already formed associations and even built what they called tabernacles, thus replicating the practice of the Jews, newly liberated from Egypt, who carried the ark of the covenant on their forty-year journey and housed it in a tent.[47] There is no statistical evidence that shows the pace of these exclusions and resignations, but as deadlines approached and fervor mounted the rhetoric and recriminations rose accordingly. Disappointment certainly fueled the animosity, scoffers' ridicule goading condemnation in response. The failure of the August 1840 prediction was followed by dashed hopes at the spring equinox in March 1843, again at the arrival of the new year 1844, and most seriously by the passing of the spring equinox that March.

As early as February, Miller agonized over the ferocity of the attacks against them. "We would ask in the name of our dear Master Jesus Christ, by all that is holy, by the fellowship of the Saints, and the love of the truth, why you cast us off as if we were heretics?"[48] He saw himself, of course, as orthodox — Bible-centered, Christological, primitive — and he had long expected that the clergy would see these qualities in his message and support them, even if they could not accept his predictions. Criticism was bad enough, but condemnation

46. Knight, *Millennial Fever,* 127.

47. Knight, *Millennial Fever,* 151-53.

48. "An Address to Believers in Christ of all Denominations," *Advent Herald and Signs of the Times* [hereafter cited as *Advent Herald*] 7, no. 146 (February 14, 1844), 9. The paper's name changed from the *Signs of the Times* with this volume.

and exclusion were shattering. Still, he long had cautioned forbearance. Responding to the old charge that he was seeking, like Joseph Smith, to create a new sect, he had called to witness "thousands, and even tens of thousand more" that he had "begged of you to make no divisions in your churches or sects." Quite the opposite — he had "advised all men of every sect not to separate from their brethren, if they could live among them and enjoy christian privileges." Henry Dana Ward had privately advised Miller similarly to use his influence "in subduing the passions, & restraining the vexed spirits of others, whose feelings are smarting under the undeserved wounds of their friends."[49]

That might have had an effect on the Millerites of the 1830s, for whom Father Miller's spiritual paternalism was direct and intimate, but to the Adventists of the 1840s Miller's "fatherhood" was abstract, idealized, incapable of parenting such a protean mass movement. Animosity was kindling awaiting a spark, and in July 1843 Charles Fitch struck it. An 1838 convert to Millerism, Oberlin graduate, perfectionist, and friend of Charles Grandison Finney and William Lloyd Garrison, Fitch was a rising star in both reform and evangelism. In the war against Satan, he took no prisoners. An early leader in Millerism, he was responsible for perhaps its most enduring visual legacy, the Great Chart, a large wall hanging depicting the "Man of Sin" from Nebuchadnezzar's dream with head of gold, torso of silver, legs of brass, and feet of clay, a metaphor for the four kingdoms that would endure until the second coming. Miller himself used a chart like this in his lectures to help auditors follow his complicated chronology.

But Fitch could also be controversial; in 1844 he preached George Storrs's annihilationism, discrediting himself in the process. Six months before that, though, he had given form to the fermenting resentment of persecuted Adventists by calling on them to separate from their churches. By rejecting Miller's predictions, all the denominations had shown themselves to be daughters of the whore of Babylon, and the Scriptures required the faithful to flee

49. "Wm. Miller's Address to the Believers in the Second Advent Near, Scattered Abroad," *Midnight Cry,* vol. 1, no. 2 (November 18, 1842), 9; Ward to Miller, October 29, 1841, Miller Letters.

from that city lest they be partakers of the destruction that awaited it. True Christians were Adventists, and the test of faith was removing oneself from Antichrist. If you are a Christian, Fitch wrote, "*come out of Babylon!* If you intend to be found a Christian when Christ appears, come out NOW!"[50] Many did, often publicly and loudly, particularly after Himes endorsed the call. In September Himes wrote in the *Advent Herald* (formerly the *Signs of the Times*), "It is death to remain connected with those bodies that speak lightly of, or oppose, the coming of the Lord. It is life to come out from all human tradition, and stand upon the word of God, and look daily for the appearance of the Lord."[51]

Miller remained noncommittal on this point. In April he drafted a letter to Elon Galusha, a leading Millerite in western New York, expressing concern about come-outerism: "I fear the enemy has a hand in it, to divert our attention from the true issue the midnight cry, 'Behold the Bridegroom cometh." Besides, scriptural precedent suggested not fleeing from corrupt churches but cleansing them by excluding the corruptors. Like St. Paul, Miller was "very loth to say to any of Gods people 'come out of the churches.'"[52] The letter was unfinished, unsigned, and probably unsent. One wonders if he intended it for publication (such strong statements made to an important and connected man could not have remained private) but changed his mind. Clearly it represents his thinking about this important subject, but he made no public pronouncements. It was controversial, dividing older from newer leaders.[53] Perhaps that is why in this, as with other issues, he preferred to stay out of the fray and let matters take their course. But later, after the final failure of predicted time, he strongly condemned the come-outer movement, now giving vent publicly to his private doubts. Its effects proved that it was, as he thought at the time, "a perversion of the word of God,—a wresting of Scripture." The hostility it created prevented people from heeding his warning; it separated Adventists from their own churches; worst, it divided Adventists by creating a test of faith se-

50. Charles Fitch, *Come Out of Her, My People* (Boston: J. V. Himes, 1843), 18. On Fitch's life and Millerite career see Knight, *Millennial Fever,* 105-13, 153-58.

51. Vol. 8, no. 177 (September 18, 1844), 53.

52. Miller to Galusha, April 5, 1844, Miller Letters.

53. Knight, *Millennial Fever,* 156-57.

cessionists used to judge those who stayed in their churches. But, he added defensively, it was "brought about by unforeseen circumstances." It was a result "which I never desired, nor expected."[54]

A more honest appraisal would have led him to admit that his silence on such an important issue contributed to the debacle. And he ignored the extent to which his own hostility to the churches encouraged the mood of retribution, which he shared. As we have seen, opposition from those he expected to support him, the clergy and religious editors, provoked Miller to judgment and condemnation. The Portland reporter who wrote such a flattering description of his public presentation also noted he was "disposed to make but little allowance for those who think differently from him, on the Millenium [sic]; dealing often terrible denunciations against such as oppose his peculiar views on this point." Professor George Bush, whom Miller described as his "most gentlemanly" opponent, similarly pointed out to him, "You will scarcely deny that there has been no small measure of denunciation on [your] side" stemming in part from Miller's habit "of charging that a dissent from your views was identical with a total neglect or utter ignorance of the whole subject of prophecy." Miller, as well as others, had engaged in "wholesale condemnation of the rejecters of your opinions." So given Millerites' complicity in fostering hostility, their persecution "does not present a problem very difficult to be solved."[55]

Indeed, Miller's sardonic wit and peevishness (as he once put it)[56] could produce counterattacks so vitriolic it concerned even his supporters. Henry Dana Ward had already cautioned him against returning ridicule with vitriol. Another Millerite wrote anonymously, "[A]mong your best friends, those who are most anxious to have you succeed are much concerned[,] fearful that saying the ministers are all liars &c &c does turn away the minds of some from your teaching." No doubt they treated him badly. "But the might of meekness is the armor of Christ. Try it once."[57]

54. Miller, *Apology and Defense,* 25. Miller dictated his apology to Sylvester Bliss in August 1845, and it was first published the following year.

55. "Prof. Bush to Wm. Miller," *Advent Herald* 7, no. 149 (March 6, 1844), 39.

56. Miller to Himes, April 5, 1842, Miller Letters. "I think my cold makes me peevish," he said.

57. A friend to Miller, December 17, 1842, Miller Letters.

He couldn't. The stakes were too high. Corruption now crept into the very sanctuary that had always protected him. Kittredge Haven, a Universalist in nearby Shoreham, Vermont, gathered evidence about Miller's personal life and finances to impeach both his character and belief in his own predictions, making him out to be not only a thief but a cynical liar. Miller used money raised by lecturing to increase the size of his farm, said Haven; he paid bills in cash, no doubt garnered from auditors; his children all lived more richly than their neighbors; he has bought a new stove and built new stone walls, all proving that he expected to be around for a long time. After Haven's article appeared in the *Universalist Trumpet,* William S. was warned that "spies are busy sent from different parts of our Country" talking to neighbors to verify the stories.

Knowing what his children had to endure on his account, Miller was solicitous and eager to be justified. Soon they would all meet, he wrote his son from Philadelphia, "where no scoffing Priest will ever mantle your cheek with a blush for what your father endures at their unholy remarks, and where no lying editor will ever have a part in polluting the character, or misrepresenting the views of your aged Parrent." He was painfully aware of "how deep must be the wounds your young, and tender and unexperienced hearts must feel, when you see the thousand and one falsehoods, which a proud & haughty Priesthood have invented, and an hireling press has circulated." For they are "engaged in the work of their master the devil."[58]

So with the passing of the spring equinox in 1844 and the failure of his predicted period, misgivings about the come-outer movement notwithstanding, he confessed to a quandary. On the one hand, God required the faithful to congregate in churches. But how could he fellowship with those who denied the truth of his teachings? "To disobey God, I dare not. And to walk with and have a good fellowship for those who by their traditions, make void the law of God, I must not." To do so would be "hypocrisy in the extreme."[59] What were his followers to make of that? Try as he might, despite his sickness and relative detachment from Adventism's leaders, there was no extri-

58. William S. to Miller, December 18, 1843; Miller to "Son" (probably William S. Miller), February 2, 1843, Miller Letters.

59. "Letter from Mr. Miller," *Advent Herald* 7, no. 157 (May 1, 1844), 97.

cating himself from responsibility for the effects of Millerite radicalism in this case or in the matter of definite time.

Besides, by then the personal stakes went much deeper than anguish over his children's hurt feelings. By the end of 1843 the Hampton Church had shattered over its patron's apocalyptic predictions. Miller and his many children along with the extended family of siblings and cousins comprised the majority in the congregation. Controversy over the new measures opened a fault line in the 1830s; some wanted an up-to-date revivalist ("a quick gab," as Miller put it), while Old-School Miller wanted a traditional preacher ("a quick understanding").[60] Adventism widened the split. Not surprisingly, the large majority supported the Adventist message and its being preached, though not all accepted the predicted date. A minority opposed it and, again, the dispute soured searches for a new preacher.

After the departure of the Millerite Isaac Sawyer, the pastorate of the Baptist church became unstable. Miller made it difficult for a minister to stay who did not fully agree with his millenarian views, while others wanted a non-Adventist message. In April 1835 the church engaged a preacher who, Miller said, was "opposed to my Millennium violently, but I will conquer him." He must have, for two years later the preacher was gone. S. B. Thompson arrived in 1840, but he left in March 1841, ostensibly because the salary was too low. But it was also true, said William S., that he was "not much of a millennium man." A licensed Millerite layman, Alfred D. Low, served with them for a while; by November they were looking again. They tried to persuade a previous pastor, Leman Andrus, to return because he was "good on doctrine," but they were "sort of split over who to call."[61] Instability led to decline. In 1833 Hampton sent a messenger to the Washington Union Baptist Association annual meeting who reported 113 members, but the church sent no mes-

60. Miller to Hendryx, November 17, 1832, Miller Letters.

61. Bliss records a letter Miller wrote to a Bro. Parsons on April 7, 1847, in which he says the Adventists favored Elder Jones while the anti-Millerite minority favored Elder Dillaway (*Memoirs,* 288-89). That letter does not appear in the Miller Letters. As we will see, Dillaway assisted with a revival in the congregation in 1843, and that seems incongruous given his later strong opposition to Miller. It is likely he was, like so many other evangelicals, willing to nurture the fruit of renewal even though he objected to its source.

sengers again until 1839, when the congregation numbered only 90. The tallies decreased regularly: 87 in 1840, 85 in 1841. One can question the Hampton messenger's report that year, "Union prevails," though there is little doubting the claim, "They have an interesting Sabbath-school and Bible-class."[62]

Ironically, revival strained the fault line to the breaking point. It all happened while Miller was absent. On December 31 he was in New York, beginning a ten-week lecture tour. That night the Hampton Baptists gathered in their church for prayer, "on Watch tour" until after midnight "at the comm[encement] of the year 43 so long lookd for by many an anxious soul." An awakening in a nearby Methodist Church "though not on the 2d advent Doctrine" persuaded William S. "the spirit is manifestly calling in the last of the scattered sheep into the fold of our great shepherd." Night prayer meetings continued, until two weeks later son William could shout "Bless the Lord O My Soul for his great mercy that he is transporting in our place." Elder Dillaway was there to help them out, and the savior's spirit "was felt in every hart." Even his brother was swept up, and anything that could "bring Satterlee on his knees to beg for mercy must be more than man can do." Then George was converted, proclaiming himself "a minute man now ready to go, or do as the Lords spirit & duty direct." Robbins, too, became an active worker for the movement, distributing literature and writing a testimonial letter that the *Midnight Cry* published in March. Their father, overjoyed with the news, wrote from Philadelphia thanking God, "who has saved all my children."[63]

Euphoria did not last. The shaking had done more than drive young people to their knees. Anti-Adventists actively attacked Millerite preaching in their midst. William S.'s cryptic comment that "the family duties are attended daily at the old place by prayers

62. Miller to Hendryx, April 28, 1835; William S. Miller to Hendryx, February 21, 1837; William S. Miller to Himes, March 28, 1841; William S. to Miller, November 27, 1841; see also A. L. Low to William S. Miller, January 25, 1841, Miller Letters. *Minutes of the Washington Union Baptist Association,* 1841, 13.

63. William S. Miller to Miller and Himes, January 8, 1843; William S. to Miller, January 22 and February 9, 1843, Miller Letters; "Letter from a Son of Bro. Miller," vol. 6, no. 9-10 (March 21, 1844), 9; Miller to William S. Miller, February 2, 1843, Miller Letters.

rather by Mother or some of the Boys" suggests physical separation had already occurred. What the letters do not reveal is a simmering dispute that came to full boil by the end of the year. In December 1843, neighbor Paulinus Millard quit the church because "there is so much 2d Advent as we have," and two weeks later William S. lamented "our Elder Brethren remain in their cottages, and we are left a verry small remnant indeed."[64] Elder Dillaway had assisted the congregation during their recent refreshing, but the fact that he used an anxious bench might have been a warning of trouble to come. When the Millerite majority hired a sympathetic Elder Jones to be their preacher, the minority championed Dillaway. Both could not occupy the pulpit at the same time, so the minority removed themselves to the schoolhouse close by the Miller farm. When Jones's year-long agreement ended, the Adventists willingly changed places, hoping to avoid an open dispute. That expectation, like others, would be in vain; soon a more shattering Adventist disappointment would give their opponents the opportunity to strike.

In late March 1844 all the predicted periods for Christ's second coming had passed uneventfully — August 1840, the spring equinox of 1843, the end of the calendar year 1843, and the spring equinox of 1844. Publicly Miller had refused to settle on a particular day, though as we have seen he engaged in private musings. The passing of each landmark left him disappointed, but he continued to expect the end of the world sometime during the "Jewish year" 1843. Erysipelas mercifully focused his attention on convalescence at the beginning of the prophetic year, but January 1, 1844, provided a symbolic blow when the page of the calendar no longer read 1843. Still, he reassured followers, "Never has my faith been stronger than at this very moment. I feel confident that the Savior will come, and in the true Jewish year." I. E. Jones reminded Miller that he had said in one of his lectures that "the whole time would expire before Christ would come." Besides, the last phase of the process of parousia would be a time of trial. Before the light, there must first be darkness.[65] But

64. Miller to William S. Miller, February 9, 1843; William S. Miller to George Miller, December 18, 1843, Miller Letters.

65. "Address to Second Advent Believers," *Advent Herald* 6, no. 144 (January 31, 1844), 195; I. E. Jones to Miller, February 9, 1844, Miller Letters.

when the next spring equinox also failed, and March melted into April, Miller was badly shaken. Apparently in despair he wrote to Chilion Wines, asking, what shall we do? "Why ask you that question," Wines replied. "Why not go to Gods Bible" where it says "it is for an appointed time[;] though it tarry[,] wait for it." As to what *Miller* might do, he could not say. "[W]hether you are to assist in this cry God only knows. He will manage his own cause in his own way." Indeed, Miller had collected himself by the time he received Wines's advice. To Elon Galusha he wrote, "I now am looking every day and hour for Christ to come, my time is full, the end of days are come, and at the end the vision shall speak and will not lie." Like Jonah sitting under the fig tree and bemoaning God's saving Nineveh, Miller now wondered if the Lord had some final act of mercy, or vengeance, in mind. "If God should give a few days or even months more as probation time, for some to find salvation, and others to fill up the measure of their cup, before they drink the dregs, and wring them out in bitter anguish. It is my saviors will."[66] All the signs were fulfilled, so now the duty of the faithful was to wait and watch.

It was, indeed, the tarrying time, a time of testing. Scoffers ridiculed them virulently, churches expelled recalcitrant Adventists, and the steadfast streamed out of the churches. Miller lectured only once in April and very sporadically in May and June. Some Adventists set about recalculating the prophetic timetable, which forced Himes to disavow all such efforts publicly. "Mr. Miller has no other time for the termination of those periods than about the Jewish year A.D. 1843," and he still "looks for the savior this jewish year."[67] But following his own statement Himes published an article on prophetic time by Samuel S. Snow, a new name in the movement. Like Miller, Snow had been a militant agnostic, but reading Miller's lectures converted him, and when he heard Miller preach at the East Kingston, New Hampshire, camp meeting he committed all his labors to spreading the message. Like many in the movement, Snow heeded the call to study Scripture for himself, and, again like Miller, found in exegesis a startling truth. Calculating the prophetic peri-

66. Wines to Miller, April 4, 1844; Miller to Galusha, April 5, 1844, Miller Letters.

67. "Prophetic Time," *Advent Herald* 7, no. 153 (April 3, 1844), 68.

ods according to the Jewish calendar, Snow computed that the real termination of the prophecies would take place in the fall of 1844.[68]

Adventist leaders paid little attention to him at first, but in February 1844 Southard and Himes published an article by Snow detailing his calculation in the *Midnight Cry.* Himes had been careful to keep discussion of time in the papers focused on Miller's "Jewish year 1843," and Snow had not yet acquired a following that would have forced him on their attention as had other controversial voices. But Himes had not fully accepted the idea of definite time, and the vernal equinox was rapidly approaching. Perhaps he wanted to have some "fallback position" should it fail. The leaders had no intention of endorsing Snow's position, so accompanying the letter was a disclaimer by L. Delos Mansfield of Portland, undoubtedly inserted at the editors' request: "It is possible that Bro. S., may be correct; but we cannot see it in the light that he does."[69]

Still, Snow preached his views wherever he appeared, and as the tarrying time waxed so did interest in his prediction. A camp meeting at Exeter, New Hampshire, in August provided the catalytic opportunity. As George Knight tells the story, Joseph Bates was speaking to a listless crowd on old ideas that had failed to come true and now failed to arouse their interest. A Mrs. John Couch interrupted him and pointed to Samuel Snow who had a new message for them to hear, thus paving the way for him to address the audience. By now he had refined his calculations to a specific date in the fall of 1844, the Jewish day of atonement that occurred on the tenth day of the seventh month. Converting from the Jewish calendar, the day would fall on October 22. The spirit at this camp meeting was particularly enthusiastic (or fanatic, as Himes would put it).[70] Inevitably the new prediction was greeted as a new charism, a revelation to faithful souls who had endured much. Jesus had tarried long enough. Now he was certainly coming.

This "true midnight cry" spread like a prairie wildfire. George Storrs, who had developed a sizeable personal following with his annihilationist views, now took up this new message and helped to

68. Knight, *Millennial Fever,* 192, 193, 188-89.

69. *Midnight Cry,* vol. 6, no. 5 (February 22, 1844), 243-44.

70. Knight, *Millennial Fever,* 187-89.

popularize it. The first sign of excitement in the *Advent Herald* was a reflection by Josiah Litch in the August 21 issue; he did not deny the significance of the seventh month but did not see it as clearly nor as certainly as others. A month later, though, the paper printed articles regularly on the seventh month, explaining its significance in the Jewish liturgical calendar and demonstrating when it actually would fall. At the end of September Himes became directly involved. Enthusiasm for the message was not his motivation; indeed, he confessed to Miller that the "question is not yet clear to my mind." Still, "the fruits are glorious." It was not its effect in converting sinners that most impressed him, but its impact on Adventists. "It has done away all Fanaticism, and brought those who were given to extravagance into a sober discreet state of mind. 43 never made so great, and good an impression as this has done upon all that have come under its influence." He was sure the Lord would come in the fall, "And for ought I know he may come on the 7th month & 10th day."[71]

Himes's real agenda in writing to Miller was to involve him in the discussion: "Never was there a time when we needed you more." Clarity of the message required it, no doubt. But more was at stake than that. Miller had remained silent about the "true cry," and his silence created the vacuum that others were now filling. Snow had published his own newspaper *The True Midnight Cry* (for only one issue as it turned out) and was gaining influence rapidly. More serious, George Storrs seemed to be using the true cry to further his own influence. I. E. Jones, Josiah Litch, and Nathaniel Whiting had recruited Miller to use against him and his annihilationist views in April, arguing then that "he virtually wields from our silence, the whole, or almost the whole Advent influence."[72] This time it was Himes who worked to involve Miller in the dispute, sending pointed questions about the atonement and its prophetic significance. He put it directly: "Was the attonement, which was made by the priest on the 10th day of the 7th mo. a type of Christ's second coming as to time. . . . Why may we not look for the return of our High Priest to bless his people at that time."[73]

71. Himes to Miller, September 30, 1844, Himes Letters.
72. Jones, Litch, and Whiting to Miller, April 6, 1844, Miller Letters.
73. Himes to Miller, September 30, 1844, Himes Letters.

At first Miller remained characteristically aloof, preferring to let the others joust in the lists. The spring disappointment had left him publicly expectant but privately moody. Scoffing and ridicule had been merciless, and while some supporters encouraged him, many did not, even in his own family. Brother-in-law Joseph Adams, a Universalist, urged him to give up preaching. "[Y]ou must be aware that the folks in general will not believe what you say," for "what you believd as you thought the bible taught has fai[led] to come to pass."[74] Defending himself against the charge of fanaticism, Miller had clung tenaciously to the fact that he had never predicted a specific day. He had already confessed to a mistake in "the exact time of the event," but in August the *Advent Herald* published an additional "Confession and Correction." Misrepresentations of his views were leading people astray, both believers and nonbelievers, endangering souls in the process. Some have claimed he did not expect to see Jesus come until a distant future, perhaps fifty years away, but he reiterated his firm faith that the prophecies were all satisfied and the end could happen at any moment.[75] How difficult it must have been for him, then, to consider endorsing a specific day and month at all, one not only from another's calculating but based on the conclusion that Miller's had been fundamentally wrong. No wonder he remained silent.

But the established leaders required him to stand with them, and with increased publicity and their persistent urging for "light" from him, Miller's reservation began to crumble. In a September 11 statement in the *Advent Herald* Miller assured supporters, "We are as confident as faith in the blessed word can make us, that we are now at the very door, and soon our wondering eyes will be ravished by all the beauty, splendor, pomp and glory of our descending King." No matter that it was the same hope he had always expressed; in the context of the true midnight cry it sounded like an expectation of imminent realization. On October 9 the editors pointed out that as early as May 17, 1843, Miller himself had described the particular significance of the tenth day of the seventh month in Scripture. It was on that day that Noah's ark came to rest; it initiated a

74. Joseph Adams to Miller, August 4, 1844, Miller Letters.

75. Vol. 8, no. 172 (August 14, 1844), 14.

week-long period of cleansing according to Leviticus; it was the day established for blowing the jubilee trumpet and for the priest to emerge from the sanctuary to bless the people. So, as he thought out loud, it seemed to him then that "we shall not see his glorious appearing until after the autumnal equinox." The editors found "considerable force" in the idea at the time but averred that "it would be impossible to fix positively on any one [date]." Now, less than two weeks from the deadline, they reprinted his May letter and added a new concluding comment. "[I]t is our deliberate conviction that the institutions of the seventh month — the feast of trumpets on the *first* — the day of atonement on the *tenth* — and the feast of tabernacles on the *fifteenth* will be honored by the great events of the end of our probationary state."[76] The positions of Snow and Storrs now theirs, the leaders' articles now began appearing prominently in the paper.

All that remained was a firm endorsement from Miller. On October 3, Sylvester Bliss applied the pressure. He was convinced "the Lord will be here in a few days." Surely the hand of God was in the true midnight cry. "We take our stand that the anniversaries of the seventh month, will bring His glorious appearing." It was time for Miller to commit himself: "We want you to look the question over . . . & give us all the light possible." The stakes were enormous. "It will be glorious to go into the kingdom so soon, but O how awful to be left. Give us your prayers that we may be guided aright in this important crisis." Miller complied. On the sixth he penned the letter that appeared in the *Herald* six days before the deadline. "I see a glory in the seventh month which I never saw before," he wrote. "Although the Lord had shown me the typical bearing of the seventh month, one year and a half ago, yet I did not realize the force of the types. Now, blessed be the name of the Lord, I see a beauty, a harmony, and an agreement in the Scriptures, for which I have long prayed, but did not see until to-day." The new light left him enraptured: "I believe it, yes, I love it. Oh, the glory I have seen to-day." Ever the Old School evangelist, he wished "he could shout. But I will shout when

76. "Letter from Wm. Miller," vol. 5, no. 107 (May 17, 1843), 86; vol. 8, no. 180 (October 9, 1844), 79-80. The editors reprinted Miller's 1843 letter, their responses to it, and then a second, updated response in the next issue.

the *'King of kings comes.'"* His greatest dreams were about to be fulfilled. "I am almost home. Glory! Glory!! Glory!!!." Bliss's reply three days later, barely legible, was just as excited. "Praise God Praise God. May we all be ready & meet in the skies. May God grant it."[77]

Miller was at home. Though Bliss expected to see him in Boston, illness prevented him from leaving, Miller said. But it is unthinkable that he would have left his family as the day of jubilee approached. Stories of their activities those last few days are legion, and often legend. There is no doubt that many Millerites, as reported, gave away or sold their possessions, stopped working, paid off debts, and settled old quarrels. Randolph E. Ladd wrote to Himes on October 22, apologizing for slights he may have committed toward him. "I hope you have laid up nothing against me but will overlook and forgive all that has seemed like wickedness & want of love towards you in me."[78] Mystics and perfectionists were active, particularly in Philadelphia, adding enough grist to the media mill to brand the movement's reputation permanently. But for most Adventists the tenth day of the seventh month was a time to gather with friends and cobelievers in tabernacles, meetinghouses, or home parlors and prayerfully await whatever God was going to do.

Miller was at the farm with his family, though how many were there we do not know. Among the group were Sally Nichols and her husband, probably cousins, from New Hampshire, and there undoubtedly were other extended family members from closer to home. Himes, fearing the potential for violence against him in Boston and wanting to experience the glorious event with Miller, arrived with his wife Alice. One can imagine them gathering to sing Adventist hymns and visiting with Father Miller in the east study as the hours ticked away. Family tradition holds that they waited praying on a large, flat outcropping just west of the farmhouse, today known as Ascension Rock. That makes sense, since it has a wonderful view to the east, by ancient tradition the direction from which the New Jerusalem would descend. But if so, they unfortunately

77. Bliss to Miller, October 3, 1844, Himes Papers; "Bro. Miller's Letter, on the Seventh Month," *Advent Herald* 8, no. 181 (October 16, 1844), 88; Bliss to Miller, October 9, 1844, Himes Letters.

78. Ladd to Himes, October 22, 1844, Miller Letters.

would have provided a tableau like the one scoffers have always projected — Millerites crowding the tops of hills and roofs of barns to be closer to Jesus when he appeared. Mercifully, in his only mention of "the ninth day," the eve of the predicted date, Miller never mentioned the rock. "We held meeting all day and our place of worship was crowded to overflowing with anxious souls apparently."[79]

That last word denotes the psychic boundary Miller and the others crossed one at a time at some point that night or the next day. So long as all were expectant they shared the exciting, terrifying, hopeful, anxious experience of being watchers on the walls of Zion. But doubt slowly crept into their midst. First to falter were the hangers-on who were there covering their bets, more fearful than hopeful. The night had not yet ended when they began to say "Christ would not come on the morrow."[80] These were the anxious souls "apparently." But eventually even the most faithful, those who yearned for Christ to come, even Miller himself, had to confront reality. Painfully, at their own time and in their own way, each had to confess to themselves and then, later, admit to each other: Not now.

79. Sally Nichols to "The Family," December 21, 1844, Miller Letters.
80. Miller to I. O. Orr, December 13, 1844, Miller Letters.

CHAPTER EIGHT

Our Hearts Are Growing Weary of Thy So Long Delay

For Miller and many of his followers, the world did indeed come to an end on October 22, 1844, not melted in divine fire but dissolved in bitter tears. Hope did not necessarily die, but expectation did. Previous predictions had been sufficiently vague or contingent that the disappointed could renew their confidence in the face of prophetic recalculation based on "new light" on the Scriptures. But this "true midnight cry" offered no escape. Jesus was to have come back to earth, the righteous dead raised from their graves, and the world consumed by fire on *that day* — and nothing happened. Failure was undeniable to any reasonable person, and a scoffing world, unsparing in its ridicule, would allow no waffling. Mobs that had harassed Adventists on that day in Boston and elsewhere could be aroused at any time; some former supporters were lashing out at the Millerites in anger and frustration; reputations were suffering from charges of insanity and chicanery. Those who had left jobs and fields untended faced real distress in the coming winter if they did not quickly return to their daily occupations.

The situation required immediate action, wrote Nathaniel N. Whiting to Miller two days after the disappointment: nothing less than a public acknowledgment from Millerite leaders that they had been wrong. "Any shuffling on this point will authorize the community to say that we are not only credulous but absolutely *dishonest.*" (So concerned was he about the public mood that he sent his letter to Miller's son George, fearing that it might be intercepted and opened.) Confessions and apologies appeared quickly, first from

George Storrs and Joshua Himes on November 6, then in a joint statement from the movement's leaders published in the Advent newspapers a week later. Explanations of what went wrong ranged from the rational to the bizarre. Himes and Litch defined the error as too strong a reliance on a definite time that had no clear scriptural base. Those, like Himes, who had always been hesitant to believe and preach that Scripture revealed the time of the end had no difficulty discarding the principle of revealed time now. Samuel Snow, whose prediction had fomented the latest excitement, waited until the end of December to confess his error; not giving up on revealed time, he remained confident the Lord would come within five years. Storrs thought the fervor had been the product of "a mesmeric influence."[1]

For more than a month, Miller remained publicly silent. The safe world he had known and to which he had always returned for refreshing and healing was irretrievably shattered. On the 23rd "it seemed as though all the demons from the bottomless pit were let loose upon us. The same ones and many more who were crying for mercy two days before, were now mixed with the rable and mocking, scoffing and threatening in a most blasphemous manner."

Some indication of the rebuke he faced appears in a letter from a neighbor written anonymously on the 27th (though Miller easily identified him as "Old Baxter"). "I should be ashamed to have my head seen in Publick had I sayed as much as you have and have it all prove false." Miller was responsible for "more suicide and more insanity in the course of 5 or 6 years than has ben known for 50 or 60 years before, you have bin one of that Class of things that has crept into houses and led astray silly wimin laden with sins . . . you have bin the means of men leaving their business and letting their Crops stand out and not gathered them saying they should not kneed them" and much more. All this reminded him of that "Certain time in your life when you lived in Poultney" and denied "in my hearing that [the Saviour] died for your salvation." Now, with his prophecies shattered, it was time for Miller to "believe in Jesus Christ [and]

1. Whiting to Miller, October 24, 1844, Miller Letters, Jenks Memorial Collection of Adventual Materials, Aurora University, Aurora, Illinois; see issues of the *Advent Herald,* November 6, 13, and December 26, 1844.

Convince the Neighbours and the world that you mean to be a man and a Christian."

Miller returned fire. "That you are deceitful is evident," he wrote, "for to my face you have pretended friendship, but I have heard much from you behind my back." He had come into their prayer meeting supposedly for "light" but his real purpose was "to find fault, and you have improved it to the entire satisfaction of your master and his children." To Baxter he ascribed the gossip Hazen had published, about making money and building the stone wall "and many things more equally as untrue." Since the judgment was near, "I am thankfull yourself as well as myself will meet our just reward."[2]

Failure of the date finally encouraged opponents in the Low Hampton Baptist Church to take action. On November 10, twenty-four anti-Millerites, all neighbors, including Paulinus Millard, lodged formal complaints against the Adventist majority with the Washington Union Association, asking to be recognized as the legitimate Baptist Church of Low Hampton. The Adventists, they said, had proclaimed "doctrines which time has proved to be false" and were guilty thereby of sowing "dissension and discord among brethren." Specifically, they had employed an Adventist preacher "contrary to our expressed wishes," excluded people who could not abide such preaching, established belief in the Second Advent in 1844 as a test of membership, and "denounced as Babylon" any church or brethren who disagreed with them and "calumniated [the ministry generally] in the most slanderous manner." They thus demonstrated their intent to "change the character of this church into that of a Second Advent church." In January Miller learned that a council of elders was to meet with the minority to consider the charges and asked to be included, making what had been intended as an *ex parte* council *mutual.* This meant that they would have to accept the council's decision, and that predictably went against the Adventists. Finding every charge against the majority sustained, the council

2. Anonymous to Miller, October 27, 1844; Miller to Old Baxter, November 5, 1844, Miller Letters. Miller probably copied his reply and sent it to Himes, since it includes the long story about the master and his servants that appeared in his first published statement since the Great Disappointment, discussed below.

proclaimed the minority to be "the regular Baptist church in Hampton."[3] The Millers were no longer Baptists.

So, not surprisingly, when Miller did speak, he was far from apologetic. Seeing himself as a victim, Miller was in a combative mood, reflecting his now-familiar unwillingness to take responsibility for contributing to difficulties that flowed in the wake of his preaching: "If I have erred, it has been on the side of charity, the love of my fellow man, and my conviction of duty to God." Despite long-standing worries about the effects on people's faith should he be proven wrong, now Miller averred he "could not see that I should harm my fellow men"; ignoring his wholesale condemnation of the clergy and sects, he denied even "a distant thought of disturbing our churches, ministers, religious editors"; and while he had consistently claimed developing his exegesis independently, he now cited authority for his views "from the vast biblical commentaries or rules which had been recommended for the study of the scriptures." All the evil results were the product of forces "over which I could have no control." Beginning with the Universalists in 1839, opponents unleashed "a war of extermination" against "the Advent faith" with "[o]dious names and cruel epithets." In defense, followers had responded by calling true Christians to come out of Babylon, and if, "I am sorry to say it," they attached that label to all denominations indiscriminately, still, "in *too many* instances it was not unjustly applied."[4]

All this justification, attack, and complaint obscured, but did not hide, the real source of Miller's anguish: God had not acted. Humans failed, to be sure, but Scripture never said that fulfillment of promise depended on humanity's proper response to God. Indeed, as the memoir he had penned only three years before had demonstrated,

3. Reports of these proceedings appear in the *Advent Herald and Signs of the Times* [hereafter cited as *Advent Herald*] 13, no. 322 (July 3, 1847), 174-75 and in *Minutes of the Washington Union Baptist Association,* 1844 and 1845. Elder Dillaway wrote to Himes requesting an opportunity to present his side of the story (August 23, 1847, Joshua V. Himes Papers, Massachusetts Historical Society, Boston, Massachusetts [hereafter cited as Himes Papers]), but no such letter appeared in the paper. The *Advent Herald* did include Miller's account, written in response to a request from James Parsons in Rochester, New York. See Parsons to Miller, April 14, 1846, Miller Letters.

4. *Advent Herald* 8, no. 186 (November 27, 1844), 127-28.

humans were incapable of living in right relationship with God. Vowing to "be good" as a boy failed because Miller could not be good of his own will; seeking to understand God failed because God was not comprehensible; merely obeying God blindly failed because Miller was rebellious, proud, and ambitious. But this eighteenth-century, anthropomorphic, Old School Baptist God of justice could accomplish through grace what humans could not achieve. He touched Miller's soul and transformed his heart, enabling him to live as a faithful son with his loving Father. The message and the mission to warn the world were God's gifts through which Miller could achieve all he had dreamed. By fulfilling his obligation Miller would be good; by first studying and then explaining the prophecies, Miller would find God to be reasonable; by humbly accepting all the trials that came with his public career, Miller would learn obedience, humility, contentment. "We have thus far done all we could," he said. God chose not to return as expected for a reason, "to humble, purify and prepare us for an admittance into his blessed kingdom." In fact, far from being disheartened, he was encouraged: "I have now much more evidence that I do believe in God's word; and although surrounded with enemies and scoffers, yet my mind is perfectly calm, and my hope in the coming of Christ is as strong as ever."[5]

Nevertheless, undercurrents of complaint caused ripples on the surface. "I have been waiting and looking for the blessed hope," he pointed out, though he had been "twice disappointed." He had done his part; "I must now wait and watch untill he is graciously pleased to answer the 10,000 prayers that daily and nightly ascend his holy hill, 'come, Lord Jesus, come quickly.'" Waiting may have been the faithful response to disappointment, but it was also painful. The Millerite hymn expressed it well: "How long, dear Lord, our Savior/Wilt thou remain away?/Our hearts are growing weary/of thy so long delay."[6] What

5. *Advent Herald* 8, no. 186 (November 27, 1844), 127-28.

6. Miller to Orr, December 13, 1844, op cit; the hymn, sung to the tune of "Stand up, stand up for Jesus," first appeared in the 1842 edition of Joshua Himes's *Millennial Harp, or Second Advent Hymns; Designed for Meetings on the Second Coming of Christ* (Boston: Joshua V. Himes, 1842), 6-7. Its appearance as one of the first songs in the book suggests its popularity. Jane Marsh Parker, late in life, remembered singing it as a Millerite child. See "A Little Millerite," *Century Magazine* 11 (November 1886–April 1887), 316.

more could God require? Miller used a parable about a master who leaves his servants, telling them how long he would be gone but not revealing the hour of his return. The faithful porter and a handful of others watched on the appointed night. Three times they detected what they thought were signs of his approach and sent up an alarm, only to be disappointed. The other servants became angry, first scolding, then beating them, and finally, after the third false alarm, shutting them out of the house. But on the fourth watch, the master came back. Which of these servants, Miller asked, loved the master the most? Obviously, those who waited and watched. Pointedly he asked Brother Himes, "[G]ive us the signification of the word WATCH."

This query to Himes betrayed a certain impatience. Dating the beginning of Millerism's troubles to 1839 and 1840, ignoring all the hostility he had received before that, Miller laid them at the door of the managers who assumed operating control of it that year. Their apostolic gifts had wrested authority from his hands, rendering the message abstract and impersonal where before it had been concrete and intimate. The effect had been theological innovation and emotional overreaction. By limiting preaching to people he knew either directly or by extension in the 1830s, Miller had been able to control the message and the movement. Now it seemed the leaders were taking Adventism in another dangerous direction, by rejecting revealed time. That God had written clues to the time of the end into Scripture was the strongest evidence of God's mercy and reasonableness. Jesus himself had promised "that day will not come upon you as a thief; you will see and know the sign of the Son of man." October 22 had failed, but he now fixed on another time, "*To-day,* TO-DAY, and TO-DAY."[7] Besides, the Jewish year was not yet over, and since he had relied on fallible historians for his chronology, who could know when it really ended or, for that matter, when the entire prophetic period terminated? A historian's error could relocate the end four or five years into the future. Thus he clung to the slippery raft of time in the broiling seas, avoiding the obvious conclusion that he was wrong. Thinking it over, he wrote to I. E. Jones, "I cannot see why we are not right."[8]

7. *Advent Herald,* November 27, 1844; he used virtually the identical words in his December 13 letter to I. O. Orr.

8. Miller to I. E. Jones, *Advent Herald* 8, no. 190 (December 25, 1844), 154.

Miller's vacillation encouraged others who now searched diligently for the "true" date — April 1845, July, perhaps the tenth day of the seventh month but a year later, no later than the end of 1846, then 1847. Himes was determined to quash such "visionary nonsense." Portland Adventists were focusing on the Passover and the Pentecost "and then, if things continue, the 7th month is to be got up again, and so on etc. I am not willing to humbug myself, or be instrumental in leading others astray in this way." Miller seemed to agree with Himes, making fun of Samuel Snow and Apollos Hale, the two most prolific chronologizers. But, he added, "to be sober, any theory which will prove Christ near, and the nearer the better, therefore I like Bro. H. views more than I do Bro Gross or Marsh, because it is sooner."[9] Once again, it was difficult to tell exactly where Miller stood.

Isolation in Low Hampton had left him detached from the immediate influence of the Boston and New York leaders, alone with thoughts and feelings that he coddled in the context of a protective family. With the church divided, he no longer had to hear complaints from hostile neighbors in the congregation (there are "no wicked to molest us," he wrote at the end of November), but loving and supportive children and grandchildren were available to affirm his faith. So as weeks passed he was able to achieve a certain peace. In December he claimed more "calmness of mind" and "resignation to the will of God, and patience" than he had enjoyed "within a few weeks past." For years, he said, he had suffered "a spirit of impatience for Christ to come" and "a spirit of fretfulness and a mind full of impatience." But now his faith was stronger than ever, which he found "somewhat remarkable, when I reflect on the disappointment I have met, in my former expectations." Anyone who asked for advice from him received the same reply: patience. We won't need it long, he said, "[no] longer than the farmer waits for the precious fruits of the earth, and hath long patience for it until he receive the early and latter rain."[10]

9. Himes to Miller, March 12 and November 26, 1845, Himes Papers; Miller to Himes, November 15, 1845, Miller Letters.

10. *Advent Herald* 8, no. 190 (December 25, 1844), 154; *Advent Herald* 8, no. 189 (December 18, 1844), 147. Miller's mood illustrates the condition of cognitive dissonance, strengthened commitment to predictions even when they have been proven to be wrong, though it should be pointed out that the theory has received extensive

Himes, Bliss, and Litch could not afford patience. While Miller was protected from the storms swirling about the movement, they were in the thick of it, and they needed his help. Millerism was not only exploding, it was imploding as well. While they were publicly confessing that their date had failed, other Adventists were claiming victory. Something momentous *had* happened on October 22, they claimed, but not in the manner they had all expected. Jesus had returned to the world spiritually, said some, and separated the saved (themselves) from the wicked (everybody else). Their salvation placed them in the New Jerusalem and imbued them with power to judge others and perform miracles. Drawing from the extreme tendencies of perfectionism, they gathered around charismatic "prophets" forming cults that licensed all kinds of "ultraist" behavior — sexual promiscuity (spiritual wifery), attempts to raise the dead, "promiscuous" feet washing, judging the world, and threatening violence against their enemies. The popular press loved to report their antics, thus keeping alive Adventism's reputation for religious and mental aberration.[11]

Miller learned about these prophets firsthand from his family in Oswego County, New York, who reported their activities to him in detail, and from time to time these believers communicated their peculiar visions and prophecies to him directly. Rebecca Marshall in Philadelphia said that on the 22nd she had shut up her shop and warned all her friends to get ready "as if on my death bed" and then had fled the city with many other Millerites "thinking the cities would be destroyed first, thought I if no one goes I go." Far from admitting defeat, she claimed to have been cleansed "and translated as Paul says into the Kingdom of Gods dear son. I think we then commenced the new dispensation."[12]

Another group of spiritualizers was more dangerous to the

---

criticism. See Leon Festinger, Henry W. Reicken, and Stanley Schlachter, *When Prophecy Fails: A Social and Psychological Study of a Modern Group That Predicted the Destruction of the World* (Minneapolis: University of Minnesota Press, 1956).

11. George R. Knight, *Millennial Fever and the End of the World* (Boise: Pacific Press Publishing Association, 1993), 245-66.

12. Silas Guilford to Miller, February 23 and March 17, 1846; Rebecca T. Marshall to Miller, December 29, 1844, Miller Letters. See also Household of Faith to Miller, May 14, 1846; J C S S to Miller, June 4, 1846, Miller Papers.

movement's unity and to Himes's leadership. In January 1845 Apollos Hale and Joseph Turner published their view that on October 22 Jesus entered into the sanctuary in heaven, separated the saved from the wicked, and shut the door of mercy, closing probation and the possibility of salvation for sinners. He thus had fulfilled the prophecies but not in the expected manner, spiritually rather than physically. The idea caught fire and recruited many leading Adventists, including Samuel S. Snow, Enoch Jacobs in Cincinnati, and the strong Millerite congregation in Portland, Maine, headed by John Pearson and Emily C. Clemons. This contradicted the established leaders' view that nothing had happened on October 22. When the "shut-door" advocates began to publish their own newspapers popularizing their ideas, they drew support and scarce revenues away from the *Advent Herald* and the *Morning Watch,* in effect creating a rival organization that warred with the triumvirate of Himes, Bliss, and Litch. They seemed to be winning. The *Herald* was already suffering from the loss of subscriptions after October; at the end of January 1845 Himes told Miller it was sinking.[13]

Throughout the crisis Miller did nothing to help, and Himes was upset. "I have had to toil almost alone, against all the contrary winds, and besides some of my best friends have given countenance to the opposing influences, raised against the best interests of the cause."[14] Indeed, since the Great Disappointment Himes had suffered personal attacks from the press, charges brought against him by his congregation, and the threat of lawsuits for financial chicanery in raising money through Millerism and using it to enrich himself.[15] He had so far survived all that, but now enemies from within were getting ready to finish him off. Most galling to Himes, among those "best friends" who had contributed to the enemy's cause, he thought, was William Miller.

Those who preached that Jesus had returned to earth spiritually

13. On the shut-door movement see Knight, *Millennial Fever,* 236-42; Himes to Miller, January 28, March 29, June 27, and July 30, 1845, Himes Papers.

14. Himes to Miller, April 22, 1845, Himes Papers.

15. The best discussion of these events is David Tallmadge Arthur, "'Come Out of Babylon': A Study of Millerite Separatism and Denominationalism, 1840-1865" (Ph.D. dissertation, University of Rochester, 1970), especially chapter six, "Conflict of Personalities," 234-78.

never attracted Miller. They were too much like perfectionists who innovated all sorts of liturgies and theologies, and, as he said to Himes, "You know how I feel towards these kind of religionists." On the other hand, as George Knight informs us, Miller had always believed that the closing of probation would take place simultaneously with the second coming of Christ. He published that idea in his book and had preached it in 1839 and 1840 when predicting the fall of the Ottoman Empire.[16] Not surprisingly, Adventists had begun asking his views on the closing of probation soon after the October disappointment, and in November he expressed his support for it in no uncertain terms: "We have done our work in warning sinners, and in trying to awake a formal church. God, in his providence has shut the door; we can only stir one another up to be *patient;* and be diligent to make our calling and election sure."[17]

But Himes, Litch, and Bliss were saying that nothing happened on October 22, so why did Miller believe the door of probation shut on that day? In part it was comforting to believe that *something,* even something unexpected, might have happened on October 22. When he reconsidered the chronology of events, the possibility became a probability. It appeared they had all miscalculated by not providing sufficient time by October 22 for the stages indicated in Matthew's parable of the ten virgins. The events of the last day were there, carefully staged — preparation for the bridegroom to come at the end of the day, virgins going to get oil for their lamps because the night was coming, a false warning that he was coming, a tarrying time waiting for the true cry, five foolish virgins letting their lamps go out, and then the groom's actual return finding the other five virgins waiting faithfully. As Miller saw it, the period between the spring disappointment and the tenth month in the fall was the tarrying time, as the prophecy predicted, but there had been insufficient time to accomplish the remaining required events. Unbelievers were not ready because they had never accepted the bridegroom's invitation to attend his banquet in the first place.

16. Miller to Himes, November 15, 1845, Miller Letters; Knight, *Millennial Fever,* 237-38.

17. Nathaniel Hervey to Miller, November 28, 1844, and Clarkson Goud to Miller, January 4, 1845, Miller Letters; "Letter from Bro. Miller," *Advent Herald* 8, no. 188 (December 11, 1844), 142.

So the problem was not with the world, but with Adventists. There had to be a time for testing Adventists, to allow the foolish among them to show their faithlessness. And so they did. In so many cases Adventists' lamps had gone out. "PRIDE, FANATICISM, and SECTARIANISM" had distracted them — pride in ascribing their work to themselves rather than to God; fanaticism in adorning themselves with outer rather than inner piety and holding meetings that too often were "distinguished by noise and confusion" and "more like Babel, than a solemn assembly of penitents bowing in humble reverence before a holy God"; sectarianism in condemning *"all but Adventists"* as Babylon and "raising up a sect of our own." For all of that, he prayed, "may God forgive us." But there was hope, for "the experience which we have passed through, from the beginning of the present year" is surely "the beginning and preparation of the final *cleansing of the sanctuary.*"[18]

Miller seemed to be blaming Adventists for Jesus' failure to return, and some of the leaders found his censure offensive. Elon Galusha, for one, feared the public would apply his "unguarded expressions" to Adventists in general and not just to the few. "[W]e must *discriminate* — else we shall prove our own slanderers." Surely it was saying too much, echoed L. Delos Mansfield, for Miller "to say *we,* in such epithets, thus including himself and all his brethren in the cause." Miller had to backtrack, apologizing for what he confessed were "unguarded remarks." The fault indeed lay in his use of the pronoun *we* instead of *they,* thus overgeneralizing. On the other hand, he had "no thought of trying to escape censure myself, and let my brethren bear alone the burden," but rather sought to share in it.[19] What they missed in Miller's critique was his dark insinuation that God was tarrying to allow unbelievers, including faithless Adventists, to get caught in a trap — or "snare," as one Millerite put it — so they might be damned.[20]

Schadenfreude, a glorying in the misfortune of others, colored much of Miller's thinking. Ridiculed by many of his neighbors, es-

18. *Advent Herald* 8, no. 189 (December 18, 1844).

19. *Advent Herald* 8, no. 192 (January 8, 1845), 122-73, 174; "Letter from William Miller," *Voice of Truth, and Glad Tidings of the Kingdom of God at Hand* [hereafter cited as *Voice of Truth*] 5, no. 2 (February 5, 1845), 5.

20. "Coming as a Snare," *Voice of Truth* 5, no. 3 (February 12, 1845), 9.

sentially expelled from the Baptist church by lifelong friends, he and his family suffered enormously, and they cherished dark thoughts. George was convinced "God did in the 7 month a great work among his people which we shall see in a verry few days." Unbelievers would soon shout to God for help. But "have they not refused to hear any thing about the Lords coming? have they not abused the messengers that God has sent to them and despised his work?" Yes, they had seen all that, "and because we know it and tell them of it they say [thou] shalt not Prophecy any more unto them, lest we die by there hand." There was no room in his heart for charity; "God tells me not to pray for this people, let him alone, let his anger wax hot against them. the pits that they have been diging for us they will fall into themselves. their mischief will return upon their own head." There was especially little hope for apostates, "for those who will go back to that which they have given up to the Lord."[21]

In this context, Miller's belief that God had shut the door of mercy on sinners was not only consistent with his long-standing teaching, it also made intellectual sense. And it offered George emotional comfort. "[I] am perfectly convinced that the eyes, and hearts of all those who have heard, and had the means of the light, and rejected it," he wrote, "are sealed over for final and eternal destruction. . . . [I]n my inmost soul I believe God commanded us to let them alone, for they should not taste of his supper." Perhaps this seemed "hard hearted and cruel," but "it is neither. It is the just treatment of a holy God." More, it was no more than justice to Miller: "When you will find any modern man who has sacrificed more than I have according to their means for to warn poor perishing souls of their danger, then call me cruel and hard hearted."[22]

Himes was certainly aware of Miller's feelings and point of view, but it did not become an issue for him until Hale, Snow, and the others launched a crusade against the triumvirate calling on followers to come out of this *Adventist* Babylon and leave behind these established leaders who, they said, doubted the promises of God. I. E. Jones was astounded by how quickly these ideas had become "a test by which the wise & foolish virgins were to be made apparent!! WE

21. George W. Miller to S. N. Nichols, November 28, 1844, Miller Letters.
22. George W. Miller to T. Wrightson, March 20, 1845, Miller Letters.

have therefore damned & been damned several times apiece, & yet the result is, that God is not only more wise, but mercifull than us all. . . . Tis mystery all." Miller's public quiescence once again encouraged the fratricidal warfare. He did not appear to be taking sides, which in itself was troublesome. In reality, though, he was pondering the issue, writing to both Hale and Turner discussing fine points of their theory, and to Emily C. Clemons and, through her, the shut-door Adventists in Portland.[23] He found himself caught in the middle between the longtime friends and supporters who had done so much to spread his message and more radical "newcomers" who preached views that in his heart he believed to be correct. Masonic iconography may have played a role in his thinking; the High Priest (Jesus) entering the sanctuary and shutting the door smacked of lodge liturgy. He once spoke with Bliss of the prospect of dying and going to the world of the spirits — the "upper room," as he called it — until Jesus should return.[24]

He would have liked to have avoided the shoals in these dangerous waters, but he was still the patriarch, and eventually he had to take a stand. On January 15 he wrote a letter for publication to Joseph Marsh, editor of the *Voice of Truth and Glad Tidings of the Kingdom at Hand* in Rochester, New York. A Christian Connexion preacher, like Himes, and a latecomer to the movement, Marsh had edited the *Christian Palladium* until his open support of Miller in the paper led to his removal. Miller had met Marsh during his tour of western New York and became fond of his family, particularly daughter Jane, who remembered Miller much later in life as a "gentle old man shaking with palsy" with a "rosy, kindly face, shrewd, twinkling blue eyes, which could read character unerringly."[25] He undoubtedly stayed in the house when lecturing in Rochester — as did many itinerants, according to Jane — and it was probably in their parlor that he penned an acrostic on her mother's name. So

23. I. E. Jones to Miller, February 15, 1845; Joseph Turner to Miller, January 28 and February 7, 1845; Emily C. Clemons to Miller, February 17, 1845, Miller Letters.

24. Sylvester Bliss, *Memoirs of William Miller: Generally Known as a Lecturer on the Prophecies, and the Second Coming of Christ* (Boston: Joshua V. Himes, 1853), 90n.

25. Jane Marsh Parker, "A Little Millerite," 314, and Parker, "A Spiritual Cyclone: The Millerite Delusion," *Magazine of Christian Literature* 4, no. 4 (September 1891), 323.

fond was Miller of the little girl that Himes, just before his death, sent her Miller's personal copy of the Great Chart that he used in his lectures and that Himes had kept ever since.[26] Marsh's paper had appeared sporadically, but he was planning on a weekly edition and may have recruited a statement from Miller to bolster his prospects.

Miller's letter appeared on the front page on February 5, a seemingly innocuous statement for that "little, but valuable sheet" asking followers in the West to remain faithful, and patient. He made no overt statement about the shut door, averring only his belief that "Christ is not tarrying for sinners to get ready, so much as he is to try the patience and faith of the saints."[27] The significance of his letter lay not in what he said but in its being published in a paper Himes did not control. Marsh was publishing views from all the Adventist factions — Judaizers, spiritualizers, shut-door advocates, those seeking a new definite time — and Miller's writing a letter specifically for him suggested sympathy with dissent in general just when his own papers were failing. They intended, said Himes, to "put down the 'Herald' & 'Watch' and sustain the 'Hope of Israel' and the 'Voice of Truth.' "[28]

Miller realized his friends' worst fears when he answered the questions being asked of him in "almost every part of the country": what was the significance of October 22, and did he think the door of mercy closed on that day? It was "a close point," he said. Clearly, God's "benevolent hand and wisdom was in the movement," attested by the rapt attention, the seriousness with which Adventists approached the day, and its effects in awakening piety and watchfulness. Thus he rejected Himes's view that nothing had happened.

26. The acrostic on Sarah M. Marsh's name is included in a file of correspondence between Jane (Jenny) Marsh Parker and Augustus Hopkins Strong, President of Andover Seminary in Rochester. The file also includes letters Parker wrote concerning the chart and copies of Advent newspapers she wished to sell to the seminary, since Strong was compiling a bibliography of Millerite publications. See the folder "Letters to Dr. Strong regarding Millerite chart," box 2, Augustus Hopkins Strong Papers, Ambrose Swasey Library, Colgate Rochester Divinity School. The location of the chart today is unknown. She also mentioned wooden models, probably of the Man of Sin, that Miller used, though whether she actually had possession of them is unclear.

27. *Voice of Truth* 5, no. 2 (February 5, 1845), 5.

28. Himes to Miller, March 12, 1845, Himes Papers.

Miller then reconsidered his old belief that the seventh trumpet would cease sounding and the door of mercy would shut simultaneously with the second coming of Christ, and he presented eight arguments that suggested he had been wrong. Christ had not come as he had always preached he would — in a physical body — so the tenth day of the seventh month could not have been the event that ended the 2300 days in Daniel's vision. The faithful were called upon to wait patiently. But in studying Scripture again, Miller found evidence to sustain the view that Jesus would already have separated the wicked from the saved and shut the door of mercy *before* returning, for it was at his second coming that he would reward everyone as they deserved. After all, Jesus said, "He that is unjust, let him be unjust still: and he which is filthy, let him be filthy still: and he that is righteous, let him be righteous still: and he that is holy, let him be holy still." So for all these reasons Miller now confessed, "I have done [completed] my work in warning sinners, and that in the seventh month." It was, he said, his own opinion, and, undoubtedly hoping to forestall criticism from his longtime colleagues, Miller wrote that he expected "we will have no contention on this point, for we be brethren."[29]

That was wishful thinking. The *Advent Herald* printed his letter, but Bliss added a response to it countering Miller's arguments point by point with Scriptures of his own. "We thus find," he said in sum, "that the weight of evidence greatly preponderates against the closing of the door of mercy a time before the Advent." He threw a barb at Miller personally for his inaction, declaring, "And while the worth of a single soul is of such incalculable value, the bare possibility of saving one soul should cause us to put forth our every effort, and discourage none in their efforts to obtain salvation." Himes and Bliss wrote to Miller privately as well, charging him with giving aid and comfort to the enemy. "It is very painful," wrote Bliss, "to dissent from any of your views," but responsibility required a response. Portland Adventists had told people who asked them to pray for their salvation that the door of mercy was shut "and they must go to Hell." So they went away "to where Christians would pray for them, believing that Millerites were a hard-hearted, unfeeling, unchristian

29. *Advent Herald* 9, no. 197 (February 12, 1845), 2-3.

race." This "class of ultraists are now rejoicing that father Miller is with them and against us." Himes, too, described the evil tendencies of shut-door Adventism and urged Miller to return to long-tested truths. "We have nothing to fear if we will stick by the gospel system of truth published in your 19 Lectures, with the exception of the exact time — take it as you first had it 'About the Year 1843.'"[30]

Their letters undoubtedly crossed in the mails a new missive Miller had just posted to the *Voice of Truth.* Moving beyond his February 12 statement in the *Advent Herald,* Miller now stated explicitly that the shut-door views of Hale and Turner were "in the main correct" and that Christ had indeed come "in the sense spoken of" in Matthew 25:10: "And while they [the five virgins who had let their lamps go out] went out to buy [more oil for their lamps], the bridegroom came; and they that were ready went in with him to the marriage [feast] and the door was shut."[31] Not only was Miller reversing the order of events on the last day as he had long preached, he now seemed to be agreeing with the mystics that Christ had done something spiritually rather than physically on October 22 by entering into the feast and closing the door of mercy, thus sealing the fate of every soul, living and dead.

The Millerite establishment responded with a full barrage. The day after Miller's letter appeared in the *Voice of Truth,* Himes printed his arguments against the shut door in the *Morning Watch.* The "true midnight cry" could not have been the final cry, since it was local and not universal; it came too suddenly to arouse Adventists in England. Jesus could not come spiritually because he has never been absent spiritually; he must come physically. The door of probation was not shut; Adventist preachers had been reporting many conversions since October 22.[32] Himes and Bliss devoted the next two issues of

30. Sylvester Bliss to Miller, February 11, 1845, and Himes to Miller, February 13, 1845, Himes Papers.

31. While copies of the *Voice of Truth* generally are extant, the February 19, 1845, issue does not appear to be. George Knight in quoting from the letter (*Millennial Fever,* 240) cited James White, *Life Incidents, In Connection With the Great Advent Movement, as Illustrated by the Three Angels of Revelation XIV* (Battle Creek, Mich.: Seventh-Day Adventist Publishing Association, 1868), 201-2.

32. "Is the Door Shut?" *Morning Watch and Midnight Cry* [hereafter cited as *Morning Watch*] 8, no. 165 (February 20, 1845), 64.

the *Advent Herald* exclusively to discussing and refuting the shut-door theory, publishing Apollos Hale's original article and accompanying it with long counterarguments and a reprint of Himes's article from the *Morning Watch.*[33]

Never one for defensive measures, "General" Himes now maneuvered to gain the chief prize in the battle: William Miller. First he assaulted Miller's understandable but misguided desire to retire. He had spoken of it ever since October, and while Himes understood Miller's feelings he had not encouraged the talk. "It is not right for us to set down, and brood over our disappointment, and give way to a morbid feeling, that will arise out of such a state of things." Jesus had not come yet, so "we have No right therefore to hold our peace yet." Besides, "If we do not awake, and go to the work again, God will give it to others."[34] The thought of who else might rush to the task was too dreadful to contemplate.

Following Miller's pronouncements on the shut door, his "retirement" portended to Himes something more worrisome. He obviously had succumbed to what Himes called the "no work system"; since judgment had already taken place, there was no further need to warn sinners to repent. The souls of the unconverted were at stake. So was Himes's leadership, and with it his financial investments. Shut-door Adventism "makes havoc with our publications. If things go on in this way long, I shall have to shut up both my offices!" He had no desire to dictate or to recriminate; he was "glad" for Miller's "privilege of a little rest" and hoped God would give him "much repose and blessedness." As for himself, the afflicted editor wrote, "I will lean my youthful bosom to the storm, and try to save the cause you have done so much, yes, nearly all thus far to promulgate and establish."[35]

Himes now moved to separate Miller from the dissenters. Undoubtedly at Himes's behest, on March 5 Nathaniel Whiting wrote to ask Miller directly "whether in your judgment that period during which mercy can be shown to men . . . came to a close on the 22d of October or not," following it with reasoned arguments why that

33. Vol. 9, no. 199 (February 26, 1845) and no. 200 (March 5, 1845).

34. Himes to Miller, February 13, 1845; see also January 28, 1845, Himes Papers.

35. Himes to Miller, February 13, 1845, Himes Papers.

could not be true.[36] A week later Himes continued his foray, sending a letter marked "Private, for Father Miller," perhaps concerned about son George's influence on him. *The Hope of Israel* (the Portland dissenters' paper) "will lay all in ruins, if they have time enough to do it," he said. "They are using your influence, or your name and letters to sustain themselves in this new and visionary movement." Their views are encouraging "many of the farmers to neglect ploughing" while others "are selling off their cattle saying they only want enough to last till the 23d of April. The door is shut, and the bridegroom has come, the marriage has taken place, and now they say the Lord must come. I shall clean my skirts from this matter, in a kind way. And I think if you could advise all to attend to their proper duties, in a scriptural way it might have a good effect."[37] Three days later Whiting wrote again, this time about S. S. Snow in New York, who had set up a separate meeting and launched a new paper. "They go for miracles etc. and are going into extravagance." Unfortunately, "they are doing all in their power to identify you with all their movements." There was only one solution: "I think it is time that you give a letter or word in some way that will enable us to exculpate you, from any sympathy with them in their wild movements." Wrote Himes sympathetically, "I feel deeply for you. I know you love us all in the Lord. But as you see how the case is, now, you will have no difficulty in making all right. I think you can do it in your [response] to Bro. N. N. Whiting."[38]

Finally, Himes traveled to Low Hampton and spent March 8 and 9 discussing the issue with Miller face to face, no doubt reprising all the arguments thus far — scriptural, personal, humanitarian — and appealing to Miller's strong sense of duty. The result was a letter to the *Advent Herald,* the day after Himes left. Upon consideration, Miller now believed the parable of the ten virgins did not intend "to show the exact order or time of the marriage & shutting of the door." Given their "present light" it would be impossible to "prove that the door is shut," and at present "the evidence is strong against" it. It was, after all, a matter of opinion.

36. Whiting to Miller, March 5, 1845, Himes Papers.
37. Himes to Miller, March 12, 1845, Himes Papers.
38. Himes to Miller, March 15, 1845, Himes Papers.

Facing a Faustian choice — side with those whose views fed his brightest and darkest desires, or remain loyal to those who had borne the battle with him and helped him "tell it to the world" — Miller chose the latter. In the end the requirement of consistency in his message and the well-being of his beloved Himes won him over. But, now standing above the fray, he could exercise the prerogative of a patriarch and urge peace. This was "one of those questions calculated to divide warm friends." He did not like "much I have seen published and spoken on both sides of the question," but he urged supporters of the shut-door perspective "to yield the point to our brethren of the opposite view." Finally, he urged everyone, "Let us be silent at least for two months, if Christ does not come before, and by that time I think we shall obtain more light; and if Christ does come, we shall not wish to be found contending with brethren of a like precious faith."[39]

Now it was the dissenters' turn to be stunned. "By your last letter many of them have been saved," Himes reported. They had once preached that as one of God's messengers Miller was like a herald angel, but many "are of the opinion, that Bro. Miller . . . is now a fallen man."[40] So deep was the affection "for the old man" that blame for his about-face fell not on Miller but on his *abbé grise*. "General" Himes relayed to him Emily Clemons's comment that "Mr. Miller, will be saved, as he is not a free agent, and consequently not accountable!"[41] There may be some truth in it. Himes's personal presence in Miller's house had been persuasive. It would not be the last time one of the triumvirate would journey to the farm to "help" him write a critical document. Still, Himes was undoubtedly aware that the man who had changed sides once could do it again.

His concern was well grounded. In his March 20 letter to T. Wrightson, Miller affirmed his belief in the damnation of those who had rejected God's warning, while at the same time saying he was "not satisfied that the door of mercy (as it is called) is yet shut." In September 1847 Joseph Bates circulated the news at a camp

39. *Advent Herald* 9, no. 203 (March 26, 1845), 49. That he urged silence for two months reveals his suspicion, at least, that Christ would return before June.

40. Himes to Miller, March 29, 1845, Himes Letters.

41. Himes to Miller, August 18, 1845, Himes Letters.

meeting in Champlain, New York, that Miller had once again affirmed the shut door, provoking inquiries to Miller from anxious Adventists who wanted to know if it was true. The rumors were sufficiently vexing to provoke from Miller an explicit denial and refutation of the shut door; he was, he said, "utterly ignorant of that theory" and "never understood it."[42]

Himes had worked with Miller long enough to know that keeping him in close contact and breaking his isolation, and perhaps the influence of his children, was necessary. Having won his assent to the triumvirate's interpretation of October 22 and coaxed him into assuming a leading public role once again, Himes now initiated a process that would reassert his authority and save his financial investments in the movement. On March 15 he first informed Miller, "We think to have a 'Mutual Conference' in Albany, N.Y. the last week in April." The location was calculated. The city hosted a strong Millerite group that met in its own building, the House of Prayer, whose leaders remained loyal to Miller's long-preached views. And it was a convenient journey from Low Hampton. The plan was to formulate a creed, establish a structure of authority to shut out dissenters' views, and plan for continuing the Adventist mission into the future.[43] Unfortunately for Miller, it would also require the old gentleman to support an action he had long rejected and condemned: establishing a new sect. In December he had accused Adventists, among other things, of "raising up a sect of our own" and of proclaiming "many sectarian dogmas, which have nothing to do with our message," thus distracting them from their true work. Now Himes was trying to involve him in that very enterprise.

Himes had not waited for Miller's consent. Returning to old habits, even before informing him of the plan he included Miller's

42. See Joseph Marsh to Miller, September 6, 1847; O. R. L. Crozier to Miller, September 20, 1847; Ezra Shepherd to Miller, September 26, 1847, Miller Letters; *Advent Herald* 13, no. 341 (November 13, 1847), 119. In this light George Knight's belief that Miller's March 1845 statement was a sign that Himes had "brought him around at last" (*Millennial Fever,* 241) appears to be an overstatement.

43. Himes to Miller, March 15, 1845, Himes Letters. Once again the best narrative of these events is George Knight's *Millennial Fever,* 267-73, though my interpretation of them will differ.

name in the *Morning Watch*'s call for the conference.[44] Miller's assignment was to prepare an address that would repeat the story of how he developed his views, present the "bible position as to time now," and advise based on Scripture "how we are to occupy till Christ comes." Getting him to do it was another matter, requiring the same mix of empathy and cajolery that had always worked in the past. "[I]t will be of the greatest importance," he insisted. "Now this will not be a hard thing to ask of you. I do ask this with all my soul." If he didn't come to Himes's aid, "I shall sink and fail," for this is "the trying time and the crisis — the last in our office." But "God is with us still, and now we will put shoulder to the wheel, and the work will be accomplished."[45]

Extremists were winning the day, Himes argued: "You can have no conception of the evil, that is resulting from this new view of the 'virgins,' 'door,' 'Bridegroom having come,' etc. It leads them to neglect all work, live in continual association in exciting, and social meetings, which has degenerated into fleshly, and selfish passions." Partly to blame for all this were Miller's previous letters; the extremists "have made more of them than they had any right to do." Miller's refuting the shut door had helped, but they continued to be "the bane of the cause at this time, and unless we set our face against them, we shall be ruined, with all we have done." So Miller needed to give "one more letter in which you will in a general way, utterly disavow, and condemn all such movements. You know that these things are not the fruit of your labour — nor of your sentiments. Why then should you bear it. Why should we." Two days later he repeated the call: "In view of these things you will have to stand by us, and defend the great principles, or we are gone." All depended on Miller's being there. "Do you go to Albany to Lecture. [finger pointing] You will go to the Conference of Course. And No Mistake!! [multiple underlinings]"[46]

Miller went, but the fire was gone. Bliss quotes a letter (unfortunately not extant) that, despite the frequent ellipses, shows a man

44. Vol. 8, no. 12 (March 20, 1845), 96.

45. The date of this document is unclear, but it appears in the Himes collection between letters dated March 15 and March 29 (Himes Letters). It is probably a planning sheet he included in the March 15 letter.

46. Himes to Miller, March 29 and March 31, 1845, Himes Papers.

doing his duty most reluctantly. True, he said, many Adventists had fallen into fanaticism and were trying "to lead away followers after them." These were "wandering stars," some of whom "emit only twilight." But, he reminded Himes, "we must learn to have patience." That he "was sick of this everlasting changing" could have applied to Himes's actions as well as to theirs. "You know, my dear brother," he told Himes, "there was a time when you and I, with a few choice brethren stood alone. . . . We acknowledged our weakness, and claimed no superiority over our fellows. We provoked no one to combat, and made no attack on the prevailing or popular institutions of the day; yet they began to be alarmed. Why? Because as the people began to hear the foolish reports of our enemies, they became more and more anxious to know what these things meant." But what was there to fear with God on their side? "I often think, when I hear a brother judging and condemning another, what an excellent Pope he would make. Therefore, fear them not; for if we judge and condemn our brother, we are making ourselves 'judges of the law, rather than doers of the law.'"[47]

Yet to be "judges of the law" was the purpose of the Albany Conference, to establish a structure for future action, a creed to establish orthodoxy, and an authority to evaluate what was genuine and false in Adventist faith and practice. Miller chaired the Committee of Twelve that prepared the "plan of future operations" and presented the "declaration of principles" that would guide discussions "respecting our future association." It was not Miller, though, but Josiah Litch who presented the committee's report and guided the resolutions. At the end of the conference they had agreed on a set of ten principles that defined authentic Adventist doctrine, instituted ordination of Adventist ministers, defined an Adventist congregation as "believers who habitually assemble for the worship of God, and the due observance of the Gospel ordinances," anathematized practices of the dissidents that had so discredited Adventism, and cautioned against the excessive use of camp meetings, which had done so much to encourage and broadcast their ideas and liturgies.[48]

47. Bliss, *Memoirs*, 298-99.

48. *Proceedings of the Mutual Conference of Adventists, Held in the City of Albany, the 29th and 30th of April and 1st of May, 1845* (New York: Joshua V. Himes, 1845).

It was a complete apostolic success, even proclaiming the value of Sunday schools and publishing a set of questions based on Daniel to use as a text. One wonders how Miller's Old School heart fared after years of declaiming against such practices and urging gospel liberty as the basis for communion. Nevertheless, he recognized the threat that mystics and cultists posed to the life of Adventism. He was able to provide a strong cautionary in his address to the Albany Conference: "Our present difficulties arise more from the multiplicity of masters and leaders among us (some of whom are governed by carnal motives), than from any want of light." Often "weak and silly," they "bring a stigma on the blessed Book, confuse the mind of the inquirer after truth, and divide the children of God." Adventists must learn "to judge men and principles by their fruits" rather than by "expositions which may be presented by every pretender to wisdom and sanctity." How hurtful it was to hear people "murmur against those who have been pioneers in the war"; rather they must "frown on the man who attempts to cause division." Finally, responding to the warfare among the newspapers, Miller advised again that it was time for all to return to their Bibles, to commit themselves to "more study of the Scriptures, and less writing" on speculative ideas.[49]

The conference met all Himes's expectations. Adventists united on a creed; reports from the field highlighted the self-destructive effects of the dissenters' words and actions; the leaders created a reasonable program for institutionalizing the mission. Most important, Miller was now walking with them, equally accountable for formalizing belief and practice. Coaching might still be helpful, though. Predictably, dissenters condemned the conference as dictatorial and a violation of Adventism's long-held primitive standard of personal liberty. Himes wrote to Miller, "You know that we have sought the good of all our brethren — and the cause. And that we have no desire to bind a brother conscience. We wish all to be free — and act as they shall judge best, but we cannot act together, and apart at the same time." Calling for liberty, the extremists had distracted followers, and that "cannot be of use to God's cause." As if to make sure Miller got the point, he closed with a prayer: "My God keep us united, and help us to stick to the text!"

49. Bliss, *Memoirs,* 309-13.

If Miller had any remaining reservations, dissenters' vituperation provoked him to counterattack in sentiments very similar to Himes's. He had intended to retire "and not engage in the suicidal and unnatural war going on among the once stiled adventists," but criticisms of actions taken at Albany changed his mind. Rather than organizing "an 'advent sect'," they were merely working to unite those who had been misled by "those very wolves" who now condemned them. Having enticed Adventists to withdraw from their churches ("you well know my bro, that I was opposed to that cry"), they left them with "no order, no home, no brother." It was Satan's desire to divide and scatter, so it "will be evident to every honest mind who is on the Lord's side, and who is not."[50]

His letter rehearsed arguments for a formal defense of the conference, published in the *Morning Watch* on June 12. Joseph Marsh had not attended the meeting; he condemned it as authoritarian in setting up an Adventist sect to prepare for future action. Not so, said Miller. They were merely rescuing the movement from the Babylon (and the Babel) into which dissenters had led it. They had not adopted a specific name, *Adventist* or otherwise, but affirmed that "[a]ll true churches are 'Churches of Christ.'" Nor had they established a creed as a "test of Christian character" but had merely stated what they collectively believe. It was the others, crying "Liberty," who required submission to their sentiments. As for setting plans for the future — long a sign of faithlessness among Adventists — Miller rejected the claim out of hand as "only fears of what may be done, arising out of the jealousy of the human heart." It was a dangerous time, he said; "Let us have no enemies in disguise among us" but rather "contend earnestly for the race" and "fight manfully the good fight, for they will soon win the race."[51]

It was a reasoned and effective argument, but Marsh's critique highlighted a level of inconsistency between Millerite, and Miller's, words and actions that, no matter how well justified, could not be readily explained. The message *had* promulgated revealed time and now rejected it; Miller *had* stated the door of mercy was shut and

50. Himes to Miller, May 3, 1845, Himes Papers; Miller to Himes, May 20, 1845, Miller Letters.

51. *Morning Watch* 8, no. 181 (June 12, 1845), 190-92.

now refuted it; the movement *had* encouraged followers to establish separate meetings where circumstances required it but condemned sectarianism; now the Albany Adventists *were* formalizing faith and practice while denying that was what they were doing. One could forgive friends and the public for being confused. The situation called for clarity, and only the man who had fathered Adventism could provide it. But he was, in large part, the source of the confusion.

Once again, Himes proposed a solution. Miller, unlike all the other principal leaders, had not yet published a confession and apology for the tragedies that flowed in the wake of his preaching. It was time to do that, and in the process he could provide a unified statement of his beliefs that would reconcile, or obscure, all the apparent contradictions. Himes even outlined it for him. The document would begin with a restatement of his personal history and how he developed his message, and then proceed to a recounting of his treatment by ministers, a review of principles "held up to 43" focusing on a "defense of your course," an explanation of the "failure of the exact time" and repudiation of "false theories and extravagant movements etc etc," and culminate in his "Present position" and the "Duty of the Times" as he saw it — watchfulness and warning. What Himes was proposing was more than a personal confession. If properly handled it could serve as a foundational document for the new entity that was emerging from the Albany Conference, complete with creation myth, justification, creed, and mission statement. So important was it that Himes could leave nothing to chance. As he had recently journeyed to Low Hampton to oversee his rescue from the shut door, now he proposed sending Sylvester Bliss to spend a week with Miller to help write the statement "if you wish him to do so." Apollos Hale would come shortly after "so you will have some dear friends to visit you."[52]

The fruit of their labors was Miller's *Apology and Defense*, published in August 1845 and reprinted four years later, just before Miller's death. Twenty-five of its thirty-six pages relate his personal narrative and the history of the movement as he remembered it. It is in the last ten pages that Miller justified the actions at Albany and dissociated himself from the "erroneous views connected with the

52. Himes to Miller, June 30, 1845, Himes Papers.

doctrine" that had arisen since the Great Disappointment: sectarianism, bigotry, disorder in church government, use of terms and ideas not contained in Scripture (including both Calvinism and Arminianism), the shut-door theory, spiritualizing the second coming of Christ, annihilation of the souls of the wicked, the call to come out of Babylon. As to his own mistakes: "That I have been mistaken in the time, I freely confess; and I have no desire to defend my course any further than I have been actuated by pure motives, and it has resulted in God's glory." But he could not reproach himself "for having preached definite time." If he had known 1843 would pass without the fulfillment of the promise he would not "have so done," but "not knowing that it would, I feel even now more satisfaction in having warned my fellow-men, than I should feel, were I conscious that I had believed them in danger, and had not raised my voice." Still, apology was in order for "my indiscretions and errors," though he did not enumerate them.[53]

It was a summation, not a consideration, of all he had done and said, at times inconsistent and factually wrong as we have already noted. But it is not as history or apologia that the document achieves its significance. Through it Miller was claiming a personal legacy and passing it on to a new generation. "My labors are principally ended," he said. "I shall leave to my younger brethren the task of contending for the truth. Many years I toiled alone; God has now raised up those who will fill my place. I shall not cease to pray for the spread of truth."[54] And what was that truth? Miller would have said truth is God's promise that Jesus would return the way he left, in a physical body, at a time of which God will warn us by signs and portents. As the promise was true so also were the words that conveyed it, the Bible, whose meaning God makes clear to faithful people. That faith was possible was also true. His lonely toil had demonstrated that, making it the greatest witness he could leave for others. Maybe he could see in it also the assurance that he had indeed fulfilled his youthful promise to God to be good.

The load now began to lighten, but there was work yet to do. The Albany Conference strengthened traditionalists in the movement

53. *Apology and Defense* (Boston: Joshua V. Himes, 1849), passim.

54. *Apology and Defense*, 34-35.

but did not destroy the dissidents. Himes still had to struggle to save his newspapers. In July he combined the two under the one banner, *Advent Herald,* thus adding a thousand subscribers from the *Morning Watch* to its roles. Miller was growing feeble, but Himes still asked him to write letters for the *Herald,* and pointedly *not* to write letters for the other papers.[55] So he did, though infrequently and often simply to update readers on his health and his continuing faith. He continued to lecture, with family or Adventist leaders accompanying him, mostly in nearby venues, occasionally returning to old hustings. In May 1845 he accompanied Himes on a tour to Boston and then to Portland, where dissidents continued to hold out against them. A year later he returned to New York, Philadelphia, Providence, and Boston. September and October he lectured in Canada, staying with his now-widowed sister Anna, but illness kept him confined to her house for three weeks. In May 1847 he lectured in Boston for the last time, and that fall at a camp meeting in Ferrisburg, Vermont, Miller made what was undoubtedly his last public appearance.[56]

Already he had become something of a curiosity. The public attended his lectures along with longtime and new Adventists, hoping to get a glimpse of this man of whom so much had been said. Rowdies still disrupted meetings. There was talk of tar and feathers in Sandy Hill before his appearance there, and in Vermont the public was particularly restive. In Morristown Miller and Hale "had the honor of being rejected" by spiritualizing Adventists, while at Stowe "fire crackers, squibs, and home-made rockets" escorted their procession to the speakers stand. A critic in Waitsfield had already warned Miller not to come to town unless he confessed his errors and preached "Jesus & him Crucified Leaving Entirely out of the question your notions of the Second Advent, for it is well known to yourself & to the world that you are very ignorant of that matter." In South Troy their meetinghouse was pelted with eggs, clubs, and rocks, one landing on the desk in front of Miller, who wondered aloud, "Is this Vermont, the state that boasts of its freedom, of its re-

55. Himes to Miller, July 30, 1845, Himes Papers.

56. Miller to [?] Wiggins, October 31, 1846, Miller Letters; on his illness see Bliss, *Memoirs,* 353, 358.

publicanism. Shame on Vermont!"[57] Obviously, the harassment rekindled some of his old fire.[58]

That he attracted such attention, albeit often negative, attests to his continuing stature as Adventism's creator, guide, and mentor. It was to him that homegrown exegetes sent long commentaries on the prophecies — sometimes reasoned, sometimes babbling — asking for his imprimatur on their "light" or to assist in getting them published.[59] His name appearing on a roster of speakers could still guarantee large audiences, and what Father Miller believed was still, for most Adventists, either their standard or the focus of their dissent.

From many came expressions of affection and gratitude for their awakened faith. Henry Buckley wrote responding to Miller's typically proudly-humble statement that he been nothing: "I think it would be a hard matter to convince the world that you are 'Nothing' and should they be convinced they must be awfly mortified to learn that they had made so great a cry about 'nothing.' By the grace of God you are what you are. And I thank him for bestowing so much grace upon you, for when I was spiritually blind you opened my eyes to see glorious things in [G]ods cause." Wrote Miriam Beckley, "O my dear Brother how much I owe to you under God for what he has done for my Soul" since becoming a Millerite. "I view you as my second spiritual Father and if I am faithful to the end I shall be a bright gem in your crown of rejoycing when we meet to part no more."[60]

No one looked to Miller more as a father than Joshua Himes. In the midst of controversy, when purported friends and real foes were pulling the movement apart and all their work seemed in vain, he said, "I have no change of views, or feelings. I have to thank God to

57. Ira Fancher to Miller, January 11, 1846, and "Waitsfield" to Miller, October 15, 1846, Miller Letters; "Meetings in Vermont," *Advent Herald* 10, no. 237 (November 19, 1845), 117-18; Bliss, *Memoirs*, 353-54.

58. Volume 13, no. 322 (July 3, 1847), 174-75.

59. See particularly C. Reuben to Miller, May 4, 1847; Charles Burlingham to Miller, October 11, 1846; George Sterling to Miller, July 4, 1845; J. Randall to Miller, October 16, 1846. Letters in the collection from 1846 and later are often very dark, possibly resulting from the new wood pulp paper that was rapidly replacing rag paper.

60. Buckley to Miller, March 12, 1847; Beckley to Miller, January 16, 1848, Miller Letters.

day, that I ever saw you, and still feel to prosecute this work you began, and have by your labours done so much to carry forward." In 1846 Himes finally undertook the mission to England he and Miller had discussed years before, though without his aging mentor. Sailing home, he had not yet landed before writing, "I shall make you a visit as early as possible after my return home. I want to see you, and your dear family, almost as much as I do my own." Even to the end he could affirm, "I am still yours, 'A Millerite' indeed, in whom there is no change."[61]

The relationship between the two men was controversial. Dissidents accused Himes of dictating belief and policy to Miller, a charge easily sustained by a shallow reading of their correspondence. But Miller, who might have defended himself by laying all the blame on Himes, strongly denied it, asserting that he had "never been dictated to by Bro. Himes; nor has he, to my knowledge, ever tried to direct me." He publicly testified to the quality of Himes's leadership in the *Advent Herald,* saying to him directly, "I am satisfied that you have pursued a course in accordance with the will of God." So, "Go on, then, my dear brother." Fortunately for them both, the public never saw the letter Himes had written to Miller two weeks before, suggesting such an endorsement. He even concocted a question for Miller to use as a text: "Do you approve of the general course of the Eld. J. V. Himes in the general management of the Advent cause?" If he were to include that question in his response he could use as a signature "An early believer."[62] Miller did not, perhaps suspecting the public would not readily be fooled by such an obvious ploy.

Rather than marionette and puppeteer, the two men described their relationship as that of father to son. Himes referred to himself as Miller's "son in the gospel of the Kingdom 'at hand.'" As the months passed and he saw less and less of Miller, Himes became nostalgic. "I often think of you in your retirement, and loneliness," he wrote. "But one thing remember, that you have one friend on

61. Himes to Miller, August 18, 1845; November 15, 1845; November 25, 1848; June 12, 1846, Himes Papers.

62. *Advent Herald* 14, no. 341 (November 13, 1847), 119; no. 334 (September 25, 1847), 63; Himes to Miller, August 18, 1847, Himes Papers. Himes's purpose was to give Miller the opportunity to condemn the apparent sectarianism of Joseph Marsh, but Miller's response was general and not focused on that issue.

earth, as well as one in heaven. I trust I shall never forget, or forsake, Father Miller." Miller reciprocated, treating him the same way he had treated his own sons. When decreasing subscriptions to the newspapers threatened to drive Himes into bankruptcy, Miller assisted with sizeable loans. William S. Miller informed Himes years later that "Father Miller claimed you to be his stout son in the gospel" while he could "claim to be his stout son in the flesh."[63] To be sure, Himes was directive, and Miller allowed himself to be managed, up to a point. But his reticence, indecision, and resorting to silence and retreat to the farm made him impossible to manipulate. It was Miller, after all, who decided to reject the certainty that the door of mercy was shut and to come out fully in support of the traditional leaders. His criticisms of all those who were waging war in the movement applied to Himes and the traditionalists as well as the dissidents. Ultimately he charted his own course.

In the summer of 1846 chronic illness and family events combined to further restrict Miller's activities. A growth appeared on his shoulder that doctors variously diagnosed as a "fatty tumor" or a rose cancer. While it does not seem to have incapacitated him, the Advent newspapers kept readers apprised of its progress, once again provoking prayers and homeopathic advice from worried admirers. He purchased a "magnetic machine" from Philadelphia (at a discounted price, thanks to Josiah Litch) to help with his tremors, and he thought it cured him. So he applied it to his tumor, and it cured that as well. But more important were the prayers, "better for me than the hurrahs of the millions for an Alexander, a Caesar, or a Bonaparte." They raised his spirits because they showed that "You love me still."[64]

Their comfort came as his family dispersed. Son George married in 1846 and moved to Fort Ann to live near his wife's family, and the following February, much to everyone's surprise, Bellona wed at the age of 40, disproving one of her father's pet predictions that she would die single. Less than a year later Satterlee married as well.

63. Himes to Miller, June 12, 1846, and January 12, 1848; William S. Miller to Himes, May 14, 1864, Himes Papers.

64. "Letter from Bro. William Miller," *Advent Herald* 12, no. 278 (September 2, 1846), 30; William C. Neff to Miller, July 30, 1846, Miller Letters.

One must wonder if they all waited until all the predicted dates had passed, reluctant to take such a bold step toward future life while expectation of an imminent apocalypse remained alive and nosy scoffers spied on their personal lives. Joy at these nuptials was tempered by loss, too, in the death of an infant grandson. Thus the cycles of life underscored the reality of Christ's continuing delay.[65]

It was at this moment of bereavement that new rumors of Miller's having accepted the shut door, attacks on Himes as Miller's puppet master, and insinuations of his incapacity appeared in the newspapers, requiring his denial of the charge and endorsement of Himes. These critics were former friends he once "loved in the gospel" who had become "like the obscene fowls of the air, who live only on carcasses and putrid flesh." It produced in him another deep despondency that mirrored his depression in 1816. He could not "bear the trials, perplexities, and evils, to which we are all subject, more or less, as I once could," he wrote. "[W]hether it is owing to my age, infirmities, or for the want of my former activity, I cannot tell," but it "produce[s] impatience, uneasiness, and the like." He had lost "all confidence in men, and all love for them," and he was "about to believe in the total depravity of all men, and the certainty of all profession of religion being nothing but hypocrisy."

Just at this moment, again reliving old history, Miller had an experience "which may pass for a dream." In it God gave Miller a "curiously wrought casket" filled with beautiful jewels. Thinking that duty called him to share the sight with others, he placed the casket on a table where all could see the treasure and enjoy it. But the crowds who came to see threw in counterfeit coins and false jewels, jostling the casket until it crashed to the ground, shattering the chest and scattering the jewels around the room. Weeping for his loss, he suddenly remembered God "and earnestly prayed that he would send me help." Suddenly a man entered the room, cleaned up the mess, and made the false coins disappear. He then produced a new, larger casket, and when Miller opened it the treasure was even more dazzling than before. He shouted with joy, and the shout

65. Phillip Phelps, Miller Family Genealogy. See Miller to [unnamed son], copy of an original letter, October 21, 1847, Miller Collection, Center for Adventist Research, Andrews University, Berrien Springs, Michigan.

awakened him. "The effect of this on my mind has been extremely consoling and happy," he wrote.[66] He invited readers to send him their interpretations.

They did, providing him with the last flurry of responses he would receive. Some mystics thought it was not a dream at all, but a vision, and they were eager to know if he had experienced it while asleep or awake. To avoid creating the wrong impression, when Bliss included this story in the *Memoirs* he carefully noted that Miller, "no more than others, placed any reliance on dreams," although Bliss had already prominently featured two other dreams that shaped Miller's story. Others saw it as God's sending comfort to Miller and assuaging his suffering in old age, infirmity, and deep disappointment. From this they took solace themselves, and some were inspired to send him poems expressing their strong feelings. Nobody saw it as Miller undoubtedly intended it, as an allegory justifying himself (the receiver of the gift) and Himes (the man who came to clean up the mess) and condemning those false friends he had just been describing who betrayed them and the movement.[67] Perhaps fittingly, Miller's last gift to the movement was a source of misunderstanding.

In February 1848 Miller's eyesight began to dim. The family sought medical help in Boston, but travel was required for him to receive it, and by now that was out of the question. One can trace the progress of blindness through the handwriting in letters that became increasingly illegible, finally deteriorating into a scrawl running diagonally down the page. On April 10, 1849, he tried to set some thoughts on paper for an unknown recipient despite the fact, he said, that "I can not see." One of the children, again unidentified, came into the room and "found Father writing and it is with so mutch difficulty that he does it that I have seated myself to assist him."[68] Dropsy was taking its inevitable toll, his body filling with fluid. For months old friends came to say goodbye. Bliss found him

66. *Advent Herald* 14, no. 349 (January 8, 1848), 182. Bliss reprinted the story in toto in the *Memoirs,* 360-63.

67. For examples of poems associated with the dream see Bliss, *Memoirs,* 364-66. The letters are dated generally in January and February 1848, with scattered comments arriving as late as July.

68. Miller to unidentified, April 10, 1849, Miller Letters.

melancholy over the "expected sufferings attending the dissolution of the body," though his faith in Jesus' promises did not falter.

In November it seemed to everyone, including Miller, that the end was near. William S. wrote to Himes, "[W]e look upon him as almost gone."[69] He rallied for a few weeks, but in mid-December death approached, and Himes journeyed to the farm to be with his mentor at the end. Poignant stories recount the deathbed scene. Miller lay on a couch in his east room study, surrounding children and friends singing his favorite hymns repeatedly, terms of endearment passing between father and gospel son — "Elder Himes has come — I love Elder Himes." As his breathing faltered and the end approached, he was able to shout out lines from his favorite hymns. Just after three o'clock on the afternoon of December 20, he died. Himes, standing beside the couch, bent over the body and closed his eyes.[70]

The funeral was a journey through the scenes of Miller's life. The Adventist congregation had built a chapel replacing the Baptist church they had been forced to vacate,[71] on land Miller donated near the house and the grove of trees that had played such important parts on his journey, and he wanted the funeral service to take place there. But the crowds were expected to be large, and when the Congregational church in Fairhaven opened its doors for the funeral, the family decided to hold it there. After prayer and a hymn in the house, they took the casket down the hill to the soil his father had first dug to bury William's sibling more than sixty years before. There they laid him to rest in a grave next to his parents as they sang one of his favorite hymns, "Happy the spirit released from its clay." Standing beside the open grave, Himes succumbed to sorrow and was held up by William S., fatherless sons clinging to each other, weeping. The mourners then formed a procession of sleighs, more

69. William S. Miller to Himes, November 4, 1849, Miller Letters.

70. Himes recounted these events in a series of letters published in the *Advent Herald* 4 (new series), no. 452 (December 29, 1849); see also Bliss, *Memoirs,* 376-78.

71. On December 4, 1849, Miller and Melancton Kilburn signed an agreement allowing Adventists to build a chapel on "their" land "about half way from William Miller's house to Seth Peck's north east corner bounds." The deed was not recorded until 1920. Washington County, New York, Miscellaneous Records of Washington County, Fort Edward, New York, book 6, page 142.

than one hundred, to travel the two miles over packed snow to the church, the same way four-year-old William had journeyed to the wilderness farm with his pioneering parents. Himes was able to collect himself sufficiently to preach the sermon; after three hours, they departed. Much had been said and shared about William Miller, but it was Himes who most appropriately summarized what would be true of future generations' assessment: "Mr. Miller's character and abilities have not been understood by the church or the world."[72]

72. The quote is from Bliss, *Memoirs,* 173; "Funeral of Father Miller," *Advent Herald* 4, no. 453 (January 5, 1850), 184.

EPILOGUE

This Work, This Strange Work

After the funeral, family and friends distributed the estate. Miller had entertained the hope that Jesus would return before he died,[1] but as his body deteriorated he came to accept the likelihood that he would not be among the living saints who would join Jesus in the air at the second coming. So in April 1848 he wrote a will. Lucy received all the furniture and lifelong use of the house and land. To the children, beyond what they had already received, he left money, most to be paid immediately, another sum to follow their mother's death, totaling $5100. It was a sizeable figure that might have provoked further comment from the public about Millerism being a moneymaking scheme had they known of it. But the money was to come from land he had sold to Warren Bartholomew, undoubtedly the same man who later married Lucy Ann. Bellona, long the only daughter, and George, the rebel, received $100 more than the others.

Youngest son John inherited everything else — house, land, farm buildings, livestock, tools.[2] Of all the children, his name appears least often in the written record, but it was John who managed the farm along with his mother while the movement captured his father's time and attention and his siblings were building lives away from home. Soon, perhaps immediately but more likely after his mother's death in 1854, he set out to "modernize" the Federal-

1. Sylvester Bliss, *Memoirs of William Miller: Generally Known as a Lecturer on the Prophecies, and the Second Coming of Christ* (Boston: Joshua V. Himes, 1853), 90.

2. Will, Washington County Records, book E, page 159, Fort Ann, New York.

style house, giving it the Greek Revival appearance[3] that was all the rage in Hampton but elsewhere was already giving way to more romantic Gothic Revival and Italianate styles. He thus unintentionally maintained the family's tendency to be somewhat behind the times.

More important than money and property was Miller's spiritual legacy, and in 1850 that was problematic. Himes undertook to define it by preparing the memoir that he intended would inform the world of Miller's true character and contributions. Much material was already on hand — Miller's letters to him and to the newspapers, manuscripts of articles and lectures, his text books in which he recorded his lecture and preaching itinerary and the Scripture texts he used from October 1834 to June 1844, the small notebook containing his "Statement of Belief" from 1822, sheriff records from Poultney and Hampton, Bibles, commentaries, and personal artifacts. But much more needed to be gathered. To that end Himes advertised in the *Advent Herald* asking people to send in letters or copies of letters Miller had written to them, anecdotes about him, clippings of newspaper articles reporting his lectures, tributes and obituaries from friends and foes.

People responded. Lucy did not follow convention and burn her deceased husband's papers, at least not all of them (one wonders if there had been letters she wrote to him). She (or the children) sent her husband's poems, acrostics, essays, and drafts of early speeches delivered before the debating society. Sister Anna provided letters Miller had sent to Joseph urging him to abandon Universalism. Another sister, Stella Miller Adams, sent the letter William had written to their mother while encamped at Burlington, announcing his intention to return to Hampton and to her maternal guidance. A cousin, another William Miller, sent genealogical information. Old friend Truman Hendryx gave Himes an entire collection, though he withheld one letter "which is confidential and of no importance to your object." William S. had written notes at the bottom of some of his father's letters, so Hendryx removed them "when I could do so

3. Adventist Historic Properties, Inc., "A Preservation Plan for the William Miller Farm, prepared by Crawford & Stearns, Architects, and Doell & Doell, Landscape Architects," Syracuse, N.Y., October 1987, 3.

without injury." Hendryx hoped they would be judicious in their use of the material: "I need not tell you our familiarity has occasioned many expressions which he would hardly have been willing to have go to the publick and some remarks which you may not understand. I however have no fear of your using these improperly."[4]

The task of sifting all the material and creating a narrative from it fell to Apollos Hale, Miller's traveling companion in his last years, and Sylvester Bliss, co-editors with Himes of the *Advent Herald.* After he finished the first three chapters other duties "interfered" with Hale's continuing with the project, so Sylvester Bliss, who helped rescue Miller from the shut-door dissenters (among whom Hale was originally numbered), completed it. Miller himself had already provided the core of the story in the brief autobiographies he wrote for the inaugural issues of the *Advent Herald* in 1840 and the *Morning Watch* in 1842, repeated, though not copied, in the *Views of the Prophecies* and again in the *Apology and Defense.* Himes wrote an introduction and published the three men's combined efforts in 1853 as *Memoirs of William Miller, Generally Known as a Lecturer on the Prophecies, and the Second Coming of Christ.* Miller, while well known, had been "diversely regarded," wrote Himes. One purpose of the book, therefore, was to afford the "impartial" public an opportunity to "form a just estimate" of him. In this way the book would be "an act of justice to Mr. Miller."[5]

Of course, the public was not impartial. By 1853 it held Miller to have been at best misguided, at worst crazy and crooked. Most did not consider him at all; other personalities and issues had taken center stage as the nation lurched from one crisis to another on the road to civil war. Himes's actual investment in the memoir was personal. He was fulfilling filial duties to his spiritual father, no doubt genuinely desiring to rescue Miller's reputation. But the book was also ammunition, one last chance for Miller's life to advance the cause, not the old crusade to warn the world but the new battle to save Adventism and keep it on track. The Albany Conference had

4. Joseph Adams to Himes, December 22, 1850; D. E. Atwood to Himes, February 13, 1850; William Miller to Apollos Hale, March 20, 1850; Truman Hendryx to Himes, April 14, 1850, Joshua V. Himes Papers, Massachusetts Historical Society, Boston, Massachusetts.

5. Bliss, *Memoirs,* iii-iv.

settled some issues, and some scores, but new theologies were attaching themselves to old principles. Expectations among Adventists were growing again, this time focusing on 1854. Surely it was helpful to remember old frenzies and the mistakes to which belief in definite time was prone. The view that the souls of the wicked would be destroyed (annihilated) rather than raised to eternal punishment (the second resurrection) was also finding new life among Adventists. Others were promulgating the doctrine that souls were saved only on condition that they had faith in Christ, thus denying God's providence and the sovereignty of God's grace. So again it would be helpful to remind Adventists that in his last conversation with Himes, on his deathbed, Miller denied both of these ideas and affirmed the intermediate state of the dead.[6] At the end, the memoirs had as much to do with contemporary ecclesiastical politics as with informing the public about Miller or salvaging his reputation.

It availed Himes little. Miller's theological heirs were carving up Adventism and laying claim to their particular patrimony. The "Albany regulars" rooted themselves in the Miller who preached the vague "sometime in 1843" rather than the precise "true midnight cry" and the visible, historic work of God that led inexorably from Daniel to the end of time. In 1858 they formed the American Evangelical Adventist Conference. Annihilationists and conditionalists followed suit, though laggardly. Because they added ideas to Miller's essential principles rather than denying any of them, they too could claim to be his legitimate spiritual heirs. In 1860 they organized what came to be known as the Advent Christian Church. Soon they divided, and a new body, the Life and Advent Union, arose from those who overtly denied one of Miller's core precepts, the second resurrection. Joseph Marsh led a fourth group, Age to Come Adventists, away from the Albany consensus with his Judaizing belief that a portion of the Jews would return to Israel before the end. Its radical libertarianism kept it from organizing effectively until others led it in a new direction. George Storrs, the annihilationist who was

6. George R. Knight, *Millennial Fever and the End of the World* (Boise: Pacific Press Publishing Association, 1993), 283-86; Himes first reported the details of Miller's remarks on the intermediate state of the dead in the report of his visit to Miller published in the *Advent Herald and Signs of the Times* [hereafter cited as *Advent Herald*] on December 29, 1849, and reprinted in the *Memoirs*, 377.

deeply connected with most of these developments, also influenced the young Charles Taze Russell, founder of the *Watchtower* and the Jehovah's Witnesses.[7]

Independently of all these developments, the Portland enthusiasts accomplished what Miller was unable to do. Emotionally he could not accept that he was wrong about definite time, but rationally he had to confess that during his predicted period nothing happened *on earth* that fulfilled prophecy consistent with the simultaneous judgment, cleansing of the world (i.e., the sanctuary) by purifying fire, and parousia. Joseph Bates, James White, and others developed a theology that accepted the validity of Miller's principle of definite time. His error, they said, was to identify the earth as the sanctuary; actually, the sanctuary was a chamber in heaven. On October 22 Jesus acted not by returning to earth, but by moving into that sanctuary, closing the door to his first act of salvation of forgiving sins through his blood, and beginning the work of blotting out the sins of the saved and cleansing the sanctuary of those who were not. Only when that work is completed would he return physically to earth. In this way, unlike the Albany regulars, they affirmed all of Miller's teaching except for his identification of the sanctuary. By 1850 a belief that Saturday was the true sabbath was merging with this new theology. According to James White, a founder of Seventh-day Adventism, Lucy Miller attended one of their sabbatarian lectures, and when asked what she thought of their views she ostensibly remarked that "she did not know but the Sabbath which [they] taught was right." Whether accurate or not, the story attests to the enduring power of the Miller name to authenticate.[8]

7. George Knight summarizes this complicated story in *Millennial Fever,* 283-89. The fullest discussion of Adventist sectarianism is David T. Arthur, "'Come Out of Babylon': A Study of Millerite Separatism and Denominationalism, 1840-1865" (Ph.D. dissertation, University of Rochester, 1970). Marsh connected with a Virginia millenarian, John Thomas, who was active at the same time as William Miller, giving a Millerite connection to what became the Christadelphians. According to Knight it ultimately produced the Church of God of the Abrahamic Faith in 1921.

8. See Ronald L. Numbers, *Prophetess of Health: Ellen G. White and the Origins of Seventh-day Adventist Health Reform* (Knoxville: University of Tennessee Press, 1992), and George Knight, *Millennial Fever,* 295-325. The quote from Lucy Miller appears in *Millennial Fever,* 312.

Miller's familial and spiritual progeny walked their own paths through this maze. Most of the children stayed close to home. The names of Robbins, Lucy Ann, and Bellona appear with aunts, uncles, and cousins among the charter members of the Advent Christian congregation that built the chapel near the farmhouse. Whether they remained Adventists is unknown. Of the children, only Bellona is buried in the family cemetery.[9] Ironically, it was the rebel, George, who followed most closely in his father's footsteps. At Andrews University is a family Bible that Himes gave to Lucy, who subsequently presented it to George in 1852, two years before her death, with the inscribed text, "Her children will arise up and call her blessed." In it appears a license dated June 27, 1868, so much like the ones his father carried with him, authorizing George to minister in the Minnesota Annual Conference of the "Christian Advent" Church. For his part, Himes affiliated variously with the Evangelical Adventists and the Advent Christians, but disputes with other leaders, particularly Miles Grant, led to charges of sexual impropriety that finally drove him out of the Adventist movement by 1876. In 1879, like Miller, he returned to spiritual roots by rejoining the Episcopal church in which he had been baptized as a child. Ordained a priest in 1879, he served in Elk Point, South Dakota, until his death in 1894.

Just before he died, Himes provided one more service to Miller, and to posterity. Through his movements in and out of Adventism, Himes had kept Miller's traveling trunk, and in it the collection of documents he had gathered to produce Miller's memoirs. Now, approaching the end of his life, he organized them, writing brief labels on the back of the letters indicating the date and the name of the sender, and shipped the trunk to J. M. Orrock in Boston, last editor of the *Advent Herald.* In 1895 the paper ceased publication, and all its property, including the trunk, ended up at the office of *The World's Crisis,* ironically the newspaper of Miles Grant's Advent Christian Church. Orrin Roe Jenks, earnest collector of Adventist materials, found it there and asked for it. The editors gave the collection to him, and he took it to the Advent Christian college at Au-

9. Carolyn F. McCullen and Daniele L. Roberts, *Set in Stone: The Cemeteries of Hampton* (Fair Haven, Vt.: New York Sleeper Books, 2002), 28.

rora, Illinois, where he served as its seventh president. There it resides today, much augmented.[10] In the end, Himes had the last laugh on Miles Grant: before shipping the trunk he removed his own letters. Eventually they ended up at the Massachusetts Historical Society.[11]

Thanks to Himes, the Jenks collection affords us another, unintended opportunity. It would have troubled Miller to know, first, that time continued long enough for scholarly reflection on his work and, second, that oft-condemned learned professors and doctors would be responsible for assessing it. Actually, he had little to fear and might have been pleased. Academic gaze, particularly in the last twenty years, has focused so intently on the movement, the collective experience of Millerites,[12] that Miller hardly ever appears, as though he were still ensconced in Low Hampton taking comfort at the farm. Two exceptions, Wayne R. Judd and George Knight, continued to view Miller through the Millerite lens, rarely moving beyond Adventist sources, forcing us to deduce the man from the effects of his actions.[13] Having wished for anonymity in life, Miller virtually found it in death.

Jonathan Butler has interpreted Miller's work more broadly, situating the man between the classicism, empiricism, and determinism of the eighteenth century and the romanticism, sentimentality, and Arminianism of the nineteenth. In promulgating his views, Miller had the advantage of open borders that political, economic, and cultural earthquakes created from 1800 to 1830. His career flourished in this cultural boundlessness, fed by millennialism, voluntarism, perfectionism, and revivalism before settling into the

10. The story of the Jenks Collection is told by Moses C. Crouse on the Aurora University Web page, http://www.aurora.edu/museum/jenks1.htm (Aurora University, 2004). One of the late David Arthur's great loves was carefully shepherding this collection. Its maintenance owes a great deal to his stewardship.

11. While its provenance is unclear, the collection probably passed to Himes's son, William Lloyd Garrison Himes, and through his descendants to its current repository.

12. An excellent review of recent Millerite historiography is Benjamin McArthur, "Millennial Fevers," *Reviews in American History* 24 (1996): 369-82.

13. In Ronald L. Numbers and Jonathan M. Butler, eds., *The Disappointed: Millerism and Millenarianism in the Nineteenth Century* (Knoxville: University of Tennessee Press, 1993), 17-35.

new consolidation of values Seventh-day Adventism came to represent.[14] In this interpretation Miller stands silhouetted starkly against the backdrop of his cultural context. The view clarifies Miller's relationship to that matrix, rendering him more understandable, perhaps even more conventional, than popular memory and public reputation would have had it. What remains indistinct and debatable is the man himself.

That is not surprising. Boundlessness is a temporal condition that enables something new to emerge. Miller was more about endings than beginnings. His impact on the religious culture of his day was largely negative, analogous to the Scopes trial's effect eighty years after the Great Disappointment. Then, the publicity surrounding attacks on evolution short-circuited fundamentalism's dynamic growth, discrediting it in the eyes of many and driving it beneath the surface of mass culture, where it steeped, imperceptible to the gatekeepers, not to find significant public expression for decades.[15] While we should be careful not to overstate his influence, Miller clearly did something similar to premillennialism. True, denominational expressions would sustain Adventism to the present day, but only with principles he had rejected. And true, he sparked the most significant popular millenarian mass movement in American history, but it was the only one of its kind. A product of the day's folk culture, as J. F. C. Harrison suggests,[16] Miller had much in common with political and social millenarians in revolutionary France, seventeenth-century England, and nineteenth-century China, as well as cargo cultists in Melanesia and Africa and Native American ghost shirt dancers. But unlike other leaders — the cultic Joseph Smith, the intentionally sectarian Alexander Campbell, or even the utopian Mother Ann Lee — Miller failed to provide his millennial views with an institutional expression that would guarantee their survival. His historicist hermeneutic was already archaic, as Paul

14. "The Making of a New Order: Millerism and the Origins of Seventh-day Adventism," in Numbers and Butler, *Disappointed,* 189-208.

15. See Edward J. Larson, *Summer for the Gods: The Scopes Trial and America's Continuing Debate over Science and Religion* (Cambridge, Mass.: Harvard University Press, 1998).

16. *The Second Coming: Popular Millenarianism, 1780-1850* (New Brunswick, N.J.: Rutgers University Press, 1979), 192-203.

Boyer notes.[17] Dispensationalism, born in England the same decade Miller began preaching, would have to wait until the end of the century before it could find traction again, this time in the work of Cyrus I. Scofield.

Enthusiastic revivalism suffered the same fate. It had largely dissipated when Miller's apocalyptic rhetoric, essentially a new measure, stirred the embers to full flame. His call to piety, voluntarism, and sacrifice as the end approached provoked the radical come-outerism and what even he called fanaticism that sealed revivalism's doom. By the mid-1840s the Albany Adventists joined other evangelicals in a call to eschew measures, especially protracted camp meetings, that provoked extreme responses.[18] Sinking with it was nascent Pentecostalism. The holiness movement was born the same decade as both Millerism and dispensationalism when its principal founder, Phoebe Palmer, hosted Tuesday sanctification meetings in her New York home. Inevitably the public tarred her perfectionist spirituality with the brush they used against the Millerites.[19] It was decades before Pentecostalism could again test the boundaries between the Spirit and the Word. Even today, despite Miller's contributions to them, neither fundamentalists nor Pentecostalists have claimed the patrimony of the man whose memory they largely had to outlive.

So from the standpoint of broad long-term influence, Miller's legacy appears grim. But Miller never set out to reshape this world — only to prepare souls for the next. His goal was not to promote millenarianism, revivals, or biblicism for their own sakes, but for their capacity to inculcate lives devoted wholeheartedly to God in

17. *When Time Shall Be No More: Prophecy Belief in Modern American Culture* (Cambridge, Mass.: Belknap Press, 1992), 82.

18. Timothy P. Weber states, "To say the least, by 1845 premillennialism had fallen on hard times, as far as American evangelicalism was concerned." *Living in the Shadow of the Second Coming: American Premillennialism, 1875-1925* (New York and Oxford: Oxford University Press, 1979), 16.

19. On Phoebe Palmer's career and influence see Mark A. Noll, *America's God* (New York: Oxford University Press, 2002), 359-62. The New England Centenary Commission in 1866 credited Millerism as one of the causes for significant decline in growth of Methodist membership generally in the 1840s. See Melvin Easterday Dieter, *The Holiness Revival of the Nineteenth Century* (Metuchen, N.J.: Scarecrow Press, 1980), 48.

love and trust, not in some far-off fulfillment of promises, but here and now. More than anything else, Millerism was about conversion.[20] At that Miller was enormously successful, because he was conveying to audiences his own experience of faith through struggle and darkness. The logic of his computations and charts only partially accounts for his remarkable capacity to persuade people to accept the self-evidently odd ideas he promulgated. At its inception, this "strange work" began with God's transforming of Miller's own heart, the gift of metanoia and the effects it created in him. Having come to faith through it, Miller was able to lead others to hope, because in him and his testimony they could see evidence already of transformation, rejuvenation, God's shattering and then rebuilding of one man's life. Why couldn't the same thing happen to them? Indeed, this changing of lives was his ultimate task, and his greatest success.

20. Paul Boyer makes this point explicitly, stating that "Miller's message promoted conversion," though he did not necessarily see this as its defining quality (*Time*, 83).

Bibliography

Archives and Public Records

Cooke, Rollin H. Pittsfield Families. Berkshire Athenaeum. Pittsfield, Mass.

Halstead, Vera C. Letter [re Elnathan Phelps]. Misc. File #1125. Vermont Historical Society. Barre, Vt.

Himes, Joshua V. Papers. Massachusetts Historical Society. Boston, Mass.

Holden, Clarence H. Whitehall, N.Y., Scrapbooks, 1910-1927. New York State Library and Archives. Albany, N.Y.

Knurow Collection. Berkshire Athenaeum. Pittsfield, Mass.

Millard, Paulinus. Day Book. Del E. Webb Memorial Library. Loma Linda University. Loma Linda, Calif.

Miller Family. Bible. Miller Chapel, William Miller Farm [Adventist Heritage Ministry]. Hampton, N.Y.

Miller, William. Collection. Center for Adventist Research. James White Library, Andrews University. Berrien Springs, Mich.

———. Collection. Ellen G. White Estate. Silver Spring, Md.

———. Collection/Military Papers. Vermont Historical Society. Barre, Vt.

———. Diary and Book of Fortune. Vermont Historical Society. Barre, Vt.

———. Justice Record, 1831-1834. William Miller Farm [Adventist Heritage Ministry]. Hampton, N.Y.

———. Muster Roll. William Miller Farm [Adventist Heritage Ministry]. Hampton, N.Y.

———. Papers. Jenks Memorial Collection of Adventual Materials. Aurora University. Aurora, Ill. [Manuscript writings, poems, text books, Statement of Belief, and other archival materials in addition to Miller's correspondence.]

———. Resignation Letter from the Masonic Lodge. William Miller Farm [Adventist Heritage Ministry]. Hampton, N.Y.
———. School Book with Problems, 1798-1804. William Miller Farm [Adventist Heritage Ministry]. Hampton, N.Y.
———. Sheriff's Blot Book, 1809-1811. Jenks Memorial Collection of Adventural Materials. Aurora University. Aurora, Ill.
Millerites and Early Adventists, Ann Arbor, Mich.: University Microfilms, 1977.
Miscellaneous Records of Washington County. N.Y. State Library and Archives. Albany, N.Y.
Offensend, Dorothy. Miller Genealogy. Washington County [N.Y.] Historian. Fort Edward, N.Y.
———. William Miller, Prophet in the Wilderness. Washington County Historical Society. Fort Edward, N.Y.
Phelps, Phillip. Miller Family Genealogy. Nd.
Poultney, Vermont. Assessment. Vermont Historical Society. Barre, Vt.
Strong, Augustus Hopkins. Papers. Ambrose Swasey Library, Colgate Rochester Divinity School. Rochester, N.Y.
U.S. Government. Bureau of the Census. Manuscript Census. Hampton, N.Y., 1790-1850.
———. Poultney, Vt., 1810.
———. Whitehall, N.Y., 1810.
Washington County, N.Y. Deeds. Fort Edward, N.Y.
———. Miscellaneous Records. Fort Edward, N.Y.
———. Wills. Fort Edward, N.Y.

Published Sources

Adams, Andrew N. *History of the Town of Fair Haven, Vermont.* Fair Haven, Vt.: Leonard & Phelps, 1870.
Adventist Historic Properties, Inc. "A Preservation Plan for the William Miller Farm, prepared by Crawford & Stearns, Architects, and Doell & Doell, Landscape Architects." Syracuse, N.Y., October 1987.
An Appeal to the Common Sense of the People, or the Miller Delusion!!! Boston: I. R. Butts, 1843.
Arthur, David Tallmadge. "'Come Out of Babylon': A Study of Millerite Separatism and Denominationalism, 1840-1865." Ph.D. dissertation, University of Rochester, 1970.
Austin, Aleine, *Matthew Lyon, "New Man" of the Democratic Revolution, 1749-1822.* University Park: Pennsylvania State University Press, 1981.

Bibliography

Barton, A. S. *Millerism Refuted by History, in a Series of Letters to a Friend.* Windsor, Vt.: Joseph Fairbanks, 1842.

Bellesiles, Michael A. *Revolutionary Outlaws: Ethan Allen and the Struggle for Independence on the Early American Frontier.* Charlottesville: University Press of Virginia, 1993.

Benedict, David. *A General History of the Baptist Denomination in America and Other Parts of the World.* New York: Sheldon, Lamport, and Blakeman, 1855.

Bliss, Sylvester. *Memoirs of William Miller: Generally Known as a Lecturer on the Prophecies, and the Second Coming of Christ.* Boston: Joshua V. Himes, 1853.

Bloch, Ruth H. *The Visionary Republic: Millennial Themes in American Thought, 1756-1800.* Cambridge: Cambridge University Press, 1985.

Bottskill [Baptist] Association. *Bottskill Association Minutes, 1831-1832.*

Boyer, Paul. *When Time Shall Be No More: Prophecy Belief in Modern American Culture.* Cambridge, Mass.: Belknap Press, 1992.

Bressler, Ann Lee. *The Universalist Movement in America, 1770-1880.* Oxford: Oxford University Press, 2001.

Broadhurst, Dale R. Dale R. Broadhurst's Sites Dedicated to Mormon History. http://www.sidneyrigdon.com/dbroadhu/index.htm (accessed 26 September 2006).

Brown, J. Newton, ed. *The Encyclopedia of Religious Knowledge.* Brattleboro, Vt.: Brattleboro Typographic Company, 1838.

Brown, Raymond. *The Churches the Apostles Left Behind.* New York: Paulist Press, 1984.

———. *The Community of the Beloved Disciple.* Mahwah, N.J.: Paulist Press, 1979.

Brown, Richard D. *Knowledge Is Power: The Diffusion of Information in Early America, 1700-1865.* New York: Oxford University Press, 1989.

Bullock, Steven C. *Revolutionary Brotherhood: Freemasonry and the Transformation of the American Social Order, 1730-1840.* Chapel Hill: University of North Carolina Press, 1996.

Bushman, Richard Lyman. *Joseph Smith: Rough Stone Rolling.* New York: Alfred A. Knopf, 2005.

Campbell, Alexander. *Delusions, An Analysis of the Book of Mormon with an Examination of its internal and external Pretences to Divine Authority.* Boston: Benjamin H. Greene, 1832.

Casey, Richard P. "North Country Nemesis: The Potash Rebellion and the Embargo of 1807-1809." *The New York Historical Society Quarterly* 64 (January 1980): 45.

Clark, Christopher. *The Roots of Rural Capitalism: Western Massachusetts, 1780-1860.* Ithaca, N.Y.: Cornell University Press, 1990.

Cohen, Patricia Cline. *A Calculating People: The Spread of Numeracy in Early America.* Chicago: University of Chicago Press, 1982.

Condarcure, Steve. Steve Condarcure's New England Genealogy. http://newenglandgenealogy.pcplayground.com/sjc.htm (accessed 2005).

Connors, Richard, and Andrew Colin Gow, eds., *Anglo-American Millennialism, from Milton to the Millerites.* Leiden and Boston: Brill, 2004.

Corey, Allen. *Gazetteer of the County of Washington, New York.* Schuylerville, N.Y.: n.p., 1849.

Crocker, Henry. *History of the Baptists in Vermont.* Bellows Falls, Vt.: P. H. Gobie Press, 1931.

Cross, Whitney Rogers. *The Burned-Over District: The Social and Intellectual History of Enthusiastic Religion in Western New York, 1800-1850.* Ithaca, N.Y.: Cornell University Press, 1950.

Crouse, Moses C. Welcome to The Jenks Memorial Collection of Adventual Materials at Aurora University. http://www.aurora.edu/museum/jenks1.htm (accessed 2004).

Davidson, James West. *The Logic of Millennial Thought: Eighteenth-Century New England.* New Haven, Conn.: Yale University Press, 1977.

Dieter, Melvin Easterday. *The Holiness Revival of the Nineteenth Century.* Metuchen, N.J.: Scarecrow Press, 1980.

Dimmick, L. F. *The End of the World Not Yet: A Discourse Delivered in the North Church, Newburyport.* Newburyport, Mass.: Charles Whipple, 1842.

Everest, Allan S. *The War of 1812 in the Champlain Valley.* Syracuse, N.Y.: Syracuse University Press, 1981.

Everts and Ensign. *History of Washington County, New York.* Philadelphia: Everts and Ensign, 1878.

Farmer's Library. Fairhaven, Vt.

Feldman, Jay. *When the Mississippi Ran Backwards: Empire, Intrigue, Murder, and the New Madrid Earthquakes.* New York: Free Press, 2005.

Festinger, Leon, Henry W. Reicken, and Stanley Schlachter. *When Prophecy Fails: A Social and Psychological Study of a Modern Group That Predicted the Destruction of the World.* Minneapolis: University of Minnesota Press, 1956.

Finke, Roger, and Rodney Stark. *The Churching of America 1776-1990: Winners and Losers in Our Religious Economy.* New Brunswick, N.J.: Rutgers University Press, 1992.

Finney, Charles Grandison. *Memoirs of Rev. Charles G. Finney, Written by Himself.* New York: Fleming H. Revell, 1876.

Fitch, Charles. *Come Out of Her, My People.* Boston: J. V. Himes, 1843.

Fortin, Dennis. "'The World Turned Upside Down': Millerism in the Eastern Townships, 1830-1845." *Journal of Eastern Townships Studies* 11 (Fall 1997): 39-53.

Frisbie, Barnes. *History of Middletown.* Rutland, Vt.: Tuttle & Company, 1867.

Froom, Leroy Edwin. *The Prophetic Faith of Our Fathers.* 4 vols. Washington, D.C.: Review and Herald Publishing Association, 1946-1954.

Gaustad, Edwin S., ed. *The Rise of Adventism: Religion and Society in Mid-Nineteenth Century America.* New York: Harper and Row, 1974.

Gilmore, William J. *Reading Becomes a Necessity of Life: Material and Cultural Life in Rural New England, 1780-1835.* Knoxville: The University of Tennessee Press, 1989.

Goodman, Paul. *Towards a Christian Republic: Antimasonry and the Great Transition in New England, 1826-1836.* New York: Oxford University Press, 1988.

Graff, Harvey J. *Conflicting Paths: Growing Up in America.* Cambridge, Mass.: Harvard University Press, 1995.

Gribbin, William. *The Churches Militant: The War of 1812 and American Religion.* New Haven: Yale University Press, 1973.

Hambrick-Stowe, Charles E. *Charles G. Finney and the Spirit of American Evangelicalism.* Grand Rapids: Eerdmans, 1996.

Harrison, J. F. C. *The Second Coming: Popular Millenarianism, 1780-1850.* New Brunswick, N.J.: Rutgers University Press, 1979.

Hassell, Cushing Biggs, and Sylvester Hassell, *The Church of God, from the Creation to A.D. 1885; including especially the history of the Kehukee Primitive Baptist Association.* Middletown, N.Y.: Gilbert Beebe's Sons, 1886.

Hatch, Nathan. *The Democratization of American Christianity.* New Haven: Yale University, 1989.

———. "The Origins of Civil Millennialism in America: New England Clergymen, War with France, and the Revolution." *New England Quarterly* 31, no. 3 (July 1974): 407-30.

Haven, Kittredge. *The World Reprieved: Being a Critical Examination of William Miller's Theory.* Woodstock, Vt.: Haskell and Palmer, 1839.

Hazen, Craig James. *The Village Enlightenment in America: Popular Religion and Science in the Nineteenth Century.* Urbana and Chicago: University of Illinois Press, 2000.

Herald of Vermont. Rutland, Vt.

Himes, Joshua V., compiler. *Millennial Harp, or Second Advent Hymns; Designed for Meetings on the Second Coming of Christ.* Boston: Joshua V. Himes, 1842.

———. *Views of the Prophecies and Prophetic Chronology, Selected From Manuscripts of William Miller With a Memoir of His Life.* Boston: Joshua V. Himes, 1842.

Jackson, G. A. "Some Early Hampton, New York, Residents." *Washington County, New York.* http://www.rootsweb.com/~nywashin/hampton.htm (accessed 2006).

Johnson, Curtis. *Redeeming America: Evangelicals and the Road to Civil War.* Chicago: University of Chicago, 1993.

Johnson, Herbert T. *Roster of Soldiers in the War of 1812-14.* St Albans, Vt.: Messenger Press, 1933.

Johnson, Paul E., and Sean Wilentz. *The Kingdom of Matthias: The Story of Sex and Salvation in Nineteenth-Century America.* New York and Oxford: Oxford University Press, 1994.

Joslin, J., B. Frisbie, and F. Ruggles, *A History of the Town of Poultney, Vermont, From its Settlement to the Year 1875, with Family and Biographical Sketches and Incidents.* Poultney, Vt.: J. Joslin, B. Frisbie, F. Ruggles, 1875.

Kerry, Walter S. *Rational Infidels: The American Deists.* Durango, Colo.: Longwood Academic, 1992.

Kett, Joseph. *Rites of Passage: Adolescence in America 1790 to the Present.* New York: Basic Books, 1977.

Kittel, Gerhard, ed. *Theological Dictionary of the New Testament.* Geoffrey W. Bromiley, translator and editor. 9 volumes. Grand Rapids: Eerdmans, 1964-74.

Knight, George R. *Millennial Fever and the End of the World.* Boise: Pacific Press Publishing Association, 1993.

Lambert, Byron Cecil. *The Rise of the Anti-Mission Baptists; Sources and Leaders, 1800-1840.* New York: Arno Press, 1980.

Larson, Edward J. *Summer for the Gods: The Scopes Trial and America's Continuing Debate over Science and Religion.* Cambridge, Mass.: Harvard University Press, 1998.

Lepore, Jill. *The Name of War: King Philip's War and the Origins of American Identity.* New York: Vintage Books, 1998.

Levy, Morris. *Map of Washington County, New York.* Philadelphia: James D. Scott and Robert Pearsall Smith, 1853.

Lippincott, J. B. *History of Washington County, New York.* New York: J. B. Lippincott, 1873.

Little, J. I. "Millennial Invasion: Millerism in the Eastern Townships of Lower Canada." In *Anglo-American Millennialism, from Milton to the Millerites,* ed. Richard Connors and Andrew Golin Gow, 177-204. Studies in the History of the Christian Tradition. Leiden and Boston: E. J. Brill, 2004.

Ludlum, David M. *Social Ferment in Vermont, 1791-1850.* Reprinted New York: AMS Press, 1966.

Marsden, George M. *Jonathan Edwards: A Life.* New Haven: Yale University Press, 2003.

McArthur, Benjamin. "Millennial Fevers." *Reviews in American History* 24, no. 3 (1996): 369-82.

McCullen, Carolyn R., and Daniele L. Roberts. *Set in Stone: The Cemeteries of Hampton.* Fair Haven, Vt.: New York Sleeper Books, 2002.

Midnight Cry [renamed *Midnight Cry and Morning Watch*]. New York, N.Y.

Miller, William. *Apology and Defense.* Boston: Joshua V. Himes, 1845.

———. *Evidence from Scripture and History of the Second Coming of Christ, about the year 1843: Exhibited in a Course of Lectures.* Troy, N.Y.: Kenble & Hooper, 1836. Subsequent editions: Troy, N.Y.: Elias Gates, 1838; Boston: B. B. Mussey, 1840; Boston: Joshua V. Himes, 1842.

———. *Evidence from Scripture & History of the Second Coming of Christ about the year A.D. 1843, and of his personal reign of 1000 years.* Brandon, Vt.: Telegraph Office, 1833.

Moorhead, James H. "Searching for the Millennium in America." *Princeton Seminary Bulletin* 8 (1987).

National Park Service. "Rokeby," in *Aboard the Underground Railroad: A National Register Travel Itinerary.* http://www.cr.nps.gov/nr/travel/underground/vt1.htm, nd.

New York State. Agricultural Census. 1825.

Newcomer, Lee Nathaniel. *The Embattled Farmers: A Massachusetts Countryside in the American Revolution.* New York: Russell & Russell, 1953 and 1971.

Nichol, Francis D. *The Midnight Cry: A Defense of the Character and Conduct of William Miller and the Millerites.* Washington, D.C.: Review and Herald, 1944.

Nolan, Lewis. *Nolan-Miller Family History.* Memphis: Highland Press, 1997.

Noll, Mark A. *America's God: From Jonathan Edwards to Abraham Lincoln.* New York: Oxford University Press, 2002.

———. *The Work We Have to Do: A History of Protestants in America.* New York: Oxford University Press, 2002.

Numbers, Ronald L. *Prophetess of Health: A Study of Ellen G. White.* Grand Rapids: Eerdmans, 2008.

Numbers, Ronald L., and Jonathan M. Butler, eds. *The Disappointed: Millerism and Millenarianism in the Nineteenth Century.* Knoxville: University of Tennessee Press, 1993.

Paine, Thomas. *Age of Reason: Being an Investigation of True and Fabulous Theology.* Reprinted. Cutchogue, N.Y.: Buccaneer Books, 1976.

Parker, Jane Marsh. "A Little Millerite." *Century Magazine* 11 (November 1886–April 1887), 310-17.

———. "A Spiritual Cyclone: The Millerite Delusion." *The Magazine of Christian Literature* 4, no. 4 (September 1891): 321-25.

Phelps, Oliver S. and Andrew T. Servin, *The Phelps of America and Their English Ancestors.* 2 vols. Pittsfield, Mass.: Eagle Publishing Company, 1899.

Pickering, George. *Creative Malady: Illness in the Lives and Minds of Charles Darwin, Florence Nightingale, Mary Baker Eddy, Sigmund Freud, Marcel Proust, Elizabeth Barrett Browning.* New York: Oxford University Press, 1974.

Potash, P. Jeffrey. *Vermont's Burned-Over District: Patterns of Community Development and Religious Activity, 1762-1850.* New York: Carlson Publishing, Inc., 1991.

Proceedings of the Mutual Conference of Adventists, Held in the City of Albany, the 29th and 30th of April and 1st of May, 1845. New York: Joshua V. Himes, 1845.

Richards, Leonard L. *Shay's Rebellion: The American Revolution's Final Battle.* Philadelphia: University of Pennsylvania, 2002.

Roth, Randolph A. *The Democratic Dilemma: Religion, Reform, and the Social Order in the Connecticut River Valley of Vermont, 1791-1850.* New York: Cambridge University Press, 1987.

Rowe, David L. "Comets and Eclipses: The Millerites, Nature, and the Apocalypse." *Adventist Heritage* 3, no. 2 (Winter 1976): 10-19.

———. *Thunder and Trumpets: The Millerites and Apocalyptic Thought in Upstate New York, 1800-1850.* Chico, Calif.: Scholars Press, 1985.

Rutland Herald. Rutland, Vt.

Sandeen, Ernest R. *The Roots of Fundamentalism: British and American Millenarianism 1800-1930.* Chicago: University of Chicago Press, 1970.

Sears, Clara. *Days of Delusion: A Strange Bit of History.* Boston: Houghton Mifflin Company, 1924.

Signs of the Times [renamed *Advent Herald and Signs of the Times*]. Boston, Mass.

Silberger, Julius. *Mary Baker Eddy: An Interpretive Biography of the Founder of Christian Science.* Boston: Little Brown, 1980.

Skeen, C. Edward. *1816: America Rising.* Lexington: University Press of Kentucky, 2003.

———. *Citizen Solidiers in the War of 1812.* Lexington: University Press of Kentucky, 1999.

Skinner, Otis A. *The Theory of William Miller Concerning the End of the World in 1843, Utterly Exploded.* Boston: Thomas Whittemore, 1840.

Smith, James Edward Adam. *History of Pittsfield (Berkshire County) Massachusetts From the Year 1734 to the Year 1800.* 2 vols. Boston: Lee & Shepard, 1869.

Smith, John Howard. "'The Promised Day of the Lord': American Millennialism and Apocalypticism, 1735-1783." In *Anglo-American Millennialism, from Milton to the Millerites.* Ed. Richard Connors and Andrew Colin Gow. Leiden and Boston: Brill, 2004.

Spalding, Arthur Whitefield. *Pioneer Stories of the Second Advent Message,* revised edition. Brushton, N.Y.: TEACH Services, 1995.

Stagg, Charles Anderson. *Mr. Madison's War: Politics, Diplomacy, and Warfare in the Early American Republic, 1783-1830.* Princeton, N.J.: Princeton University Press, 1983.

Stone & Stewart. *The New Topographical Atlas of Washington County, New York.* Philadelphia: Stone & Stewart, 1866.

Stout, Harry S. *The New England Soul: Preaching and Religious Culture in Colonial New England.* New York: Oxford University Press, 1986.

Taves, Ann. *Fits, Trances, and Visions: Experiencing Religion and Explaining Experience from Wesley to James.* Princeton, N.J.: Princeton University Press, 1999.

Underwood, Grant. *The Millenarian World of Early Mormonism.* Urbana and Chicago: University of Illinois, 1993.

Vermont [Baptist] Association. *Minutes of the Vermont [Baptist] Association, 1792, 1817, 1819, 1824, 1829, 1831, 1833, 1835.*

Vermont Telegraph. Brandon, Vermont.

Voice of Truth, and Glad Tidings of the Kingdom of God at Hand. Rochester, N.Y., n.p., n.d.

Walters, Kerry S. *The American Deists: Voices of Reason and Dissent in the Early Republic* Lawrence: University of Kansas Press, 1992.

Washington [Union] Baptist Association, *Minutes of the Washington Baptist Association, 1827, 1828, 1829, 1831, 1832, 1841, 1844, 1845.*

Weber, Timothy P. *Living in the Shadow of the Second Coming: American Premillennialism, 1875-1925.* New York: Oxford University Press, 1979.

White, James. *Life Incidents, In Connection With the Great Advent Movement, as Illustrated by the Three Angels of Revelation XIV.* Battle Creek, Mich.: Seventh-day Adventist Publishing Association, 1868.

———. *Sketches of the Christian Life and Public Labors of William Miller, Gathered from His Memoir by the Late Sylvester Bliss, and From Other Sources.* Battle Creek, Mich.: Seventh-day Adventist Publishing Company, 1875.

Young, Alfred. *The Shoemaker and the Tea Party: Memory and the American Revolution.* Boston: Beacon Press, 1999.

Index